OBAMA'S WAR

OBAMA'S WAR

Avoiding a Quagmire in Afghanistan

JAMES GANNON

Potomac Books, Inc.
Washington, D.C.

Library of Congress Cataloging-in-Publication Data
Gannon, James, 1931–
  Obama's war : avoiding a quagmire in Afghanistan / James Gannon. — First edition.
    p. cm.
  Includes bibliographical references and index.
  ISBN 978-1-59797-537-7
1. Afghan War, 2001–2. Obama, Barack, 1961– I. Title.
  DS371.412.G36 2011
  958.104'7—dc22

                                                              08|11

                                          2010048447

Printed in the United States of America on acid-free paper that meets the American National Standards Institute Z39-48 Standard.

Potomac Books, Inc.
22841 Quicksilver Drive
Dulles, Virginia 20166

First Edition

10 9 8 7 6 5 4 3 2 1

To Sheila
and the millions of other powerless people
who believe that war is a bad way to settle differences

Contents

Prologue: That Awful Day ix

Preface xix

Introduction: A More Nuanced Folly xxiii

1   A PARADOX OF POWER 1

2   THE ROOTS OF ISLAMISM 15

3   THE ENEMIES 35

4   INSIDE THE SURGE 49

5   SHADES OF RAMBO 73

6   GLOBAL TERRORISM 93

7   NUCLEAR JIHADISM 123

8   THINKING THE UNTHINKABLE 139

Notes 151

Bibliography 171

Index 185

About the Author 191

Prologue

That Awful Day

They invoked the name of Allah in a crime against humanity. They committed murder by suicide and called it martyrdom. They used modern technology as a double-edged sword against the modern world. The deed was stunning for its audacity and scope, and in its execution, they humbled the world's most powerful nation, killing nearly three thousand innocent people. Thus, nineteen deeply committed but otherwise unremarkable Arabs made history on the morning of September 11, 2001. With the advantage of surprise and armed with only box cutters, they commandeered four commercial jets in a coordinated assault on two prominent symbols of America's financial and military dominance—the World Trade Center and the Pentagon—causing the total destruction of one and severe damage to the other. They had targeted another unknown landmark, perhaps the White House or Congress, but the effort failed when a few unarmed Americans challenged them in the face of near-certain death in a struggle for control of the fourth aircraft.

Americans capable of thought and feeling on that day surely remember what they were doing when they heard the news. The tragedy invites comparison with the date that "will live in infamy," December 7, 1941, when the Japanese raided Pearl Harbor and sucked the United States into World War II. But the two are not equivalent. The later date was more infamous by far. At Pearl Harbor the Japanese navy attacked clearly defined military targets. Civilian casualties were incidental to the main objective—"collateral damage" in subsequent military jargon. By contrast, the Arab hijackers of September 11, 2001, did not represent any nation. They belonged to a shadowy, extranational, loosely controlled, extremist alliance, which distorts Islam by teaching hatred—of the United States and Israel, in particular—and evinces a depraved indifference to the slaughter of innocents.

THE ATTACK

Because of its significance as a major watershed in history, the horror of September 11 deserves to be briefly relived. It began at 8:15 a.m., Eastern Standard Time, sixteen minutes after American Airlines flight 11 to Los Angeles lifted off from Boston's Logan Airport. Five hijackers among the eighty-one passengers sprang from business- and first-class seats, brandishing their knives in a cacophony of threats and battle cries. They most likely shouted "Allahu Akbar" (God is great), as instructed in a letter from an unknown source found among a hijacker's belongings, because that would supposedly "strike fear in the hearts of nonbelievers." The letter advised each to "make your knife sharp" in order "not [to] cause the discomfort of those you are killing."[1] Indeed, these zealots proved quite adept at slashing the throats of unarmed people.

The plane veered west-northwest during the one-sided struggle, and at 8:29, over Amsterdam, New York, and with the hijackers in control, it turned sharply south. Flight attendant Betty Ong, hearing no answer from the cockpit, contacted the American Airlines Southeastern Reservations Office in Cary, North Carolina. She reported that a passenger in business class and two flight attendants had been stabbed. Flight attendant Amy Sweeney, who was in touch with the American Airlines Flight Services Office in Boston, described the hijackers as Middle Easterners and relayed three of their seat numbers for identification.[2]

The hijackers' division of labor consisted of combatants and specialists, some to quell the passengers and crew, and one or two to occupy the cockpit. Authorities believe that thirty-three-year-old Mohammed Atta, the probable overall coordinator of the four hijackings, had taken over the controls of AA11. An Egyptian with a privileged background and fluent in Arabic, English, and German, Atta did not fit the terrorist mold of a robotic, underclass youth induced to commit a self-destructive act. His father was a successful lawyer with the financial wherewithal to own a Mercedes and a second home on the Mediterranean shore. Two sisters were or had been university professors. Mohammed Atta earned a bachelor's degree in architecture at Cairo University and a postgraduate degree in urban planning at the Technical University in Hamburg, Germany.[3] There he formed a tight cell of Arab men who began planning this atrocity long before they carried it out. Counterterrorism experts and the Bush administration linked Atta to al Qaeda, the global terrorist network led by Osama bin Laden.[4] Atta learned to fly small airplanes in the summer of 2000 at Huffman Aviation International in Venice, Florida, and later practiced commercial flying on a flight simulator. He knew enough on this day to guide the Boeing 767 in his control, but not how to land it (which would have been superfluous, anyway, in light of his intention).

It was a clear day. Atta would have been able to see the Hudson River on his left and follow it downstream. As he neared the gleaming steel-and-glass 110-story twin towers at the southern end of Manhattan, his heart must have pounded for joy at the thought of destroying an American skyscraper. For his thesis at the Technical University, he wrote about the degradation of the *souk* (marketplace) in Aleppo, Syria, by the proliferation of multistory tourist hotels and fast-food restaurants. Now he would take his revenge against the West.

At the same time, he must have been conflicted by the fantastic promise of Islam. "The gardens of paradise are waiting for you in all their beauty," said the aforementioned letter, "and the women of paradise are waiting, calling out, 'Come hither, friend of God.'"[5] Bin Laden made martyrdom seem even more attractive in his 1996 declaration of war against the United States. "A martyr will not feel the pain of death," said bin Laden, quoting a Muslim holy man. "Martyr privileges are guaranteed by Allah. . . . he will be shown his seat in paradise, . . . decorated with the jewels of belief, . . . wedded to seventy-two of the pure [beautiful ones of Paradise] and his intercession on the behalf of seventy of his relatives will be accepted."[6]

It seems unlikely that Mohammed Atta, a hard-core misogynist, could have fallen for the lure of heavenly women. The earthly kind, at least, left him cold. At his degree ceremony in Hamburg in August 1999, he refused to shake hands with the women on his review committee.[7] In his will, dated April 11, 1996, he instructed that no women attend his funeral or visit his grave.[8] What was it, then, that led him to the gleaming tower ahead: the call of paradise or his palpable hatred of the United States? Whatever motivated him, he became a "martyr" (and committed murder) that day.[9]

At 8:44 a.m., Amy Sweeney told Michael Woodward, the office manager in Boston, "Something is wrong. We are in rapid descent." Woodward asked her to look out the window. She reported, "We are flying low. We are flying very, very low. We are flying way too low," and after a pause, "Oh my God, we are way too low." Then the phone went dead.[10] At 8:48, AA11, loaded with fuel for the transcontinental flight, crashed in a huge ball of fire into the north tower of the World Trade Center.

A similar scene played out on United flight 175, another Boeing 767 bound for Los Angeles, which followed AA11 out of Logan by a quarter of an hour. While other hijackers subdued the passengers and crew, Marwan al-Shehhi settled into the pilot's seat. Shehhi, a native of the United Arab Emirates, had paid a hefty $4,500 for a first-class ticket that would prove more costly to the airline—indeed, to the entire airline industry—by orders of magnitude. At twenty-three, he was ten years younger than Atta and appeared to be the older man's protégé. He had been part of the Hamburg cell and Atta's constant companion at the Huffman flight school. Shehhi held course bearing west-southwest until, at 8:47 over northern New Jersey, he banked left and turned the plane back toward Manhattan. UA175 hit the south tower at 9:03, as the world watched the television coverage of the raging fire from the impact of the first plane on the north tower.

The intense heat from the burning jet fuel softened the skyscrapers' steel girders. In less than an hour the south tower buckled and then collapsed in a ghostly gray blob of dust and debris that, after consuming the hundreds of victims trapped inside, stalked the terrified people running from the scene on the streets below. Giant chunks of the falling wreckage damaged several nearby buildings. A half hour later the other tower collapsed, creating similar havoc, and a few hours after that, the next tallest building, forty-seven-stories high and known as Tower Seven, also crashed, although no plane had hit it. At day's end, the once-vibrant World Trade Center lay in ruins, leaving a deep wound in the heart of the world's financial capital.

American flight 77 to Los Angeles, a smaller Boeing 757, left Dulles Airport outside Washington at 8:21 a.m. Forty minutes later it had climbed to a cruising altitude of 35,000 feet. As it entered Ohio airspace, five more hijackers acted with the characteristic violent surprise that made them so deadly efficient. Hani Hanjour, a twenty-nine-year-old, slightly built Saudi Arabian, took the wheel. He was the only one of the four presumed pilots who reportedly did not belong to Atta's European cell. Hanjour had singularly failed since 1996 to impress any of his several American flight instructors with his aptitude for flying,[11] but in this acid test he did not fail. He turned the plane around and headed back to Washington. As AA77 approached the city, it appeared headed for the White House, where the Secret Service burst into Vice President Dick Cheney's office in the West Wing and hustled him to an underground shelter. Cheney said later he felt his feet leaving the ground as the agents hurried him along. (President George W. Bush was in Florida at the time plugging his domestic agenda.) The plane eventually banked right, circled smoothly, and plunged into the Pentagon at 9:45 a.m., virtually destroying one section of the five-sided edifice and damaging part of another.

A fourth hijacked plane crashed in its own epic tragedy, but less disastrously than the other three. United flight 93 left Newark for San Francisco at 8:43 a.m., five minutes before the first jet hit the World Trade Center. As the Boeing 757 gained altitude and swung west, its occupants probably did not see the explosion and fire on the north tower across New York Harbor. But they learned about it soon enough from cell phone connections to the outside. The hijackers—this time only four—swung into action about fifty minutes after liftoff, as the airliner approached Cleveland at cruising altitude. Ziad Samir Jarrah of Lebanon, an engineering student in Hamburg and another close associate of Mohammed Atta's, took over the controls. Jarrah, reportedly the most skilled of the four presumed pilots, turned the plane around and headed back east, his exact destination unknown.

The circumstances on this aircraft differed from those on the other three in at least one important respect. On AA11 and UA175, the passengers could not have known the hijackers' intentions. On AA77, if they knew, they lacked either the time or the presence of mind to react. On UA93, they found out in good time about the New York attack and realized a similar fate was most likely in store for them, so the more proactive among them quickly huddled to discuss how they might thwart the assailants. If they did nothing, they would surely die; if they acted, they would probably die anyway but might save other potential victims and a national symbol as well.

In the absence of surviving eyewitnesses, all that is known about what happened inside the airliner is what passengers told people on the outside by phone. Todd Beamer of Cranbury, New Jersey, told a GTE operator that one of the hijackers was guarding nine passengers, including him, and five crew members at the back of the plane. Other passengers were being held in the first-class section near the front.[12] Jeremy Glick of Hewitt, New Jersey, made several calls to his wife, Lysbeth. He described "three Arab-looking men with red headbands" who carried knives and spoke of a bomb. He said the cockpit was silent, and he assumed the airliner's pilots had been killed. Thomas E. Burnett Jr. of San Ramon, California, told his wife, Deena, that one passenger had already been stabbed to death.[13]

As robust men in the prime of life, all successful high-tech executives, Beamer, Glick, and Burnett had the physical capabilities to challenge the hijackers. Beamer, thirty-two, a competitive multisport athlete in high school and college, said he and others would not be pawns in the hijackers' plot. Glick, thirty-one, a muscular six foot, four inch former collegiate judo champion, told how they joked about taking on the enemy with plastic knives from their in-flight breakfast. Burnett, thirty-eight, who had played football in high school, shrugged off his wife's pleas to stay down and not draw the hijackers' attention. "No, no," he said. "If they're going to run this into the ground we're going to have to do something."[14] One other passenger probably joined them: Mark Bingham, thirty-one, of San Francisco, a six foot five former college rugby player who ran a small public relations firm. Glick, in his last call to his wife, reaffirmed his love for her and their twelve-week-old daughter, Emerson.[15] Beamer, whose wife was pregnant with their third child, said they planned to jump the nearest hijacker who appeared to have a bomb tied to his midsection. A devout Christian, he led the others in reciting Psalm 23 ("Yea, though I walk through the Valley of the Shadow of Death, I shall fear no evil . . . "). Then, with the phone line still open, Beamer called out, "Are you guys ready? Let's roll!"[16] What happened next, nobody knows for sure. An alarm on the cockpit voice recorder, recovered from the crash site, indicated that the plane was flying close to the speed of sound as it approached the ground. A voice in the cockpit was heard to shout, "They're coming."[17] As the Americans struggled to kick in the locked cockpit door, Jarrah pointed the nose down and sent the plane into an earthward dive. UA93 crashed at 10:10 a.m. in a field near Shanksville, Pennsylvania, and not into the White House.

The four airliners carried a total of 246 passengers and crew members, plus the nineteen hijackers. All perished. One hundred twenty-five more people on the ground died at the Pentagon. In New York, fires burned for weeks deep inside the rubble that once housed miracle products of high technology and modern communications. Rescuers found a few hundred bodies and more body parts. Authorities speculated that, given the extreme heat and the force of the collapse, many victims at the World Trade Center will never be found whole or in part. After years of painstaking recovery work, the New York City Office of Emergency Management reported 2,603 people in the towers or on the ground dead and twenty-four others missing and presumed dead. An estimated 14,000 to 17,400 people were inside the towers when the first plane hit. Most of those who died in the two towers were at or above the impact zone. It is believed that more than two hundred people jumped to their deaths. One woman died five months later from exposure to the dust raised in the collapse. Among the dead and missing were 411 men and women from the uniformed services, most of them firefighters who had rushed into the burning towers to save lives and lost their own lives when the towers collapsed. They and their uniformed brethren who frantically combed the rubble for survivors became the heroes of a grief-stricken nation.

THE RESPONSE

So began for Americans a new age of international terrorism. Bin Laden must have anticipated retaliation after the September 11 attack, but he could not have guessed the power and accuracy of America's laser-guided bombs. Because of the enormity of the crime, it would have been politically difficult, if not impossible, for the Bush administration to shrink from striking back. In fact, war hawks in and out of the administration were eager for the bully chase, with or without the "inherent right" to self-defense embedded in the United Nations charter.[18]

Bin Laden had every reason to feel safe in the rugged Hindu Kush, where his holy warriors had already survived the Soviet army and American missiles. He hoped an American response would unite the Muslim world against the West, but instead, it united most of the world, including Muslims, against his brand of terrorism—at least in the immediate aftermath of the tragedy. NATO, the cold war alliance that bound America to the defense of Europe, invoked for the first time the core principle of its existence—that an attack against one is an attack against all—and the European member nations pledged unanimous support for America. Old cold war enemies Russia and China, who suffer their own torments at the hands of terrorists, also supported the United States. Even Afghanistan's Muslim neighbors, Pakistan and Iran, where terrorism was taught and exported, found it in their best interests to side with America on this issue.

In a speech before Congress on September 20, nine days after the event, Bush took the sky on his shoulders and declared perpetual war. "Our war on terror begins with Al Qaida, but it does not end there," he said. "It will not end until every terrorist group of global reach has been found, stopped and defeated. . . . We will direct every resource at our command—every means of diplomacy, every tool of intelligence, every instrument of law enforcement, every financial influence, and every necessary weapon of war—to the disruption and to the defeat of the global terror network. . . . Every nation in every region now has a decision to make. Either you are with us or you are with the terrorists."[19] Earlier, in less formal remarks at "ground zero," amid the ruins of the World Trade Center, he promised rescue workers that he would "rid the world of evil."[20] In a speech to reservists called up for duty in Afghanistan, he vowed like a sheriff of the Old West to get bin Laden, "dead or alive."[21] On another occasion he referred to his war on terrorism as a "crusade."[22] On that point Osama bin Laden would agree—from the diametrically opposed perspective that the Crusades of the eleventh to thirteenth centuries were a Christian aggression against Islam.

These were all stirring words for an America stunned by the vicious 9/11 attacks. But the president promised more than he could deliver. America was capable of a powerful counterblow, combined with a more alert defense and unremitting pressure against terrorist cells and training sites using international police and special military forces. And there Bush should have left it. The problem was not in the effort but in the rhetoric that took America beyond its limits.

The counterblow came within weeks. Bush had promised to pursue not only terrorists but also state sponsors of terrorism. He promptly put his policy into effect by targeting Afghanistan, where the ruling Taliban had allowed al Qaeda to operate terrorist training camps. As powerful American forces deployed to the region, Bush demanded that the Taliban leader, Mullah Mohammad Omar, turn over bin Laden or suffer the consequences. Omar refused. The Americans attacked from the air using special operations forces deployed on the ground with the anti-Taliban Northern Alliance to direct the air strikes. Within weeks the Taliban was out of power and al Qaeda was on the run. The Americans failed to capture bin Laden or Mullah Omar, and then the Bush administration lost its way. Instead of pursuing al Qaeda and its Islamist allies, America prepared for the invasion and occupation of Iraq. President Bush, having belittled the Clinton administration's use of America's armed forces for nation building in backwater places such as Haiti, embarked on the mother of all nation-building endeavors in a highly cultured and sophisticated society.

In 2009 it was back to square one with a new president. America has agreed to withdraw from Iraq, and President Barack Obama has promised, seven years after the Islamists were run out of Afghanistan, to ratchet up the fight against them. But al Qaeda and the Taliban are no longer the defeated, dispirited downbeats of 2002. They have regrouped in the cross-border sanctuaries of western Pakistan, patched up their wounds, and reinvigorated their forces with new weapons and the creed of militant Islam, which includes *jihad* (holy war) and martyrdom (suicide bombing). Early in his administration, President Obama backed up his promise by authorizing the deployment of seventeen thousand additional combat troops to Afghanistan, where the Taliban effectively controlled some areas in the south of the country. He added four thousand support troops to train Afghan police and military forces and an indeterminate number of civilian specialists to give advice on the rebuilding of Afghan infrastructure. Obama's war seeks to punish the perpetrators of 9/11 and secure the nation and the world against further terrorist attacks. It is especially frightening to think of terrorists armed with nuclear weapons, a threat posed by al Qaeda since the 1990s and more recently the Taliban as it edges closer to the seat of government in nuclear Pakistan. But the prospective battleground in the mountainous terrain on the Taliban's home turf does not play to America's strength in firepower and mobility. Obama's war promises to be a tough grind that will test America's political will. The outcome for what is arguably the most powerful nation in history is not at all certain.

Preface

Every year since 2001 the nation has paused on September 11 to remember the victims of al Qaeda's attack on America. In three separate ceremonies at the World Trade Center site in New York, outside the Pentagon in Washington, D.C., and in Stonycreek Township, Pennsylvania, the names of the deceased are read aloud, bells toll, and silence is observed at the moments of impact of the four airliners and the collapse of the twin towers of the World Trade Center. These ceremonies reflect a nation's grief, but more than that, they honor the common decency of the American people. Most people can do little to avenge the atrocity of 9/11 other than keep the memory alive. The power to exact vengeance and secure the nation's future belongs to the elected political leaders and their advisers. The rest can only watch and wonder.

The Bush administration's response to 9/11 began with an attack on Afghanistan that was entirely justified but flawed in its execution. U.S. special operations forces were inserted to help the anti-Taliban Northern Alliance by directing laser beams at enemy targets and thereby facilitating precision bombing from the air. The Taliban and al Qaeda were routed, but their leaders escaped to friendly sanctuaries in Pakistan. At that point, many critics and experts believe, the United States dropped the ball. It failed to put American boots on the ground at the border with Pakistan to block Taliban and al Qaeda retreats. Most galling was the failure to capture the al Qaeda leaders, Osama bin Laden and his Egyptian sidekick in terrorism, Ayman al-Zawahiri. Then, before the job in Afghanistan was done, the

Bush administration shifted American resources to Iraq for an invasion and occupation that ultimately proved to be unrelated to the 9/11 attack on America.

In my last book, *Military Occupations in the Age of Self-Determination*, I compared the Iraq adventure to the great follies of the ages chronicled by the late American historian Barbara Tuchman. She defined "folly" as "the pursuit by governments of policies contrary to their own interests" despite timely advice against the erroneous policies and the availability of alternative courses of action.[1] The Iraq War fits this definition perfectly. The invasion diverted the United States from pursuing its true enemy, al Qaeda, a chorus of voices warned against it, and a less costly and virtually bloodless alternative course of action—no-fly zones—was already in place. Many said we were headed for another inglorious defeat like the failure in Vietnam. I agreed in principle, although I also maintained that no two wars are exactly the same. I have examined the record since 1945, when the United Nations adopted the principle of self-determination, and found that other great nations, foreign occupiers with great modern armies—including Britain in Palestine (late 1940s), France in Algeria (1950s and early '60s), the Soviet Union in Afghanistan (1980s), and Israel in Lebanon (1982–2000)—have lost to ragtag insurgents fighting for the freedom of their homeland. Even when they did not lose militarily, the great powers lost politically and eventually withdrew; colonial Britain, for example, retreated from Malaya and Kenya in the 1950s. As this was written, America was beginning to withdraw its combat troops from Iraq. The argument over whether the United States won or lost the war will persist. But in light of the blood and treasure wasted, it really doesn't matter.

In this book I hold the war in Afghanistan to the same light. Justification for it can be found in the rubble of the Pentagon and World Trade Center and the grieving of the victims' survivors. Equally compelling is the malevolent will of the perpetrator. Al Qaeda is in the business of organized terrorism and threatens to send civilization back to the dark ages. Since long before September 11, 2001, it has sought to acquire a nuclear bomb, presumably to blow up an American city. Weighed against the call to action in 2001 were the great-power defeats in small wars, plus the difficult Afghan terrain and the martial spirit of the Pashtun tribes that have fought off foreign intruders since ancient times. The historical odds and local realities obstructed the road to American success in the fight against al Qaeda and the Taliban. This was President Obama's dilemma in the fall of 2009 as he considered the nation's war strategy for Afghanistan.

————————

My thanks to the staff at Potomac Books for their contributions to this project: Senior Editor Hilary Claggett for sticking with it through thick and thin, Production Editor Kathryn Owens for smoothly shepherding the book through the production process, and Copy Editor Julie Kimmel for her careful editing of the manuscript, which made this a better book. All errors of commission or omission are my responsibility.

Introduction

A More Nuanced Folly

Henry Kissinger, endowed with heavy jowls and a dumpy figure, could never be mistaken for a Hollywood hunk. Yet he managed to cut quite a figure with the ladies in Washington's social circles during his time as foreign policy adviser to President Nixon, way back in the late 1960s and early 1970s. In 1971 the president sent him on a secret mission to China to pave the way for diplomatic relations with our then–bitter enemy. In his first meeting with Chinese leaders in 1971, before they delved into weighty international problems, Chairman Mao Zedong allegedly posed a question that threw Kissinger off balance. Mao, with a twinkle in his eye, asked that Kissinger explain the secret to his success with women. Quick to recover, Kissinger replied in the same spirit, his thick German accent rising with its guttural tones past a faint wry smile on his lips. "Power is an aphrodisiac," he said softly.

Power might captivate women in Washington, but it does not guarantee victory in war. America emerged from World War II as a global power, yet lost in Vietnam to an inferior enemy a quarter century later. By the new millennium America had become the greatest power on earth but was still sorely tested in Iraq. The American people should worry that the aphrodisiac of overwhelming power will make them forget that power has its limits as they seek to solve international problems by force of arms. Madeleine Albright, the European-born daughter of a Czech diplomat, is a case in point. She has made no secret of her infatuation with the America to which she escaped in her childhood, an admirable quality that can become dangerous when mixed with power. As secretary of state in the second Clinton term, she often described America as the "indispensable nation" to justify the use of force in support of American hegemony. Her thinking was summed up in a comment that went well over the top: "If we have to use force, it is because we are America. We are the indispensable nation. We stand tall. We see farther into the future."[1] Earlier at a cabinet meeting, when ambassador to the United Nations, she engaged in a testy discussion with Colin Powell about American policy in Bosnia. Powell had carried over as chairman of the Joint Chiefs of Staff in the first nine months of the Clinton administration. "What's the point," Ms. Albright asked, "of having this superb military that you're always talking about if we can't use it?" Later, Powell published a rejoinder in his autobiography. "I thought I would have an aneurysm," he wrote. "American GIs were not toy soldiers to be moved around on some sort of global game board."[2] Powell, the distinguished career soldier, is perhaps more understated than Albright, but no less patriotic.

Several observers have concluded that a broadly based militarism underlies the thinking implicit in Albright's superpatriotism. The scholar Chalmers Johnson of the University of California considered the various persuasive reasons widely cited for the U.S. invasion of Iraq—oil, Israel, and domestic politics—and concluded none of the above. The principal reason for attacking Iraq, he said, came from "the inexorable pressures of imperialism and militarism."[3] Most Americans do not openly avow such feelings, and President Obama has specifically denied it,[4] but according to Johnson, imperialism and militarism have become subtly imbedded in the American mind-set. Militarism, he said, "sprang from the varied experiences of American citizens in the armed forces, ideas about war as they evolved from one war to the next, and the growth of a huge armaments industry." Imperialism grew out of "the habitual use of imperial methods over forty years" and "became addictive."[5] Andrew J. Bacevich—a West Point graduate, Vietnam veteran, and current professor of history and international relations at Boston University—sees the Bush vow to "rid the world of evil" as comparable to a promise to destroy the devil with America's military might. "Americans in our own time have fallen prey to militarism . . . and outsized expectations regarding the efficacy of force," wrote Bacevich. "To a degree without precedent in U.S. history, Americans have come to define the nation's strength and well-being in terms of military preparedness, military action, and the fostering of (or nostalgia for) military ideals."[6]

Americans seem so enamored by the phantom of their power that they feel free to ignore the lessons of history. Since the end of World War II, great powers (not just the United States in Vietnam) have usually lost wars to assert their authority with military force outside their own boundaries. In the first decade of the new millennium, in the aftermath of the September 11, 2001, attack, America fought two such wars at the same time. The folly of invading and occupying Iraq was compounded by its strategic incoherence. The Iraq War, in fact, was a blunder of historic proportions. Good men and women died for no good reason, because in the final analysis, Iraq had no part in 9/11. In attacking Taliban-ruled Afghanistan, at least America had chosen the right enemy. The Taliban had given safe haven to al Qaeda, which then reached halfway around the globe to strike a severe blow on American soil. Afghanistan, in other words, was a more nuanced folly. But the Bush administration erred by shifting its attention to Iraq and letting its victory in Afghanistan slip away. Then, in both places it neglected the historical reality of great power futility in small wars.

From an American perspective, the invasion of Afghanistan can be justified in two ways. First, the 9/11 attack was a criminal act that demands justice for the victims and their families. Second, the al Qaeda organization that carried it out poses a threat to global security that should not go unheeded. Of the two issues, security trumps vengeance. Then it must be asked, how best to achieve security? Is the war winnable? If so, at what cost? And what is the best way to go about it? If not, how does America get out of the sinkhole? The burden of answering these monumental questions in 2009 fell on the president of the United States. Poor mortal!

By contrast, the rationale for invading Iraq depended on erroneous intelligence about weapons of mass destruction and Iraqi connections to 9/11. The Bush team promoted its case for war with loose, flashy language (e.g., "a smoking gun in the form of a mushroom cloud") and unproven allegations (e.g., mobile biological labs, imported uranium oxide) such as one might hear on the political hustings.[7] These flagrant errors cost America 4,232 troops killed and 31,021 wounded through the first month of 2009, the approximate end of the Bush presidency.[8] Iraq's losses are many times worse than America's: up to 100,591 men, women, and children killed,[9] and nearly 5 million displaced as of June 2009. One in every five Iraqis was uprooted from home. Two million fled the country, and 2.8 million were left homeless in their homeland.[10]

For these bitter results American taxpayers are being hit with a huge tab. The National Priorities Project, a nonprofit organization that focuses on federal budget priorities and maintains a wry sense of humor, keeps a website showing the running direct cost of the two wars, both together and separately, just like the running tally of the ballooning federal budget deficit. As of November 10, 2010, the total cost for both wars was running at $1.1 trillion and seemed to be going up faster than a thousand dollars a second. Out of the total that day the Iraq War was costing $741 billion, and the Afghanistan war, $363 billion.[11] Hidden costs—such as the rehabilitation of wounded troops, death benefits for surviving relatives, intelligence gathering, and funds from the budgets of agencies other than Defense that are involved in the war effort—push the outlay higher. The money comes almost entirely from borrowing, thereby shifting the burden of paying for it to future generations, which means that one can add the cost of interest to the total. According to economists Joseph Stiglitz and Linda Bilmes, the total comes to $3 trillion up to March 2008.[12] Faced with these staggering costs, the Bush administration engineered tax cuts that primarily benefitted the wealthiest Americans, who can most afford to pay for the war.

Iraq under Saddam Hussein was certainly not America's friend, but neither was it part of the Islamist jihad. The war to eliminate Saddam has done little or nothing to advance the struggle against international terrorism. Just the opposite, it has played into the hands of America's Islamist enemies, who seek to wear U.S. troops down in unconventional terrorist and guerrilla warfare. Just before the invasion of Iraq, bin Laden virtually salivated over the opportunity to engage the Americans in shadow warfare. He let his strategy be known with these words to his followers: "We advise the importance of dragging the enemies' forces to a long, exhausting, and continuous battle. The worst fear of the enemy is street and city fighting. . . . We stress the importance of martyrdom attacks [suicide bombings] against the enemy."[13] President Bush occasionally asserted that they (the Islamists) hate us (the Americans) because we are free. Islamists do hate America, but not because the people are free. Their hatred instead stems from American power and domination of the Islamic world, so they fight back as best they can with the means at hand. On 9/11 they struck a low blow without the slightest compunction.

As the Iraq War was becoming an ugly quagmire, President Bush made his conservative supporters happy by resisting political pressure to start pulling out of

Iraq. The pressure included the Republicans' loss of their majorities in both houses of Congress in the 2006 midterm elections. Bush took what author Thomas E. Ricks has called a "gamble" by sending reinforcements to perform an operation known as (and misnamed) the "surge."[14] With the cooperation of Sunni tribes and the suspension of terrorist activity by a troublesome Shia militia, the reinforced Americans scored one victory after another over Islamist fighters and reduced the river of U.S. military and Iraqi civilian blood to a smaller stream.

Neoconservatives both inside and outside the administration who had sold Bush on the Iraq War jumped on this improvement as a vindication of their broken policy, even though people were still dying—at a lower rate, to be sure—from terrorist bombs. During the year from September 2006 to August 2007 American troops were killed at an average rate of ninety per month, and Iraqi civilians at 2,594 per month; during the following twelve months, after the surge took effect, the monthly violent-death rates declined to 40 and 958, respectively.[15] But an uptick in violence after U.S. forces were scaled back to the pre-surge level still cast the ultimate outcome in doubt.

Whatever gains can be attributed to the surge, the Bush administration cannot easily erase the terrible cost of an unnecessary war inflicted on the American and Iraqi people. In the words of David Kilcullen, an Australian military strategist and a top adviser to Gen. David Petraeus, commander of coalition forces during the surge, "In my view the [Iraq War], in grand-strategic terms, was a deeply misguided and counterproductive undertaking, an extremely severe strategic error, and a model of exactly how not to do business. In 2007 we seem . . . to have saved ourselves [through the skill and bravery of the troops] from some of the more egregious consequences of the bad decision to invade in 2003."[16]

The war in Afghanistan against al Qaeda and the Taliban has always been the war that really mattered, so much so that key NATO allies share a burden there that they refused to shoulder in Iraq. It is obviously in the West's interest to hold global terrorism in check. Afghanistan and the mountainous, semiautonomous tribal areas of western Pakistan contain the heart and nerve center of global terrorism, where young people are indoctrinated in a seventh-century ideology and trained to terrorize twenty-first-century societies. The deeper question is how to contain them, not whether to wage the fight. Obama has made it clear that, had he been president on September 11, 2001, he would have kept the focus on Afghanistan. He does not oppose war per se, he assured the nation in 2002. He only opposes "dumb wars."[17] In his view, Iraq is a dumb war, and presumably, Afghanistan is a smart war, or in his words, "a war of necessity."

Whatever its level of acuity, America faces very tough opponents in Afghanistan, the so-called graveyard of empires. Pashtun tribesmen, who seem to thrill timelessly to a fight they think they can win, harassed Alexander's army in the fourth century BC, slaughtered a British expeditionary force in the nineteenth century, and held out against a Soviet occupation in the twentieth century. The Taliban today are really two Taliban,[18] consisting of Pashtun tribesmen from both sides of the Afghan-Pakistani border fighting for control of their respective countries under separate leadership. The most zealous among them, together with their al Qaeda allies, believe that death in the cause of Islam is a ticket to paradise. For those less zealous, resentment against Western interventionism is cause enough for them to give up their lives. Either way, they are fighting the kind of war that great powers have muddled up over the past several decades.

Obama's early moves foreshadowed a different approach to war from the one-dimensional military onslaught and austere occupation that Bush originally imposed on Iraq. The core U.S. goal, he said in March 2009, "must be to disrupt, dismantle, and defeat al Qaeda."[19] A second goal is to keep the Afghan Taliban from retaking the reins of government. In effect, America is fighting a two-front war. On the al Qaeda front, U.S. and NATO ground troops do not cross the border out of respect for Pakistani sovereignty. So, the weapon of choice has become the remote-controlled, pilotless drone, which strikes from the air with deadly force. The drones have made it possible for the United States to reach through the air across the border—arguably in violation of Pakistani sovereignty without actually stepping on Pakistani soil—and inflict severe damage on al Qaeda. Drones might even become the technology that turns the war in America's favor, like the Stinger surface-to-air missiles that helped the mujahideen defeat the Soviets in the 1980s. Drone attacks began under Bush, but Obama has pounded away at militant targets in Pakistan with much more punch. Hundreds of militants, including several high-level al Qaeda and Pakistani Taliban leaders, have been killed. But these methods, which are not always so precise, have also produced civilian casualties in excessive numbers.

On the other front against the Afghan Taliban, American and NATO forces aim not primarily at killing or capturing the enemy but at isolating the fanatic Islamists from the general population. The illusory quest for decisive military victory is put aside in favor of protecting the people by strengthening security and building infrastructure, with the ultimate goal of bringing mountain and desert tribes in closer harmony with the central government. The process requires time, patience, substantial military force, and a genuine interest in the welfare of the people. The way it often works, the military moves into a village or district in sufficient force to dislodge the enemy, with or without a fight. The move yields both a political and military benefit: the Islamist influence on daily life is removed, and the isolated insurgents can then be attacked with less fear of causing innocent casualties.

Taking this course of action shifts the priority to winning hearts and minds, only part of which is a function of the Western forces. In other words, the United States can win hearts and minds, and the Islamists can lose hearts and minds. Both al Qaeda and the Taliban, imbued with Wahhabi fanaticism, are stern enforcers of sharia law. Additionally, the al Qaeda elements are alien, like the Western forces. Once the Islamists take over a village or district, they typically impose their radical seventh-century justice. They might kill community leaders, or anyone else who defies their authority,[20] and force local women into marriage with Islamist men. Thus, they rule by fear and indoctrinate by impregnation. They discriminate against women, trying to keep them homebound and uneducated. They also penalize petty offenses by flogging and punish thievery by cutting off hands or arms. That sort of enforcement wins them little love among the populace and leaves an opening for the NATO forces. However, if the West should respond to the Islamist presence by attacking the larger community, especially with reckless air raids, they risk alienating the villagers and uniting them in common defense with the fanatics. David Kilcullen, the Australian advocate of this approach, is bitterly opposed to the use of drones because it kills civilians and drives survivors into the hands of the militants. It is better, he says, to reach out to local leaders who might be looking to rid the community of the Islamists. In just that way the surge succeeded in Iraq, and that formula is being tested again in Afghanistan.[21] There is just one small hitch in Kilcullen's critique: the American side has basically adopted his approach in Afghanistan, but the drone missiles are fired primarily in Pakistan.

If Obama's war is more legitimate than Bush's, it is no less dangerous and potentially damaging to American security. If the United States stays too long in Afghanistan, Obama will sacrifice more American and Afghan lives and waste trillions more dollars. If he should withdraw prematurely, it could lead to a Taliban takeover in Afghanistan or possibly in nuclear-armed Pakistan. Al Qaeda could once again be the Taliban's honored guest, this time, perhaps, under a nuclear cloud. Then Obama could be trapped in a hole as big as, if not bigger than, the one Bush dug for himself in Iraq.

In this book, I will examine the prospects for the success of "Obama's war" by reviewing the current status of America as the world's predominant power, perhaps the greatest military power in history, albeit with an Achilles' heel that is exposed in small wars. Then I will look back at the growth of the Islamist movement, including the impact of global terrorism, and forward in more detail at how the ongoing conflict can be fought with the open hand of friendship to Islam and the clenched fist of hostility to Islamism. A chapter is also devoted to the threat of nuclear terrorism.

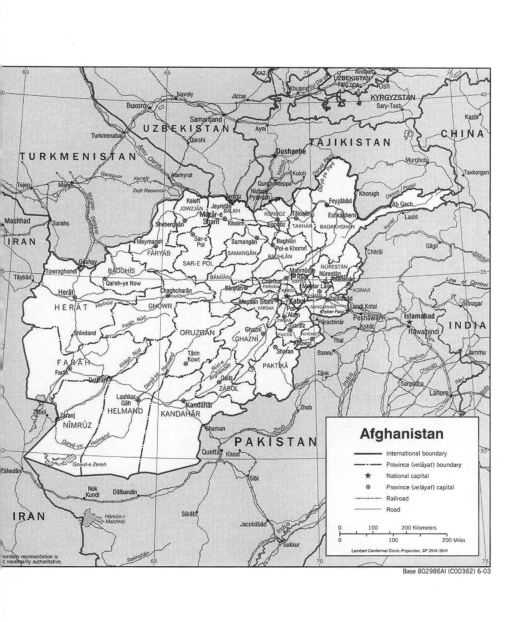

Afghanistan

- International boundary
- ·—·—· Province (velāyat) boundary
- ★ National capital
- ⊙ Province (velāyat) capital
- +++ Railroad
- Road

0 — 100 — 200 Kilometers
0 — 100 — 200 Miles

Lambert Conformal Conic Projection, SP 29 N/39 N

1

A PARADOX OF POWER

America prepared for decades to meet the mighty Soviet Union in a titanic war on a European battlefield—a war that, fortunately, did not happen. Yet, even given this preparation, America has struggled in small, unconventional wars against insurgents. Currently, the pattern is being repeated in Afghanistan. Before that it was repeated in Iraq. Earlier a similar scenario had played out in Vietnam and, going back to the early twentieth century, in the Philippines. A wise man once said, "Those who cannot remember the past are condemned to repeat it."[1] Why is it so easy to forget the pain of small wars?

The United States is not alone, if that is any consolation. Since 1945, the year the United Nations came into being and adopted in its charter the principle of self-determination, several great powers have fought losing struggles against determined insurgents. Britain and France lost their colonial empires, sometimes in bloody conflict, in restive places like Palestine, Vietnam, and Algeria. The Soviet Union occupied Afghanistan for most of the 1980s but, unable to defeat the mujahideen, ultimately withdrew. Israel invaded Lebanon in 1982 to quash terrorist attacks by the Palestine Liberation Organization and stayed as occupiers in southern Lebanon for nearly two decades before pulling out in 2000 under persistent guerrilla attacks from the Islamist Hezbollah.

Now in the seventh decade of the age of self-determination, the United States has inserted troops into Afghanistan. The richest, most powerful nation in the world has intervened militarily in one of the poorest to deflect the terrorist challenge posed by Islamist fanatics. The reader need only reflect on the 9/11 atrocity to understand. In 2001 the Taliban ruled Afghanistan and allowed al Qaeda to operate terrorist training camps. Individuals who trained there participated in attacks on America and other nations in Asia, Africa, and Europe. It is within the right of self-defense for America to do what it can to keep another attack from happening. But the struggle against al Qaeda has shaped up as a tough fight. This book will cover the details of the efforts in Afghanistan and neighboring Pakistan as the narrative goes along. In this chapter, it touches on America's great power and the quagmires created by our participation in small wars.

TWO CENTURIES OF GROWTH

The urge to expand seems always to have dwelled within the American psyche. Canada was urged to join the American Revolution in 1776–81 and again to fight against Britain in the War of 1812. Both times Canada rebuffed the American advances. The Louisiana Purchase from France in 1803 doubled the U.S. land mass and pushed the frontier to the Pacific Ocean. A later compromise fixed the northern border at the forty-ninth parallel. The sun and sands of eastern Florida were bought from Spain in 1819. Texas was first colonized by immigrants from the United States who wrested control of it from Mexico and appealed to Washington for annexation. It became the twenty-eighth state in 1845. The Mexican War, fought partly over the price America should pay for Texas, followed. After a one-sided war that brought Mexico to its knees, the United States acquired not only the Texas territory to the Rio Grande River but most of today's southwestern states for $20 million. In 1853 the United States bought a further strip of land from Mexico that fixed the present southern borders of New Mexico and Arizona. The Alaska Purchase from Russia was carried out in 1867 for about $2 an acre—more than 375 million acres at a cost of $7.2 million.

Expansion up to this point came largely through the addition of adjoining territories and the defeat of native tribes trying to defend their land. Even Alaska, though not contiguous, involved land on the North American continent. After the Civil War, the United States began its imperialist outreach by acquiring islands in the Pacific and Caribbean. Midway Island, northwest of Hawaii, became an American possession in 1867. A decade later the United States obtained the right to use the Samoan harbor of Pago Pago, and in another three decades it added the entire island of Tutuila, where Pago Pago is located. The Hawaiian Islands fell gradually into the American grasp, starting with a free trade agreement in 1875 that benefited American owners of Hawaiian sugar plantations. Mission schools there planted the ideas of Christianity and American power. In 1887 the U.S. Navy established a coaling station at Pearl Harbor, and six years later the American minister on the scene, John L. Stevens, engineered a coup d'etat against Queen Liliuokalani. Initially, Congress resisted annexation and Theodore Roosevelt lamented the legislators' "queer lack of imperial instinct,"[2] but it finally came in 1898.

After another one-sided war, this one against Spain in 1898, America gained possession of Puerto Rico in the Greater Antilles and the far-off Philippine Islands in the western Pacific. At the same time, America added tiny Wake Island and Guam, as if it were laying down stepping stones to the Far East. The American Virgin Islands east and southeast of Puerto Rico were purchased from Denmark in 1916. The Philippines turned out to be a blood acquisition. The Filipino people were pleased to be rid of Spanish colonialism but not happy to trade it for the American brand. The easy victory over Spain devolved into a bloody Filipino insurrection that took four thousand American lives and cost $600 million at a time when that was a lot of money. At least 200,000 Filipinos lost their lives in the fighting, which raged intensely for three years and resurfaced sporadically for another thirteen. In 1942 Japan captured the Philippines and occupied it until 1945, when America reconquered it, only to free it the following year. (Three generations later America easily captured Iraq and then met with a similar formidable resistance from Iraqi insurgents aided by outside Islamists. The adventure cost more than four thousand U.S. military personnel killed; tens of thousands severely wounded; hundreds of thousands emotionally distressed; millions of Iraqis killed, wounded, or displaced; and hundreds of billions of dollars drained from the U.S. treasury. American policymakers appeared to have learned nothing about imperial overreach from their Philippines experience a century earlier.)

In 1903 America sent troops to the Isthmus of Panama in support of a Panamanian rebellion for independence from Colombia, which America had stirred up. The new Panamanian state that emerged granted a ten-mile-wide strip of land from the Caribbean to the Pacific for construction of the Panama Canal, completed in 1914 and controlled by the United States until 1979. For the rest of Central America and the Caribbean Islands, the United States pursued a policy of "indirect control" through U.S. business interests and a succession of Latin American dictatorships. President Woodrow Wilson, before and during World War I, believed these neighbors could be taught democracy, but with the notable exception of democratic Costa Rica, the reality did not measure up to the wish through most of the twentieth century.

It seemed for a time that America's appetite for acquisition had been satisfied. At least, it was out of sight, if never far beneath the surface. It bubbled up during World War II, when the Pentagon drew up a list of postwar international bases that would extend American influence across the Atlantic and Pacific oceans. That war marked the beginning of American hegemony in the modern sense. America put 9 million men and women under arms; fought the war in two major theaters, Europe and the Pacific; built the atomic bomb and demonstrated its awesome power by twice dropping it on Japan in 1945; and emerged as the leader of the noncommunist world.

Possession of the atomic bomb made America the most feared nation on earth until the Soviet Union, its spies having stolen the atomic secrets, exploded its own bomb four years later. That ended the American monopoly and ignited the cold war. America first tested a more powerful hydrogen bomb in 1952, and the Soviets followed in 1955 with their own H-bomb and in 1961 exploded a fifty-megaton hydrogen bomb, the largest thermonuclear blast in history. Then the two superpowers concentrated on building their nuclear inventories and delivery systems with the capacity for either to wipe the other off the face of the earth, leading to a stalemate condition known as mutually assured destruction (MAD) in which each side held the other at bay with long-range bombers continuously airborne and nuclear-tipped intercontinental ballistic missiles pointed at strategic enemy targets. They came close to a nuclear holocaust in October 1962, when America discovered that the Soviets were installing short- and medium-range missiles in Cuba that could deliver atomic devastation to much of America. Both backed down with face-saving concessions from the other: the Soviets agreed to withdraw their missiles from Cuba; the Americans agreed not to invade Cuba and to remove their allegedly obsolete missiles in Turkey, which had been aimed at the Soviet Union.

Life went on under the nuclear cloud while the two superpowers competed to advance their respective capitalist and communist systems. Immediately after World War II the Soviet Union took what the Red Army had given it by imposing communist regimes throughout Eastern Europe. The United States reacted to the threat of further Soviet advances, first by implementing the Marshall Plan to stimulate economic recovery in war-torn Western Europe and then by forming a military alliance, the North Atlantic Treaty Organization (NATO). The Soviets countered with their own military alliance, known as the Warsaw Pact. The two powers faced off in divided Germany, with neither side willing to touch off the spark that would ignite Armageddon. They talked about whittling down their nuclear stockpiles while hurling rhetorical bombs, and they engaged in proxy wars.

In 1949 the Soviet proxy, communist China, drove the American proxy, nationalist China, off the Asian mainland to the island of Taiwan. America took no part militarily in the Chinese civil war. A year later the Soviet proxy, North Korea, invaded the American proxy, South Korea, and almost overran the entire Korean peninsula. This time America reacted by sending U.S. troops to secure a foothold at Pusan on the southeast corner of South Korea and persuaded the United Nations to condemn the attack. Joined by several of its allies under the UN banner, U.S. troops surged forward almost to the Chinese border and then fell back after Chinese troops poured across the Yalu River into Korea. Hostilities ceased with a painfully negotiated truce about where the belligerents had begun three years earlier. America did not win or lose the war, but it staved off the loss of South Korea.

In Vietnam, after France lost its colony to the communist Viet Minh in 1954, the United States stepped in to halt the "falling dominoes" of communist expansion by creating the government of South Vietnam. America handpicked the new South Vietnamese leader, Ngo Dinh Diem; taught him the trappings of democracy; supplied advisers to train his army; and blocked an election agreed to at Geneva peace talks between France and the Viet Minh to unify Vietnam. Ultimately, unhappy with its student, the Kennedy administration approved a coup d'etat that resulted, to its dismay, in Diem's murder. A communist-led insurgency carried out by the Viet Cong had welled up against Diem and his successors in South Vietnam, and as it gained momentum, America continued to increase its cadre of advisers, until in 1965 President Lyndon Johnson committed combat troops to the war effort. The force exceeded half a million at the height of the U.S. troop deployment in 1968. Despite the launching of search-and-destroy missions, the all-out bombing of North Vietnam, the use of herbicides to defoliate the forests, and the burning of peasant villages, the powerful U.S. Army and Air Force were unable to defeat the Viet Cong insurgents and North Vietnamese army. The Soviets could not have been more pleased at the American quagmire. They supplied the Vietnamese with weapons and ammunition. The United States withdrew by the spring of 1973, having lost 58,000 military personnel and with its collective ego in tatters.

Within a decade of America's departure from Vietnam, the Soviet Union fell into a similar trap in Afghanistan, which Soviet troops occupied in December 1979 in order to save it for communism. The Soviets spent most of the 1980s trying to quell a preexisting rebellion against Kabul authority. They used scorched-earth tactics against a rural population sympathetic to the rebels, creating six million refugees who fled to Pakistan and Iran. The CIA set up shop in Pakistan and supplied the Afghan fighters with weapons, including Stinger surface-to-air missiles that denied the Soviets close helicopter support of ground operations and turned the tide of battle. The Soviets withdrew in 1989, and soon afterward the Soviet hold on Eastern Europe came loose, and the Soviet Union itself fell apart.

Thus, curiously, while the two great superpowers stood each other down in central Europe, building their armaments and fine-tuning their weapons in anticipation of World War III, which never happened, each suffered defeat at the hands of local insurgents. The United States managed to cope with its adversity, but the USSR did not. After the Soviet Union broke up and its constituent states became independent nations, Germany reunited and Europe became a closer-knit free-market community. In a development that the new Russia has considered provocative, NATO expanded eastward to absorb nine countries formerly integrated into the Soviet orbit, including three small Baltic nations that were once Soviet states. America, the NATO leader, was left standing as the world's sole superpower.

MILITARY POWER

The United States, with its global presence, must now be considered one of the most powerful nations in history, comparable to the Persian, Roman, and Mongol empires (all of which, incidentally, crumbled in turn). The U.S. military force is enhanced with technological tools the great conquerors of the past could not have imagined. In the *Base Structure Report* (*BSR*) for fiscal year 2008 (beginning September 30, 2007), the Pentagon listed 5,415 Army, Navy, Air Force, and Marine Corps bases. Of these, 4,654 were in the United States and its territories, and 761 were located in 39 foreign countries, up from 702 in 38 foreign countries in FY 2003. Most of the more recent foreign sites were in Germany (268), Japan (124), and South Korea (87). That left 282 bases in 36 other foreign countries around the globe. The bases outside America varied in size from the giant Ramstein base in Germany to tiny intelligence listening posts of perhaps a half dozen personnel.[3] These cannot be exact figures because the *BSR* did not list bases in Afghanistan or Iraq, where America was conducting two unconventional wars that required several bases for American and allied forces. (Steve Coll, writing in the *New Yorker* in late summer 2008, reported 61 bases and about 250 smaller outposts in Iraq.[4]) Nor did it include bases in Central Asia for logistical support of the Afghan War or secret bases said to exist in Israel's Negev Desert.[5]

The quality of the American arsenal is even more impressive. Robert Dujarric and the late William E. Odom summed up the American performance in recent wars in their book, *America's Inadvertent Empire*.[6] Odom climbed the army career ladder to three-star general and served as director of the National Security Agency from 1985 to 1988 during the Reagan administration. Upon his retirement he became a leading scholar on the status of the U.S. military. In their book, he and Dujarric found that the superbly trained American fighter pilots totally dominated the skies over Iraq during the Gulf War (1990–91), while the bombing of strategic targets deep inside Iraq and the tactical support of ground forces were largely ineffective, despite "show and tell" videos for public consumption that demonstrated precision bombing in its early stage of development. Precision bombing in support of ground troops during the Afghan and Iraqi wars a decade later, however, was markedly improved with advances in stealth, laser, and global positioning technology.

The U.S. Navy, Odom and Dujarric concluded, is far superior to any other navy in the world, but in the Gulf War it "provided nothing essential to coalition operations." The Navy positioned three aircraft carriers in the Persian Gulf and three in the Red Sea, but carrier-based aircraft had to fly long distances to their targets, so their time in the war zone was limited. Half of their most modern aircraft, the F/A-18, flew out of a land base in Bahrain. The performance of Navy aircraft improved as they became better integrated in combined operations during the later wars. But Odom and Dujarric leave the impression that it probably would not have mattered if the Navy had not participated at all. The Navy, however, had little else to do. There have been no great sea battles since World War II, and there are none in prospect in the coming decades. For that unlikely event, the Navy is armed to the teeth.

The starring role in the 1991 Gulf War and later in the Iraq invasion of 2003 belonged to the ground forces and their modern computerized weapons. In particular, the M1A2 tank proved the most potent weapon on the fields of battle. With global positioning devices, other high-tech equipment, and the heavy 120-millimeter main gun, the M1A2 could identify an enemy tank at a distance of two and a half miles—out of sight—and knock it out at two and a quarter miles with one round. The enemy tank crew would not see their attacker or know what hit them. Other American weapon systems, including the Bradley armored vehicle, the multiple rocket launcher system, and the Apache attack helicopter, also fared well in the Odom-Dujarric appraisal. Ground and helicopter-support forces knocked out 85 to 90 percent of Iraqi tanks destroyed in the Gulf War, according to statistics presented by Odom and Dujarric. Airpower accounted for the other 10 to 15 percent at a much higher price tag.[7]

During these wars the U.S. Air Force won kudos for its airlift capabilities. After the Iraqi army overran Kuwait in 1990, posing a threat to the oil fields in Saudi Arabia, the Air Force transported seven Army divisions, two Marine divisions, two armored cavalry regiments, and an armored brigade—nearly half a million personnel, their equipment, and support facilities to meet immediate needs—from the United States and Europe to the Arabian desert, a Herculean task that equaled, if not surpassed, anything like it up to that time, including World War II, Korea, and Vietnam. Other supplies of less pressing need were brought by sea.

Just before the ground offensive began early in 1991, the Air Force secretly transported the XVIII Airborne Corps and allied ground forces to attack positions west of the main front. At launch, the U.S. tanks, blasting everything in their path, moved out at thirty to forty miles an hour, and within a few hours they were attacking the main force of Iraqi defenders from the rear. The offensive lasted less than a hundred hours and ended with the demolition of Saddam Hussein's army.

When the United States invaded Iraq in 2003, Turkey refused to allow the use of their territory to launch a second front from the north. So, with America in complete control of the skies over Iraq, the 173rd Airborne Brigade seized an airfield north of Kirkuk, which the army used as its northern "landhead." Within a week, wide-body C-17 transport aircraft, big enough to carry heavy equipment, brought in M1A2 tanks and Bradley armored vehicles, which were soon headed south to close the pincer on Baghdad. Odom and Dujarric saw this as a demonstration of a new technique for forced entry into a hostile country, which might negate the need for sea invasions such as those famously carried out in World War II.

Work on precision weapons continues. Laser-guided bombs routed the Taliban and al Qaeda in the opening drives of the Afghan War in late 2001. The Iraq invasion of 2003 began with a long-range missile bombardment of a place in Bagdad where Saddam Hussein was reported to be hiding out. The missiles hit their target from hundreds of miles distant. The target was devastated, and the system therefore validated, even though Saddam was not there. Three years later Abu Musab al-Zarqawi, the leader of al Qaeda in Iraq, was dispatched with a precision air strike on his safe house north of Bagdad.

In Afghanistan, where the political barriers to cross-border pursuit of the Taliban and al Qaeda in their Pakistan sanctuaries frustrated NATO ground troops, the Americans were putting up pilotless drones equipped with state-of-the-art intelligence gear and armed with deadly missiles to seek out and assassinate al Qaeda and Pakistani Taliban militants. The drones, guided from afar by CIA technicians in safe war rooms laden with gee-whiz electronics, have killed several high-ranking Islamist leaders. The U.S. Army and Marine Corps in Afghanistan and Iraq have been equipped with a powerful new artillery weapon called HIMARS (High Mobility Artillery Rocket System), rocket launchers mounted on mobile platforms that can fire a smorgasbord of projectiles from one big bomb to many small "bomblets" up to forty-five miles with pinpoint accuracy guided by GPS (global positioning system).[8] The *New York Times* reported in October 2010 that HIMARS helped rout Taliban forces in Afghanistan's Kandahar Province from well-defended positions, which retreated to sanctuary in Pakistan or blended in with the local population.[9]

Evidence surfaced in the summer of 2009 of heightened alarm in the al Qaeda camp. Abu Yahya al-Libi, a senior al Qaeda commander, wrote in a book titled *Guidance on the Ruling of the Muslim Spy* that the CIA was recruiting local spies and operating pilotless drones to gather intelligence and fire deadly missiles. Libi's book cited the use of electronic homing devices to guide air-launched missiles, according to Steven Aftergood of the Federation of American Scientists.[10]

Even as this book, *Obama's War*, was being written, the Pentagon was testing unmanned ground vehicles to carry out search-and-destroy missions in advance of ground troops under a $127 billion Pentagon program called Future Combat Systems, the costliest Defense Department program in history. Young soldiers were being taught to control the intelligence vehicles in a manner reminiscent of their childhood arcade games. In future wars, presumably, robots will do the fighting.

UNINTENDED CONSEQUENCES

When America emerged as top dog of the capitalist world after World War II, the acquisitiveness that peaked in the late nineteenth century gave way over time to interventionism. In fact, America's largest colonial acquisition, the Philippines, gained its independence in 1946, only a year or two later than scheduled under a timeline established by the Tydings-McDuffie Act of 1934. That did not end the Philippines' American experience, however. In 1947 the United States signed the Military Bases Agreement, which allowed it to keep twenty-three bases on Philippine territory for ninety-nine years rent free. These generous terms, which provoked outrage among the Filipino population, were pared down over the years until 1991, when the closing of Clark Air Force Base and Subic Bay Naval Base finally ended the American military presence on the islands.

While they existed, Clark and Subic Bay were part of a network of bases that contributed to post–World War II American dominance in the western Pacific. They also gave rise to a Filipino sense of insecurity and subservience to American ambition. On the seemlier side, they brought about unwelcome underground industries. The town of Olongapo, adjacent to Subic Bay, had only one business activity, euphemistically called "entertainment," with approximately 55,000 prostitutes and 2,182 establishments offering "rest and recreation" to American service personnel.[11] Angeles City near Clark Air Force Base could at the time have been considered the drug capital of the Philippines.[12]

These by-products of American hegemony could also be found at other overseas bases. Katharine Moon described the camp towns that characterize American bases in South Korea as "dimly lit alleys blinking with neon-lit bars [that] rock with loud country-western or disco music, drunken brawls, and American soldiers in fatigues and heavily made-up Korean women with their hands on each other's buttocks."[13] Chalmers Johnson took note of the "massive military facilities, post exchanges, dependents' housing estates, swimming pools, and golf courses, and associated bars, strip clubs, whorehouses and venereal disease clinics" that go with the establishment of large military bases. "They can extend for miles," he said, "dominating localities and in some cases whole nations."[14]

His prime example was Okinawa, with its heavy U.S. military presence. Johnson characterized the island as having been "occupied" by the United States since 1945, when it was captured in a bloody three-month battle at a cost of 14,000 American servicemen and 234,000 Japanese soldiers and civilians killed. Strategically located in the Ryukyu chain southwest of the Japanese main islands, Okinawa served as a vital forward base for American operations in the Korean and Vietnamese wars. The U.S. military ruled Okinawa directly until 1972 and then turned it over to the Japanese government under a security treaty that ensured continued American operation of the bases, which take up 20 percent of the island's 454 square miles of land. Through more than six decades of occupation, the American military has subjected Okinawans to fatal traffic accidents from drunken American drivers, noise pollution from military planes taking off and landing, and the rape of local women. About twice as many reported rapes per capita occur in Okinawa as in the United States. In Okinawa, according to Johnson, that figure is mostly GIs raping local women.[15] In 1995 two marines and a sailor abducted a twelve-year-old girl on her way home from shopping, beat her, and bound and gagged her. One admitted to raping her.[16] American damage control did not easily still the voices of protest. By this time the cold war was over, and the need for the American bases there and elsewhere to contain the communist powers could be called into question. Yet they remain, to protect the American people against . . . what?

Vietnam was another American tragedy. The American forces afflicted it with the usual bases, post exchanges, and dependents' housing, and attracted the usual camp towns with seedy bars, legions of prostitutes, and plagues of venereal disease. They dropped more bombs on Vietnam (North and South) than on enemy targets in World War II. They also employed napalm, fire bombs that caused horrible deaths, and Agent Orange, a carcinogenic defoliant. They set fire to villages and occasionally murdered women and children. By North Vietnamese estimates, at least 2 million Vietnamese civilians were killed on both sides of the war, plus 1.1 million North Vietnamese army and Viet Cong fighters. About 250,000 South

Vietnamese soldiers and 58,000 American service men and women also died. If Laotian and Cambodian losses are added, the total goes up by about a million.[17] The U.S. invasion of Cambodia failed militarily and led to the deranged slaughter of innocents by the Khmer Rouge. Near the end of the American involvement and after the intention to withdraw was announced publicly, the U.S. Army began to fall apart. Discipline was harder to maintain, GI drug abuse was rampant with narcotics supplied by corrupt South Vietnamese officers, and fragging incidents (attacks on higher-ranking officers) were on the rise. No one wanted to be the last to die in a lost war.

America did not long remember the lesson of Vietnam. In 2003 the Bush administration, convinced of its supremacy and the rightness of its cause, invaded Iraq for allegedly taking part in the 2001 attack on America and threatening America with weapons of mass destruction (WMDs). The premises were entirely false. Iraq did not participate in the 9/11 attack and no longer possessed WMDs. The best that can be said for the Bush team's rush to war is that it acted before it knew the facts. In reality, it twisted the facts before it acted. The Iraq experience proved two things already known to history: (1) great powers such as America can easily defeat an inferior army in conventional battle, and (2) occupying powers such as America are vulnerable when fighting local insurgents.

Every army has its camp followers, and the U.S. military is no exception. But the grievous offense given "host" countries besmears America's good name. The end of the cold war should have brought an end to the American occupation of Okinawa, and the Pentagon should clean up its act in South Korea.

The conquest of Iraq by American and British forces joined by smaller detachments from a so-called coalition of the willing took three weeks in a classic conventional campaign of superior arms and trained personnel. On May 1, 2003, about three weeks after American tanks rolled into Baghdad, President Bush was flown in a Navy S-3B Viking training jet thirty miles off the coast of California to the aircraft carrier USS *Eisenhower*, which was returning from the war zone. Striding from the plane side by side with the young pilot, he was wearing a flight suit for his photo op. In a speech on the flight deck in front of a banner that read, "Mission Accomplished," he declared, "The United States and our allies have prevailed." An insurgency in Iraq that continued to escalate for four years, until it finally started tailing off in 2007, followed. Of the more than four thousand deaths to American forces in Iraq, 98 percent occurred after the president's victory speech. The only justification left for this costly strategic blunder was to turn Iraq into a beacon of democracy in the stormy sea of Arab tribalism. That dubious experiment in nation-building was ongoing as this manuscript was being written.

Sunni insurgents, joined by outside Islamist fanatics who infiltrated though Iraq's porous borders, were the main antagonists of the occupying powers. Roadside bombs planted at night and detonated during the day as military vehicles passed proved to be the most effective weapon and caused the most American and coalition casualties. Shia militia, including the Mahdi Army of Sheikh Muqtada al-Sadr, participated off and on in the violence. Neighboring Iran gained influence inside Iraq, supplying weapons and advice to some Shia militia. The ideologically committed Islamists proved to be the most vicious, even grotesque, fighters in their pursuit of terrorism, but they were so rigid in their interpretation of the Koran that they made enemies out of the Sunni tribes in western Iraq with whom they were allied. That gave the Americans a golden opportunity to reverse the fortunes of war. This turnaround will be reviewed in a later chapter. We go back in history now to gain a better understanding of the enemy we face.

2

THE ROOTS OF ISLAMISM

Before 9/11 most Americans knew little or nothing about Islam. Since that terrifying event, they know Islam for suicide bombers who take innocent lives, roadside bombs that kill GIs, and the perverse delight exhibited by many youthful Palestinians at the murder of nearly three thousand people at the World Trade Center and Pentagon. That gives them a distorted image of Islam, a great religion with more than a billion followers, of which Islamism is a tiny radical version. Islamism is the focus here. It is unfathomable to a Western mind why someone would use suicide as a war weapon and exult in the slaughter of innocents, which is repugnant to the human conscience. These conundrums are met in the Islamist war against the West. This chapter is offered in the belief that something can be gained by examining the culture that produced the suicide bomber. It is neither an apology for nor a censure of the atrocities committed. It seeks only to understand them in their own context because, if analyzed through the prism of Western democratic standards, they are reprehensible. It is important to bear in mind, therefore, that the suicide bomber reflects the values of seventh-century tribal societies and that most of the billion-plus Muslims of the twenty-first century have accepted the concepts of equality, tolerance, beneficence, and piety preached by the Prophet Muhammad in defiance of the pagan culture of his time.

Suicide is forbidden under Islamic law, according to most scholars on the subject. The rationale goes something like this: to take one's own life violates God's will, because God, the giver of life, is the only one entitled to end it.[1] But some argue in our modern world that a person living in an oppressed society can use his/her own body as a weapon, as long as no harm is done to innocent civilians. Islamists (the radicals who leveled the World Trade Center and damaged the Pentagon) pay no heed to such rhetorical niceties. Osama bin Laden said in a declaration of war against the United States that any American is fair game. Most of those killed in the 9/11 attack were innocent civilians. So how do the Islamists get around such widely accepted prohibitions against suicide? They tout the suicide bomber as a martyr on the fast track to paradise. Martyrdom was condoned by no less an authority than the prophet Muhammad. The first Muslim martyr died on the battlefield at Badr in 624. Today, Islamists consider their struggle to be a war against the oppressors of Islam, just as Muhammad and his followers fought against the pagans arrayed against them.

Islam, which means "submission," is monotheistic, just like Judaism and Christianity. Muhammad traced its heritage back to Abraham, who, God is quoted as saying in the Scriptures, would be "the ancestor of a multitude of nations" (Gen. 17:4).[2] The Judeo-Christian line of descent came through Isaac, the product of Abraham's union with his wife, Sarah, when he was a hundred years old and she, ninety. The Islamic heritage, as Muhammad perceived it, derived from Ishmael, the son of Abraham and Sarah's Egyptian slave girl, Hagar, whom Abraham had impregnated thirteen years earlier when it appeared Sarah would never conceive. When Sarah finally had her own child, Isaac, she wanted Hagar and Ishmael out of her life. So, Abraham sent them away. God promised to make a nation for Ishmael as well as Isaac and looked after the banished mother and child as they wandered in the desert. Hagar eventually found Ishmael an Egyptian wife, and the Islamic civilization was on its way. That much is in the Old Testament (Gen. 16:1–21:20).[3]

TRADITIONAL VALUES

In the tribal societies of ancient Arabia, there was no such thing as a state. No penal code existed to punish murder. "The only protection for any man's life," wrote French scholar Maxime Rodinson, "was the certainty, established by custom, that it would be dearly bought: blood for blood and a life for a life. Undying shame attached to the man whom tradition designated as the avenger if he allowed a murderer to live. The vendetta . . . is one of the pillars of Bedouin society."[4] Such was the superiority of tribal bonds over the precise application of justice for the individual that the vendetta could be satisfied in the killing of any member of the offender's tribe, not necessarily the actual murderer. The vendetta, though not unique to Islam, has remained an essential part of Islamic culture. In a modern parallel, Osama bin Laden, resenting the American military presence in his native Saudi Arabia, sought to satisfy the vendetta by calling on his followers to kill any American, even if that person had no connection to the hated U.S. intervention.

Muhammad superimposed Islam over the values of tribal Arabia, and with the religion came the concepts of *jihad* (holy war), *shahid* (martyr), *umma* (community), and *sharia* (Islamic law). Beyond monotheism, the first principle of Islam, Muhammad taught that Muslims must engage in struggle (jihad) to achieve the perfect community (umma). "Jihad" is the generic term for struggle, internal and external, peaceful and warlike. Holy war, which Muhammad waged during most of his time in Medina, is only part of the struggle, and to most Muslims, it is not the most important part. Once, when Muhammad was returning from battle, he said, "We return from the little jihad to the greater jihad"[5]—the latter being the internal struggle against our darker human instincts. Many Muslims today see the lesser jihad, holy war, as a sacred duty. Michael Scheuer, a former head of the CIA's Bin Laden Unit, cites Dr. Mohammed Abd al-Halim of al-Azhar University in Cairo, who said, "Jihad in Islam is one of the greatest actions to repulse tyranny and to restore justice and rights."[6]

Martyrdom in the Islamic tradition goes hand in hand with holy war. "Wars come to provide martyrs and that God may prove those who believe," says the Koran. "Paradise is only to be attained when God knows who will really strive and endure."[7] The first Muslim martyrs died on Muhammad's initial battlefield, an oasis west of Medina called Badr. Muhammad declared that God would admit into paradise any of his followers who died fighting that day in 624. On hearing this, a young follower noshing dates, Umayr ibn al Humam, fully convinced that Muhammad was the messenger of God, cried out, "Is there nothing between me and paradise but to be killed by these men?" He dropped the dates, took up his sword, and plunged into the enemy line, slashing with all his fury until he died a shahid and took his trip to paradise, leaving his blood-soaked body on the battlefield.[8]

A modern martyr of note in the belief system of radical Islam is what we in the West call the suicide bomber. Suicide bombers' motivation is difficult for the secular mind to grasp, but there can be no doubt that their offer of sacrifice is a potent weapon available to Islamist leaders. It might be useful for the reader to think of martyrdom in the context of the communist revolution, which projects a competing totalitarian worldview. Suicide bombing would be an impossible weapon for communist believers because communism offers redemption, or at least uplift in this world for which suicide would be counterproductive, whereas radical Islam promises salvation after martyrdom, which no living person can refute from experience.

The modern Islamist movement, with its reverence for jihad and shahid, is in no small measure a reaction to the Muslims' direct experience with European colonialism, including Zionism. Contrary to an often-repeated misconception, the Islamist goal is not the grandeur of the Arabian empire, but the idealized realm of pure Islam, characterized by equality, justice, humility, and devotion to God. Allegedly, that realm existed for less than four decades, a tiny blip of history, from 622, the year of Muhammad's flight from Mecca, until 661, upon the death of Ali, the last of four "right-guided" caliphs who presided over Islam after the prophet died in 632. Those were the golden years of the umma, the Muslim community that Muhammad created from his conversations with God and His angels, a community divinely inspired, with equality and justice for all mankind—or so it is said. This period is also known as the True Islam of the Salaf, the Salafis being Muhammad and the first four successive caliphs, who knew him personally during his life. In modern times, the strictest adherents to Wahhabism and the most uncompromising Islamic terrorists think of themselves as Salafi.

The ideals of justice and equality remain core values of Islam. Muhammad enunciated a principle of racial equality in his last pilgrimage to Mecca: "You are all descended from Adam and Adam was [born] of the earth. . . . An Arab is superior to a non-Arab in nothing but devotion."[9] These core values go a long way toward explaining Islam's mass appeal.

When the core values of justice and equality, together with that impervious vestige of tribal Arabia, the vendetta, are held up in the light of Western dominance of the Middle East, it is easier to see the rationale for jihad and shahid. It can all be summed up in one four-letter word: rage. Islamic law, the sharia, which governs the divine kingdom on earth, is compiled from the Koran (the revealed word of God), the Sunnah (the exemplary life of Muhammad), and the Hadith (the sayings of Muhammad).[10] And though it was given to the prophet in the seventh century of the Christian calendar, Islamists do not necessarily consider it seventh-century law. They believe it is eternal, immutable, and universal, a formula for living for all mankind for all time. All the Islamist thinkers covered in this chapter—Muhammad Wahhab, Hasan al-Banna, Mawlana Mawdudi, and Sayyid Qutb—propounded a Muslim obligation to bring divine law to the entire world, Banna and Mawdudi by persuasion, Wahhab and Qutb by force. They all believed that God was on their side. Indeed, the Islamist movement has gained momentum in our time, which the West has failed so far to confront in the necessary depth.

THE ARABIAN BROTHERHOOD

Muhammad ibn (son of) Abd al-Wahhab, born in 1703 in a region of southeastern Arabia called the Nejd, studied Islamic jurisprudence in Mesopotamia and western Arabia before settling down in his homeland. In his late thirties, he worked as a *qadi*, a judge in sharia law. He was an activist judge. Following the example of the Prophet Muhammad, he renounced earthly pleasures—drinking, smoking, even prayer mats to kneel on—and led campaigns to destroy idolatrous objects, such as holy shrines or monuments to the dead. He condemned adultery, insisted that Muslims pray in the prescribed manner, and excoriated followers who showed indifference to the plight of widows and orphans. He taught, as Muhammad had taught, that no terrestrial object should come between the individual and God. In his zealotry he went beyond Imam Ahmed ibn Hanbal, who founded the strictest of four schools of Islamic law in the ninth century. Wahhab forbade his followers to pray to the saints and other holy men, including Muhammad, because he considered it polytheistic. "Pray to God and God alone," he said.[11]

About 1744 Wahhab took his rigorous brand of Islam to the oasis community of Dariyah, a few miles north of Riyadh. The tribal chief there, Muhammad ibn Saud, had heard Wahhab's message and invited him to be the qadi for the Saudi people. Thus the House of Saud and the Wahhabi sect were joined in an alliance that led twice to the conquest of Arabia. The strength of the alliance derives from Wahhabi doctrine, which turns political loyalty into a religious obligation and religious practice into political conformity. Each individual swears allegiance to the ruler to ensure redemption after death, while the ruler earns the followers' allegiance by leading according to the laws of God. The Wahhabi refer to their movement as "the call to unity" and to themselves as "the people of unity," or "Unitarians" (*muwahhidun*), out of their belief in a unified world under one God. The Wahhabi dispense with all dualities and triads, and, needless to say, all pluralities. Thus, beyond the rejection of any division between religion and politics, they refuse to recognize any class distinctions, national boundaries, or separate states.[12] If the strictest Wahhabi had their way, we would all be Wahhabi living Spartan lives focused on our obligations under divine law, or dead.

Wahhab taught jihad in the broadest sense, both the inner struggle of the individual to be worthy of God and the struggle to spread His word. Wahhab expected the Saudi tribesmen not only to purify themselves but also to reform their neighbors. If friendly persuasion failed, the jihad turned from the inner struggle to holy war. Wahhabi welcomed death in sacred battle because it offered martyrdom and a fast track to paradise. They were savage killers, yet devout Muslims. While engaged in a murderous rampage, they might stop a while for prayer and then go back to killing. They did not waste much time preaching. Anyone who refused to take the righteous path would be put to the sword. Often in their deadly zeal they did not offer even that choice.

Wahhabi tribesmen became the shock troops of the House of Saud. They made no distinction between holy war and aggression against their neighbors, and it was part of the culture to take plunder from the cities and villages they conquered. Soon they overran Riyadh, and before ibn Saud's death in 1765 they had subdued most of the neighboring tribes and extended their dominion over a large area of the interior. Zealous reformers followed zealous warriors. On the heels of military conquest, they established mosques and taught Wahhabi doctrine.[13]

Ibn Saud's son, Abdul Aziz ibn Muhammad, took over after his father's death and continued on the path of conquest and plunder. In 1801 he led his troops all the way to the environs of Baghdad, where they laid waste the town of Karbala. This was the burial place of Hussein, the Shia martyr and grandson of Muhammad slain in the seventh century for refusing to relinquish his claim to the Muslim caliphate. The Wahhabi marauders of 1801 desecrated Hussein's tomb, destroyed the temple, and butchered every male they could find, adult and child. It was their way of dealing with "polytheists."

The following year Abdul Aziz appointed his son, Saud, to lead a Wahhabi army in the invasion of the Hijaz, the region at the northern half of the Red Sea coast. First, they attacked the mile-high community of Taif, which is perched on the high ground above Mecca. As in Karbala, every male inhabitant was slaughtered, except those lucky enough to escape. From Taif the Wahhabi descended to the coastal plain and captured Mecca and Medina. When they entered these holiest of Muslim cities, they smashed shrines and icons, and dismantled a mosque consecrated to the memory of Muhammad and his family, where, to the Wahhabi, votive offerings and prayers to the saints smacked of polytheism.

One eyewitness account during this period gives a fascinating portrayal of these Islamic reformers. The witness was a Spaniard named Domingo Badia y Leblich, who assumed the guise of a Muslim and the Arab name Ali Bey al-Abbasi. In 1807 Ali Bey undertook the hajj to Mecca. It is believed that his real mission was to spy for Napoleon. While in Mecca one morning he saw about five thousand Wahhabi men enter the city twenty abreast in tight formation to perform the prescribed rites at the Kaaba, or holy shrine. "What men!" Ali Bey exclaimed in his journal. "Without any covering [other] than a small piece of cloth around their waist, except some few who had a napkin placed upon the left shoulder, that passed under the right arm, being naked in every other respect, with their [muskets] upon their shoulders, and their khanjears or large knives hung to their girdles." At the head of the column up to twenty mounted men carried lances twelve feet long. "Some uttered cries of holy joy, others recited prayers in a confused and loud voice."[14] Their performance inside the Kaaba was chaotic as they surged forward to kiss the sacred Black Rock, a meteorite that predates Muhammad and was first revered by pagans. At the Zamzam, a well with supposedly miraculous water, they grasped for the bucket and broke the system of ropes and pulleys that brings the water to the surface. So they formed a human chain down the well shaft to fetch the water as best they could.[15]

For a few years the Saudi-Wahhabi dynasty controlled most of Arabia, from Syria to Yemen, from the Red Sea to the Persian Gulf. Before long, the Ottoman Empire struck back. An Egyptian army sent by the government in Constantinople retook Medina in October 1812 and Mecca early in 1813. The Egyptians followed up with a cruel and bloody campaign to the Nejd that ended seven years later in total victory. The Saudi king, Abdullah ibn Muhammad, was taken in chains to Constantinople, and when he refused to renounce his Wahhabi faith, he was executed. Dariyah was reduced to rubble and never rebuilt. After the invaders left, the Saudis moved their capital down the road a few miles to Riyadh and carried on for most of the nineteenth century as just another desert tribe.

The fortunes of the Saud family reached their nadir in 1891. Driven from Riyadh by the Rashid, a rival tribe, the family retreated into the desert wilderness in the south and then took refuge in Kuwait. Early in 1902 Abdul Aziz ibn Abdul Rahman (better known as ibn Saud), then a strapping, broad-shouldered young lion standing well over six feet tall and later the long-reigning king of Saudi Arabia, led a few stouthearted warriors in a daring thrust to regain the family's power and pride. They crept into Riyadh in the dark of night and the next morning ambushed the Rashid governor, who was killed in the scuffle. The leaderless enemy garrison soon surrendered. Having recovered their old capital, the Saud family under Abdul Aziz carried on in the Arabian tradition of desert alliances and tribal wars. In two and a half decades they would reunite most of the Arabian Peninsula. Wahhabi holy warriors were once again the key to the re-expansion of the Saudi dynasty.

THE EGYPTIAN BROTHERHOOD

A religious movement, similar in substance to the Arabian *Ikhwan*, that sought a return to strict Muslim laws took root in twentieth-century Egypt. It started between the two world wars as a religious study group called *al-Ikhwan al-Muslimun* (the Muslim Brotherhood). Unlike the original Arabian *Ikhwan*, which was a pure desert bloom untouched by colonialism, the Egyptian movement, like Doeband-ism and the writings of Mawlana Mawdudi, represented an unambiguous rejection of Western secular values. At the time of its inception the Muslim Brotherhood urged, as an alternative to British colonialism, self-government under divine law. To a Muslim culture in the grip of imperialism, overshadowed by Western political and technological hegemony, the idea had great appeal. The unemployed and underemployed masses of Egypt shared little, if any, of the newly created wealth of modern life, and to make matters worse, the British colonial masters dominated the Egyptian government.

Hasan al-Banna, the founder of the Muslim Brotherhood, was born in 1906 in the Nile Delta town of al-Mahmudiyya, the eldest of five sons of a watch repairman and Islamic scholar-teacher.[16] Hasan was exceptionally bright and pious. It is said that he committed the Koran to memory at an early age. At twelve, in his first year of primary school, he joined the Society for Moral Behavior and soon became its leader.

When in 1919 Britain proclaimed Egypt to be its "protectorate," a euphemism for colony, Banna took part in anti-British demonstrations. When he turned fourteen, he entered primary teachers' training school, and two years later he scored highest in his class on a teacher training examination. He went on to higher education at the Dar al-Ulum (House of Sciences) in Cairo at the age of sixteen. By this time he was fully immersed in Sufism and joined the campus chapter of the Sufi Order of the Hasafiyya Brothers and attended the lectures of another religious group, the Islamic Society for the Nobility of Character. He organized students to preach at mosques, coffeehouses, and other meeting places for the purpose of bringing the faith to the people. Banna's exposure to Wahhabism came through one of his teachers, Rashid Rida, a follower of the rigorous Hanbal School of Law and admirer of the Saudi Ikhwan. Rida taught that the Muslim world had strayed from the true path of Islam, a condition that could be corrected only by a return to the Islam of the Salafi.[17] Upon completion of his courses in 1927 at the age of twenty-one, Banna promised in a graduation essay to oppose "the impact of western civilization . . . materialist philosophy, and [foreign] traditions" and to teach children and parents alike "the objectives of religion and the sources of their well-being and happiness in life." It was, he said, a "covenant between me and my God."[18]

That September he began teaching Arabic at a state primary school in Ismailia on the Suez Canal. True to his graduation pledge, he organized evening religious instruction for the parents, who, in the main, comprised lowly workers, bureaucrats, and shopkeepers. He also reached out to powerful religious and community groups. In this bustling commercial city alongside the international waterway, he grew more acutely aware of Egypt's colonial subjugation. British managers oversaw international ship traffic. British troops kept the peace. The British masters lived in luxury on the heights above the impoverished Egyptian masses.

In March 1928 he held the first meeting of the Muslim Brotherhood at his Ismailia home, with his brother, Muhammad, and five others attending. According to one account, all six were part of the British labor force in town. They came to Banna in despair at their status as "mere hirelings belonging to the foreigners" and asked that he show them "the path to the fatherland, the religion, and the nation, as you know it. . . . All that we desire now is to present you with all that we possess, to be acquitted by God of the responsibility [to find our own way], and for you to be responsible before Him for us and for what we must do." Together they took an oath to God to be "troops for the message of Islam."[19]

Their willingness to surrender their selfhood to Banna fit perfectly with his authoritarian nature. In 1945 he wrote a revised code for the Brotherhood, which required members to take a loyalty oath "to have complete confidence in [the Brotherhood's] leadership and to obey absolutely, under all circumstances."[20] While the "general guide" who assumed the leadership position had to be elected, no one doubted who that leader would be as long as Banna lived.

From the first meeting in 1928, Banna built a vibrant organization and ran it with skill and energy. Within four years fifty branches were established throughout Egypt, and Banna moved the headquarters to Cairo. By 1948, its twentieth anniversary year, the Muslim Brotherhood claimed a half million members and at least twice that many supporters.[21]

This impressive growth stands as a tribute to Banna's organizational and propaganda skills. He taught that Islam is more than a religion, that it is a total system, the final arbiter of life, all things to all people, for all time in every place, based on the revealed word of God in the Koran and the sayings of the Prophet Muhammad in the Hadith. At each branch he set up an office, a school, a mosque, a workshop, and a sporting club. He laid down three basic principles for expansion: (1) the indoctrination of followers, (2) the recruitment and organization of supporters, and (3) the implementation of the message, which is encapsulated in the motto "God is our purpose, the Prophet our leader, the Koran our constitution, jihad our way, and dying for God's cause our supreme objective."[22] He defined the "society" that he founded as "a Sunni way, a Sufi truth, a political organization, an athletic group, a cultural-educational union, an economic company, and a social idea." He created "rovers" to spread Islam and tried to organize them into "battalions," "each one equipped spiritually with faith and belief, intellectually with science and learning, and physically with training and athletics." Together they would "plunge through the oceans," "rend the skies," and "conquer every obstinate tyrant."[23] He had a way with words.

Banna was actually less militant than the slogan implies. His jihad was less holy war and more missionary zeal. He was a persuader—a spellbinder of an orator, not a military conqueror. He sought to bring around an overwhelming majority of the population so that the secular government would collapse from its loss of support and could be replaced by divine rule. Banna ran for parliament in 1944–45 and lost an election that he thought was rigged against him.

Generally he operated the Muslim Brotherhood legally and openly, but he also established in 1942 or 1943 an underground wing known internally as the "special section," which operated in small groups of no more than five. His principal motive appears to have been the protection of his organization as he steered a course on the "righteous path" that made powerful enemies. But the secret apparatus was far from defensive. It turned quickly to espionage and sabotage against the British occupiers during World War II. Notable for his close ties to Banna during this period was a young Egyptian officer and future Egyptian leader named Anwar al-Sadat, who doubled as a spy against the British.

After the war the special section continued to attack the British overlords and also targeted government figures and Jewish business leaders. The first edition of the *U.S. Army Intelligence Review*, dated February 14, 1946, reported that the Brotherhood possessed a secret cache of arms, including sixty thousand to seventy thousand rifles. The secret publication described Islam even then as "a potential threat to world peace."[24] During one week in 1946 the militants carried out four major attacks with firearms and explosives against British forces, wounding 128 people. The alleged perpetrators were tried and convicted, and eight months later two members of the special section assassinated the trial's presiding judge. As tensions escalated leading up to the formation of the Jewish state, the Brotherhood's underground wing carried out several attacks in 1947 and 1948 against Jewish businesses in Cairo. When war broke out between Jews and Arabs, the Brotherhood sent volunteers to fight in Palestine. One of them was a young, peripheral figure named Yasir Arafat.

In December 1948 Prime Minister Mahmud al-Nuqrashi accused the Brotherhood of plotting to overthrow the monarchy and issued a military decree dissolving it. Three weeks later a young militant assassinated Nuqrashi in a daring assault inside the Interior Ministry. Banna, who seemed to have lost control of his militants, condemned those responsible for the murder as "neither brothers nor Muslims." But it was too late for apologies. Banna was gunned down on a Cairo street on February 12, 1949, in a murder that is widely believed to have been carried out by government agents. By midsummer four thousand members had been imprisoned, but in April 1951 a court found the Brotherhood not guilty of plotting against the government and rescinded the ban.[25]

Whether or not the extremists' plot was real, another conspiracy was actually brewing in the Egyptian army. In 1952 the monarchy fell in a military coup known as the Free Officers Revolution. Initially, the Brotherhood was supportive, but when Gamal Abdel Nasser rose to the presidency and installed an earthly socialist regime, the Brotherhood's unrelenting pursuit of an Islamic state put it once again in opposition. In 1953 Nasser dissolved political parties in Egypt, and a year later he banned the Brotherhood. Several members were arrested. Later, in 1954 while Nasser was delivering a speech in Alexandria, Muhammad Abd al-Latif, a tinsmith enlisted by the Brotherhood, fired shots at him and missed. Nasser cracked down on the Brotherhood with all the force at his command. He meant to suppress it as part of his effort to gain total control of Egyptian society, but in the long run he stimulated its growth and further radicalization.

Thousands of Brothers were arrested. Most of the leaders were held in Tura Prison, in a southern Cairo suburb, under deplorable conditions. Several were put on trial and sentenced to death or life imprisonment. Others allegedly died while being tortured. Those who survived the long, harsh prison ordeal returned to the outside world in 1964 more fiercely at odds with the political establishment, and one of them, Sayyid Qutb, had written an Islamist manifesto that inspired new generations of Muslim radicals to fight on for divine rule.

Like Banna, Sayyid Qutb came from the Egyptian hinterland. He was born in 1906 in the village of Musha south of Cairo in the mid-Egyptian province of Asyut. Like Banna, he memorized the Koran at an early age. He later passed through the same teacher training institute, Dar al-Ulum, from which Banna had graduated a few years earlier. For the next sixteen years he worked in the Ministry of Public Instruction, first as a teacher and later as an inspector. On the side, more significantly, he made a name for himself as a writer and literary critic.

In 1945 Qutb took up political writing. These were the dying days of British colonial rule and the turning point of Qutb's career. He wrote bold anti-imperialist articles, so outspoken that King Farouk wanted to throw him in jail, but his political connections spared him. In 1948 the government sent him to the United States to study the American system of education, expecting that he would return with ideas for improving Egyptian schools. But the experience turned him solidly against Western culture. He found only lax morals and empty values. He condemned the United States for its lack of spirituality. He thought American women had too much freedom and once witnessed, disapprovingly, a church social in which men and women danced hand in hand, cheek to cheek, and body to body. Neither was he impressed by the American free enterprise system that put profit above community. Soon after he returned to Egypt he resigned his government job and joined the Muslim Brotherhood.

While in prison, though consumptive and confined for long stretches to the sickbay, Qutb still had freedom to write. He completed his largest work, a multivolume interpretation of the Muslim holy book called *Under the Aegis of the Koran.* Then he went to work on the great manifesto of radical Islam, *Milestones,* first published in 1964. *Milestones* presented a purely Islamic framework by which radical Muslims could justify terrorism. While always respectful of Banna and never directly confronting him, Qutb turned Banna's strategic formula for building God's kingdom on its head. Whereas Banna had opted for persuasion, Qutb urged jihad in the sense of holy war. Whereas Banna believed a global Islamic society would rise on its own power once the educational groundwork had been laid, Qutb would have a vanguard aggressively take over a single state as a steppingstone to total world conquest.

Qutb wrote that the ultimate goal is to "attain world leadership" so that, through Islam, God will rule the world.[26] Preaching is one way of going forward, wrote Qutb, but it is not enough. There must also be "an activist movement" led by a "vanguard," the purpose of which is to "strike hard at all those political powers" that impede the movement. "After annihilating the tyrannical force, whether a political or a racial tyranny, or domination of one class over the other within the same race, Islam establishes a new social economic and political system, in which all men and women enjoy real freedom."[27]

Qutb's prescription for a revitalized world is, of course, divine rule based on the sharia, which is the polar opposite of godless communism and incompatible with acquisitive capitalism. Islam, he declared in *Milestones,* possesses what the world at large lacks: values from God "that can restore harmony with human nature." Creating such harmony would not be an easy task, and it might take centuries to achieve because the world is in a "state of ignorance" about God's design, like the state of ignorance that existed when Muhammad began preaching to the pagans of Mecca. This ignorance, called *jahiliyyah* in Arabic, was swept away during the four decades of the umma triumphant, the golden age of Islam from 622 to 661. When the last caliph died, according to Qutb, jahiliyyah once again enclosed the world, snuffing out the kingdom of God like some great primordial ooze. So it has remained ever since. "[The] whole world is steeped in *jahiliyyah*," wrote Qutb in the early 1960s, using the present tense, "and all the marvelous material comforts and advanced inventions do not diminish its ignorance. This *jahiliyyah* is based on rebellion against the sovereignty of Allah on earth. It attempts to transfer to man one of the greatest attributes of Allah, namely sovereignty, by making some men lords over others. . . . The result of this rebellion against the authority of Allah is the oppression of His creatures."[28]

With these words Qutb adds a new dimension to the modern jahiliyyah. It is ignorance plus defiance of God. In pre-Muhammad days, the people knew no better; in the post-umma days, they have ignored God's revelations to Muhammad. No modern man-made system escaped Qutb's wrath. He condemned equally "the humiliation of the common man under communist systems and the exploitation of individual nations due to the greed for wealth and imperialism under capitalist systems" and also included the "hypocritical" secular governments in Muslim countries that do not live up to the sharia.

Members of the Brotherhood took away different meanings from Qutb's use of the term "jahiliyyah." The older generation inspired by Banna interpreted it as allegory and continued to follow Banna's prescription for preachment and social integration. Younger followers saw in it a call to armed conflict, whether against all disbelievers and apostates or merely the rulers who had strayed from the right path.[29] The power of Qutb's words demonstrates the depth of his belief. It also signals danger. He propounds a religious justification for violent action against established authority, which could hardly be more threatening to the non-Islamist world, whether religious or secular. In that sense, radical Islam rivals communism for its bold assertion of global purpose.

The Nasser regime formally dissolved the Muslim Brotherhood in 1954, but starting in 1957 scattered cells re-formed and held clandestine meetings. By 1962 *Milestones* was being piped out to the underground chapter by chapter. The initial select readership greeted it enthusiastically. But when the book was finally published in 1964, the reception from the Egyptian establishment, as might be expected, was far less positive. Nasser was not pleased either. He did not like being included in the jahiliyyah. Qutb had been set free in 1964, but the following year the government alleged a conspiracy by the oddest of the odd couples, the Communist Party and the Muslim Brotherhood, to overthrow the regime, and Qutb was caught in the police dragnet.[30] At his trial the book was used as evidence against him. He was convicted, sentenced to death, and hanged on August 29, 1966. Thus he gained the status of shahid in the Islamist movement.

THE EXTENDED FAMILY

The age of divine providence that Islamists yearn to recapture was but a fleeting moment in history—not quite four decades of dramatic Muslim consolidation and modest expansion through holy wars and earthly conquests. In its aftermath Arab Muslims conquered and instilled Islam in much of the known world from the Atlantic Ocean to the Indian subcontinent. The current struggle for Islamist reform, already more than seven decades old, goes far deeper than the terrorist network that destroyed the World Trade Center. The idea penetrates the distant reaches of the Muslim world through the instruments of education, propaganda, politics, social service, and finance, and not all of its applications are as crude as those that surfaced during the 1990s in Afghanistan and Sudan. As it passed into the maelstrom of power politics, its purity was often diluted and the ideal compromised. But it has become and will remain a force to be reckoned with in the twenty-first century. While it is important to crush the apostles of Islamist violence, no purpose is served by resisting the idea's peaceful spread. Its role in Muslim society is no less valid than that of a Christian sect in Western society.

The Muslim Brotherhood began to expand beyond Egypt's borders within a few years of its founding in 1928. It could not have been otherwise, given the Muslims' frustration over their colonial subjugation, Hasan al-Banna's personal dynamism, and the power of his message for Muslim youth. He did not leave the organization's growth to chance. When he rewrote the Brotherhood's code in 1945, it contained a section for liaison with the Islamic world, formalizing what was already taking place. Committees were established to study Islamic problems and make contact with spiritual leaders and intellectuals outside Egypt. The Brotherhood took advantage of Cairo's position as a center of Muslim learning by

inviting non-Egyptian Arab students attending Cairo universities to visit headquarters facilities and participate in the activities. There were frequent confer-
ences pertaining to Banna's "pure Islam." "Scarcely a week passed," wrote the late
Professor Richard P. Mitchell in his early English-language book, *The Society of
the Muslim Brothers*, "without witnessing the appearance at the headquarters of
one or more dignitaries and many lesser personages from all parts of the Muslim
world. . . . [Headquarters] also provided a . . . haven for . . . hundreds of 'foreign'
Muslim students at the Azhar [University] and other Egyptian schools . . . [who
were] in sympathy with the ideals of the movement."[31] The warm welcome combined with the targeted message non-Egyptian Muslims received from the Brotherhood usually reinforced their own predilections and made it more likely that
they would become effective missionaries for the cause when they returned home.
It was the sort of zealous institutional outreach one might expect from Christian
Evangelicals or Mormons in the United States.

The ideals of the Muslim Brotherhood, whether in their violent (Qutb) or
nonviolent (Banna) manifestations, spread out from Egypt in all directions. To
the east in Palestine, it spawned Hamas and the Palestinian Islamic Jihad, which
spearheaded the terrorist excesses of the al-Aqsa Intifada. To the west in Algeria, it produced a powerful Islamist political bloc, the Islamic Salvation Front,
which nearly gained control of the nation through the ballot box before a military
takeover unleashed a particularly violent six-year civil war that began in 1992. In
the north it created a popular groundswell in Turkey that lead to the election of
an Islamist politician as premier. To the south in Sudan, Islamists gained power
through the political manipulations of a seasoned legal scholar, Hasan al-Turabi.
But the creed of the Muslim Brotherhood did not have to go abroad to stir up
trouble. The Islamic Group and Egyptian Islamic Jihad were involved in the assassination of Anwar al-Sadat and a vicious terrorist campaign that included the
murder of fifty-eight innocent tourists in Luxor. Ayman al-Zawahiri, the number-
two man in al Qaeda, was sentenced to death in absentia for his alleged role in the
Luxor massacre.

DEOBANDISM

Wahhabism grew out of the desert sands of the Arabian Peninsula in the eigh-
teenth century, effectively isolated from the colonial world. Deobandism was born
on the Indian subcontinent in the nineteenth century in direct conflict with impe-

rial Britain. They came together in the late twentieth century in the Pashtun region of Pakistan/Afghanistan to produce the radical Taliban.

Historically, this merger can be considered contradictory because certain critical precepts of these two Sunni subsets were poles apart. Wahhabism derives from the Hanbali fundamentalist school of Islamic law in which God's prescription for living (sharia) is transmitted in its entirety in the Koran and the Hadith, whereas the Deobandi movement is an offshoot of the Hanafi school, which allows for bodies of Islamic scholars, *ulemas*, to reinterpret scripture to account for changing realities.

The Sepoy Mutiny of 1857 set the stage for the Deobandi movement. At the time, the British East India Company governed India. Sepoys, Indian Hindus and Muslims, served in the company's colonial army and deeply resented their lowly status. The introduction of a new Enfield rifle served as the immediate trigger for their mutiny. The Enfield came with shells encased in greased paper cartridges that the soldiers had to bite open. Muslim soldiers believed the grease they tasted originated from pork fat, which they abhorred as unclean. The Hindus thought the source was beef, the fat of the sacred cow. They rose up in unison on May 10, 1857, at the East India Company garrison in Meerut, about sixty miles east-north-east of Delhi. With support from the wider population that turned the mutiny into a revolution, they spread out over much of northern India and gained control of several communities and territories. In Delhi they installed the Mughal ruler, Bahadur Shah Zafar, as the emperor of Hindustan. It took more than a year for the reinforced company army to put down the rebellion. Retaliation was severe. Most rebels who fell into British hands were executed; some were reportedly tied to the muzzles of cannons and blown to bits.

In the wake of the Sepoy Mutiny, the British raj came down heavily on the Muslims, subjecting them to severe punishment, excluding them from public life, and leaving them to ponder how to deal with their colonial masters. Muslim reforms emerged prominently in the field of education. One movement mixed Islam with Western-style liberal arts and sciences to prepare Muslim youth for political careers and government service. In contrast, the Deobandi movement considered secular education to be un-Islamic and focused their curriculum entirely on religion. In 1867 Mohammed Qasim Nanautawi and Rashid Ahmed Gangohi founded the Dar-ul-Uloom (House of Knowledge) in the town of Deoband, a hundred miles north of Delhi. They propounded a revival of Islamic values based on education, sharia, and *tariqah* (the path). The last included the rejection of nationalism, restrictions on the role of women, the universality of Islam, and the denial of all forms of hierarchy. The Deobandi movement experienced substantial growth from its humble beginnings. By 1967 the centenary of its founding, nine thousand Deobandi madrassas were scattered throughout South Asia.[32]

Meanwhile, Deobandism influenced perhaps the most important Islamist thinker in South Asia over the past two centuries. Mawlana Abdul Ala Mawdudi was born in 1903 in the central Indian town of Aurangabad into a family that on his father's side is said to have come from a line of Sufi saints.[33] His father saw to his education, either by hiring tutors or personally instructing him in the essentials of Islam and the cultural heritage of the Arabic, Farsi, and Urdu languages. Mawlana Mawdudi's formal education was limited to three years in a madrassa.

By the time he reached adulthood, he was thoroughly immersed in a journalism career that centered on Islamic themes. He said later that he gained his basic insights about the nature of his religion from his early research.[34] In a profusion of articles and books, Mawdudi patiently defended Islam against Western and Hindu detractors, arguing that Muslims had lost their true identity by turning away from the fundamentals of their own religion. He blamed this neglect on India's Muslim leaders and the encroachment of Western secular thought.

If it can be said that Mawdudi learned from the Deobandi movement, he also blazed a divergent path that brought him closer to the more fundamentalist ideas of his contemporary, Hasan al-Banna, and his writings inspired the more radical Islamist thinker, Sayyid Qutb. Mawdudi founded a small teaching academy, the Dar al-Islam (House of Islam), and a religious order, the Jamaat-e-Islami (Islamic Society), in pre-independence India to instruct and train a leadership cadre. With these moves he hoped to build a spiritual order to lure the lost Muslim masses back to what he called the "righteous path."

He wrote against the secularization and democratization of India as it approached independence, insisting that Muslims should have an identity of their own, Islam. He roundly condemned nationalism and its democratic institutions by which the colonial powers divided the great Islamic world into smaller states.[35] But nationalism was only part of his problem; the other part consisted of India's sectarian divide. In a democracy (which Mawdudi perceived as the rule of the majority whether right or wrong), he feared that the Muslim minority would lose its selfhood and be destroyed in a Hindu-dominated society. He urged, therefore, that Muslims not participate in the struggle for independence led by the renowned Hindu Mohandas K. Gandhi. Mawdudi went a step further. He opposed the partition of the subcontinent and the creation of the Muslim state of Pakistan. It would merely encourage one form of nationalism over the other, he argued, and he opposed nationalism in any form. Islam was not to be divided by artificial national boundaries.

Mawdudi envisioned a Muslim community governed by the sharia in which all members act as God's "vicegerents" under a single ruler, or caliph, designated as their leader. With the right leader the people would live in perfect harmony and freedom under God—no tyranny, no separation of church and state, no class distinctions, no rival nations. The caliph would carry out Islamic law as God revealed it in the Koran. As Mawdudi saw it, the Muslim community was not a theocracy because no priestly hierarchy ruled.[36] God was sovereign. No king or president or caliph or human ruler of any kind stood between the individual and God. In that sense, Mawdudi could think of this kind of government as democratic. But, strictly speaking, it was not a democracy because the people did not rule. So, he coined a hybrid term to describe his ideal state, "theo-democracy."[37]

When partition of the Indian subcontinent came in 1947, Mawdudi accepted it despite his opposition to nationalism, and in 1956, after implementation of a constitution modeled after the British parliamentary system, the Jamaat-e-Islami functioned as a political party in Pakistan's government, which was alternately a secular, democratic, thoroughly nationalist state or a military dictatorship. In theory, Mawdudi used the words of a radical thinker; in practice, he worked within the system. The Jamaat appealed largely to intellectual circles in Pakistani society but never caught on with the poverty-stricken masses. It became a major player in the halls of power after Mawdudi's death. Though not a terrorist, he did not shrink from speaking out against his government. On one occasion he received a death sentence for his effrontery, but his conviction and sentence were overturned. He stepped down from the leadership of Jamaat-e-Islami in 1972 and died in 1979.

Deobandism took a much more successful turn than Jamaat-e-Islami in Pakistani politics, and this will be covered in the next chapter about al Qaeda and the rise of the Taliban.

3

THE ENEMIES

By now it has become anachronistic to speak of the Taliban as a single coherent entity. For all practical purposes the Taliban fighting American and NATO forces in southern and eastern Afghanistan and the Taliban fighting the Pakistani army in Swat Valley and South Waziristan are two different groups, united in religious fervor but with separate leadership and in pursuit of different goals.[1] Failure to understand this distinction leaves a confused picture of the separate struggles going on there. Both are Islamist and largely Pashtun, but the former are mostly Afghans led by Mullah Omar fighting to regain control of Afghanistan; the latter are largely Pakistanis who followed Baitullah Mehsud until he was killed in August 2009 by an American rocket fired from a remote-controlled drone aircraft. One can usually tell which Taliban is which from the location of the action. If there is a skirmish in the south of Afghanistan, particularly in Kandahar and Helmand provinces, one is likely seeing the Afghan Taliban in action. If an attack takes place in the mountainous east or north, it probably involves the Pakistani Taliban and/or al Qaeda, and the location is probably close to the Pakistani-Afghan border drawn by colonial Britain in 1893 cutting through Pashtun and Baluchi tribal territory, which, deep down, neither ethnic group accepts.

Although they cooperate with al Qaeda in cross-border raids, these Taliban seemed bent singularly on the conquest of Pakistan until they claimed to have added America to their target list. In May 2010 they sent an American citizen of Pakistani descent into Times Square in a failed effort to set off a car bomb that could have killed a large number of tourists. A spokesman for the Pakistani Taliban said they meant to retaliate for American drone attacks against militants in the frontier districts. Although the effort in Times Square fizzled, the odds have multiplied of future terrorist attacks on U.S. soil.

The Afghan Taliban, former rulers of Afghanistan, took refuge in Pakistan's Baluchistan Province after 9/11. They are often referred to as the Quetta Shura. (Quetta is the Baluchistan capital; the *shura* is the tribal council.) Prior to 9/11 the Afghan Taliban gave al Qaeda safe haven in Afghanistan to train terrorists, but in exile they have kept their former ward at arm's length, not out of animosity (they still share the same radical Islamic beliefs), but, probably with the advice of Pakistani intelligence, to deflect American retaliation aimed at al Qaeda. They remain fixated on the recapture of Afghanistan. They were the original Taliban led by Mullah Omar, consisting of semiliterate, mostly Afghan youth displaced in the Soviet war and taught in thousands of radical madrassas along the Pakistani side of the border. They conquered most of Afghanistan in the 1990s. Pakistan's Inter-Service Intelligence Directorate (ISI), following a perceived national interest in establishing a government friendly to Pakistan and less friendly to India in Kabul, helped the Taliban overrun Afghanistan and has continued to nurture them in their Quetta sanctuary.

The Pakistani Taliban are a post-9/11 phenomenon that emerged in the semi-autonomous Federally Administered Tribal Area (FATA) of western Pakistan. They look two ways: westward to the infiltration and harassment of Afghanistan with their al Qaeda allies, and eastward to the possible overthrow of the Pakistani government in Islamabad. They started by doing chores for al Qaeda, which had retreated from Tora Bora into South Waziristan, one of the FATA districts, in the winter of 2001–2. Jalaluddin Haqqani, a well-connected former Taliban minister in Afghanistan and the leader of a small but influential mountain tribe, played a key role in bringing the two groups together and has cooperated in their joint activities. Together al Qaeda and Pakistani Taliban raided border provinces in eastern Afghanistan, sent suicide bombers into Afghan cities, and sometimes engaged NATO and U.S. troops. The Western forces, constrained from entering sovereign Pakistani territory, pressured Islamabad to attack the militants. There followed some halfhearted army-Taliban battles ending in half-baked cease-fires as the Pakistani Taliban moved from mountain valley to mountain valley, imposing their strict version of sharia law along the way. As these Taliban edged closer to Islamabad, the Pakistani army began to realize the nation's peril and engaged them in serious combat in the Buner and Swat valleys and later in South Waziristan. The ISI found itself conflicted by its ties to the Afghan Taliban, which had no apparent designs on Islamabad, and the aggression of the Pakistani Taliban, which did.

Al Qaeda had conflicts of its own. Kept at a distance by the Quetta Shura, it may have exercised an outsized influence on the Pakistani Taliban. Islamabad is a far more attractive target for al Qaeda than Kandahar or Kabul because Pakistan possesses a nuclear arsenal coveted by Osama bin Laden. Whether an Afghan Taliban restored to power would again allow al Qaeda to train recruits for global terrorism is uncertain—better perhaps not to find out. The Taliban could regain power only if America decides to fold its tent and bring its troops home.

The circumstances dictate different American approaches to the conduct of the war, depending on the enemy, the terrain, and the political environment. Originally, al Qaeda felt justifiably safe among friendly tribesmen in the high valleys of the Hindu Kush behind the shield of Pakistani sovereignty. But the Americans began flying remotely controlled, pilotless drones across the border for reconnaissance over al Qaeda camps. Before long, the drones were armed with Hellfire missiles, which have racked up a very high success rate and have become the weapon of choice against al Qaeda in that part of the globe. Inside Afghanistan, where the enemy is primarily the Afghan Taliban, the principles identified with the surge in Iraq can be applied: isolate the enemy, defend the people, and encourage them to throw in their lot with the central Afghan government. In general, the more troops deployed, the better these tactics succeed. The war against the Pakistani Taliban behind the invisible wall of Pakistani sovereignty is left to the Pakistani army.

AL QAEDA

The organization that became al Qaeda (the Base) evolved out of a training program for non-Afghan volunteers in the mujahideen resistance to the Soviet occupation of Afghanistan (1980–89). During that war and up to the mid-1990s, Islamists commonly used "al Qaeda" to describe a function, such as the activity of the training camps or their global operations, but not a specific organization. So the transnational Islamic fighters could not be said to "belong" to al Qaeda, but they took advantage of the assets available to them, such as training, funding, transportation, communications, and weapons expertise. During these earliest years, Osama bin Laden was at best a marginal figure, one leader among many.[2]

Bin Laden and Sheikh Abdullah Azzam, his former college professor, ran one of the bases, and bin Laden, the scion of a prominent Saudi Arabian construction family, distinguished himself by bringing in heavy equipment to build base camps, enlarge mountain caves, and cut tunnels for the mujahideen fighters. Theirs was an uneven partnership and not altogether harmonious. Azzam, a respected religious scholar, firmly grasped the reins of power. Bin Laden, an impressionable, ambitious young man, was drawing closer to hard-core, anti-American Islamists like the medical doctor Ayman al-Zawahiri, the Egyptian firebrand who criticized Azzam for his cautious approach to jihad and meetings with Ahmed Shah Massoud, the Tajik warlord who had made accommodations with the Soviet occupiers.[3] Azzam died in a car-bombing murder in 1989, which several people had motive to commit, but for which no one claimed responsibility.

After the Soviet withdrawal, bin Laden returned to Saudi Arabia and then spent time in Sudan, before making his way back to Afghanistan in the mid-1990s in firm control of a small group of radical Islamists. Then in his early thirties, he required that his most loyal followers pledge devotion to him personally. The inner circle seethed with Islamist fervor and was open to big ideas, but for an Islamist outsider to gain entry the loyalty pledge was the necessary first step. Khalid Sheikh Mohammed, the self-described author of the 9/11 plot, told bin Laden of his idea to attack America with an airplane in 1996 while he was still a freelance terrorist but claimed he could never bring himself to swear his fealty to bin Laden. KSM, the acronym ascribed to him by American intelligence, was one of a hundred or so additional seasoned radicals who gravitated to bin Laden in the late 1990s. By that time the U.S. State Department had begun referring to al Qaeda as an organization. The cadre of hard-core followers had grown to about two thousand, according to Saudi intelligence, some of them concealed in sleeper cells in Europe and America.[4]

Bin Laden rose to the top because of his deep commitment to radical Islam, his political savvy in dealing with his Islamist peers, his willingness to give up the lifestyle of wealth and privilege to live in Spartan conditions, his ability to finance terrorist acts large and small out of the deep pockets of wealthy Saudi donors, and, as British journalist Jason Burke has astutely noted, his focus on the big picture.[5] Bin Laden was grievously offended when the Saudi government invited infidels to defend the country against the threat from Saddam Hussein in 1990 and outraged when American forces stayed after the Gulf War. From that time through his exile in Sudan, he condemned the royal family for straying from the true path of Islam, calling initially for reform and eventually for violent overthrow. When he moved to Afghanistan in 1996, he shifted the principal target and escalated the rhetoric. He declared war on America.

Bin Laden had been in Afghanistan only a few months when, on August 23, 1996, he delivered his "Declaration of War Against the Americans Occupying the Land of the Two Holy Places." Eighteen months later, on February 23, 1998, in a joint appearance with Zawahiri, he announced the creation of the "World Islamic Front for Jihad Against Jews and Crusaders" (the International Islamic Front, IIF), an effort to ally with other Islamic groups engaged in local jihads throughout the Muslim world. These groups, such as Lashkar-e-Toiba, Jaish-e-Mohammed, and Harkat-ul-Mujahideen in Pakistan; Abu Sayyaf in the Philippines; Jemaah Islamiyah in Southeast Asia; Ansar al-Islam in Iraq; the Moroccan Islamic Combatant Group; the Salafist Group for Call and Combat in Algeria, became partners with, but not part of, al Qaeda. Zawahiri formally became the number-two man in the new organization, although many observers see him as the dominant figure. In a new *fatwa* for the occasion, bin Laden took note of the continued American "occupation" of Saudi Arabia, the containment (at that time) of Iraq, and the "Crusader-Zionist alliance," and then set the tone for an intensified war on America: "To kill and fight Americans and their Allies, whether civilians or military, is an obligation. . . . [W]e call on every Muslim . . . to abide by Allah's order by killing Americans and stealing their money anywhere, anytime, and whenever possible."[6] The idea of killing any Americans, not just policymakers and soldiers, goes back centuries to the unwritten tribal law of the vendetta in the Arabian desert.

TALIBAN ON THE RISE

In 1947, the year Pakistan was created, the Deobandi established the Jamiat-e-Ulema-Islam (JUI, Society of Islamic Ulemas), a purely religious group on a par with Mawdudi's earlier Jamaat-e-Islami. Five years later the JUI in the North-

West Frontier Province (NWFP) turned its religious order into a political party, as Mawdudi had done after the partition. Then the Deobandi movement that had stood for Islamic unity fell apart in Pakistan, with each faction seeming to express greater militancy and more strident anti-Shiism. The most dynamic faction, the Pashtun bloc led by Maulana Mufti Mahmoud, played on populist themes to inspire an enthusiastic following. The party made a strong showing in the 1970 Pakistani elections, taking positions in favor of progressive social programs and against military rule and imperialist interference. The campaign also brought Mahmoud's JUI into defiant opposition to Mawdudi's party, the Jamaat, in a bitter conflict that has remained an open sore in Pakistani politics.[7]

When the Soviet war broke out in Afghanistan, the Jamaat was allied with the ruling junta of Gen. Mohammad Zia-ul-Haq, who had deposed and executed his elected predecessor, Zulfikar Ali Bhutto. Aid to the mujahideen went through Jamaat, which favored like-minded Islamist groups, such as those led by Gulbuddin Hekmatyar, who sought to "Islamize" modern technological society, and the Afghan Wahhabi, Abdul Rasul Sayyaf.

The JUI turned its attention to the establishment of madrassas, which rose by the hundreds in the mountainous Pashtun belt bordering Afghanistan. Many sprouted up in Afghan refugee camps. Poor Pakistani and displaced Afghan youth were given their only opportunity for a semblance of education, free of charge. It was nothing short of a cultural rebirth for the Afghans. Removed from their ancestral homes, Afghan families mingled aimlessly like a lumpen mass in the refugee camps. At the prospect of providing their children with an education, parents willingly gave them up to the madrassas, where they were boarded and cut off from their families.[8] The classroom discourse focused largely on the reading and recitation of Islamic texts, anti-West and anti-Shia lectures, and calls for militant jihad. From this controlled environment, the Pashtun Afghans and a few Pashtun Pakistanis grew up to become Taliban fighters in Afghanistan.

Persian Gulf Arabs played a significant role in the rise of the Taliban. Long before the Soviet-Afghan war, Saudi Arabia funded international Islamic organizations, such as the World Islamic League (WIL, 1962) and the Organisation of the Islamic Conference (OIC, 1969), to promote the Islamic culture. The WIL financed the building of mosques, schools, libraries, hospitals, and clinics, the training of imams, and the distribution of Korans and other religious literature. The OIC built Islamic colleges and cultural centers and created the Islamic Development Bank as a catalyst for an interest-free international Islamic banking system.[9] During the Soviet-Afghan war the Saudi kingdom matched the Americans dollar for dollar in military aid to the mujahideen and poured millions more petrodollars into the export of the Wahhabi creed, mainly through the WIL, Saudi intelligence, and the government in Riyadh.[10] One of the more popular JUI madrassas, Dar-ul-Ulum Haqqania, with 2,500 day-school and boarding students and offering master's and doctoral degrees in Islamic studies, turned out eight students who eventually became Taliban ministers in Afghanistan.[11] On a classroom wall of the Haqqania madrassa a sign read, "A Gift of the Kingdom of Saudi Arabia."[12] By the time the Soviets retreated from Afghanistan in 1989, more than eight thousand madrassas had been registered in Pakistan, and another 25,000 went up unregistered, accommodating more than half a million students.[13] But the Wahhabi-influenced courses of the Pashtun belt madrassas bore little resemblance to the classical Islamic curriculum of the original Dar-ul-Ulum Deoband, or, for that matter, to that of mainstream madrassas in modern Pakistan.

After the Soviet retreat from Afghanistan, the JUI gained greater leverage in Pakistani politics by entering into an alliance with the Pakistan Peoples Party, led by Harvard-educated Benazir Bhutto. As French professor Gilles Kepel pointed out, the woman whose lovely face adorned women's magazines of the West entered into a political alliance with an organization that wanted to hide the face of every Muslim woman behind a veil.[14] When Bhutto won the 1993 election, the JUI became part of the ruling coalition and established close ties to key government agencies: the army, the ISI (intelligence), and the Interior Ministry (police). The JUI leader, Maulana Fazlur Rehman, son of Maulana Mufti Mahmoud, emerged as chairman of the Foreign Affairs Committee in the National Assembly and gained influence over foreign policy.[15] Saudi Arabia, meanwhile, had lost confidence in the Jamaat and in Hekmatyar, leader of the Hezb-e-Islami, for supporting Iraq in the Gulf War and redirected its aid program to the JUI.[16] All these JUI gains subsequently helped the original Taliban sweep into power in Afghanistan.

During the mujahideen-Soviet war in Afghanistan, America and Saudi Arabia poured in billions of dollars in military aid for the mujahideen freedom fighters that went through the Pakistani ISI, whose favorite beneficiary was the Pashtun warlord, Hekmatyar. After the Soviet withdrawal and the defeat of the Communist regime left behind, Afghanistan emerged with a weak central government in Kabul surrounded by a patchwork of fiefdoms led by tribal warlords. While the ISI had no love for the Tajiks holding Kabul, it grew increasingly disillusioned with the pathetic military leadership of its client, Hekmatyar, whose militia was strong enough to rain artillery fire on the capital from the surrounding hills but too weak to seize it. The ISI shifted its support to the Afghan students from the Deobandi madrassas along the border in Pakistan.

The Taliban leader came out of the barren hills of southern Afghanistan. Mullah Mohammad Omar had fought against the Soviet occupation and later against the Communist regime of Mohammad Najibullah. One of four war wounds left him blind in his right eye. Known for his piety even in youth, he opened a madrassa in the village of Singesar in Kandahar Province. In the post-Communist years he gained the status of hero by mobilizing some of his dedicated followers to rescue pubescent boys and girls from lascivious warlords who wanted to use them for sexual pleasure—deeds that would make him a hero in any language. War veteran, holy man, and defender of childhood innocence, Mullah Omar rose to be consensus leader of the Pashtun students who made up the Taliban.

In 1994 the Taliban became entangled in Pakistani politics. Prime Minister Benazir Bhutto wanted to open up a trade route through Afghanistan to the former Soviet republics in Central Asia. The short way through Kabul and the Salang Tunnel was blocked by civil war between the predominantly Tajik government and the Hekmatyar militia. The longer southern road through Kandahar and Herat was encumbered only by roadblocks put up by local tribesmen and armed gangs, each of which charged a toll that collectively made the passage prohibitively expensive.

THE STUDENTS LEARN WAR

In October of that year, about two hundred Taliban fighters routed a band of Hekmatyar's tribesmen at the border town of Spin Baldak, a fueling stop on the southern route, and seized a large cache of automatic weapons, artillery, and ammunition. They went on from there with ISI support to capture Kandahar from the warlords of that region, an action that netted an even greater haul of weapons, which included dozens of tanks and other military vehicles, six MiG-21 fighter jets, and six transport helicopters leftover from the Soviet occupation.[17] Suddenly, the Taliban were armed to the teeth. The ISI and Pakistani military advisers trained by U.S. experts during the mujahideen war taught the eager young Taliban recruits how to use these weapons, and thousands of Pashtun youth, anxious to sign up with a winner, converged on Kandahar to join the army of students. By the end of the year, the Taliban army numbered about twelve thousand. Refugees continued to pour across the border from the Afghan-populated refugee camps and madrassas in Pakistan, most of them boys in their mid- to late-teens who had no sense of their tribal roots and had never seen Afghanistan at peace but who knew how to use rifles and possessed the Pashtun instincts for fighting. The students of Islamism were now students of war. Their ranks swelled by the thousands. The southern route was reopened and a single affordable toll established.[18]

In the spring of 1995, the energized Taliban army split up. One class of students drove northwest from Kandahar toward Herat, a highly cultured, five-thousand-year-old city near the Iranian border defended by a 45,000-strong militia under the leadership of warlord Ismael Khan. The other headed north-northeast toward Kabul. As the Taliban advanced on the Afghan capital, Hekmatyar's militia disintegrated. Many of its fighters joined the Taliban, which took over the siege. But both offensives ran out of steam, and the Taliban had to pull back and give up some of ground it had gained. In a neighborhood of Kabul that the Taliban had seized, it suffered a stinging defeat at the hands of the ethnic Tajik, Ahmad Shah Massoud, who was Afghanistan's best general. From Herat, Kahn, mistakenly thinking the Taliban were on the verge of collapse, launched his own drive toward Kandahar, reaching as close as Helmand Province, only to find his supply lines overstretched and vulnerable to attack. The Taliban, by this time rested and better trained, launched a counterattack. Kahn's militia crumbled, and the Taliban captured Herat. Then in the fall of 1995 the Taliban renewed its siege of Kabul. The forces guarding the capital, primarily ethnic Tajiks, held fast for ten months until the Taliban outflanked them by capturing Jalalabad and provinces north and east of Kabul. Faced with the threat of encirclement, Massoud retreated north to his stronghold in the Panjshir Valley, leaving the city undefended.[19]

Within a few hours, on the evening of September 26, 1996, the Taliban swept into Kabul. That night, a Taliban death squad entered the United Nations compound in violation of international law, seized former Communist president Najibullah and his brother, who were living there under diplomatic immunity, beat them senseless, mutilated them, shot them dead, and then hung the bloated bodies from a street post outside the presidential palace. The next day the Taliban began implementing its harsh version of Islamic law, truer to the spirit of Muhammad ibn Abd al-Wahhab than the founders of the Deobandi movement.

TALIBAN JUSTICE

Pakistani journalist Ahmed Rashid opens his informative book *Taliban* by describing the public execution of a convicted murderer that was carried out under the sharia and faithfully followed ancient tribal custom. The event took place in March 1997, and Rashid was an eyewitness to the execution amid more than ten thousand mostly Pashtun men and boys in a war-damaged soccer stadium rebuilt by UN aid agencies in Kandahar. (Females were barred from such public events.) The doomed young man in his early twenties, Abdullah Afghan, was brought into the stadium in a convoy of several pickup trucks. The convoy came to a halt at midfield, and Judge Khalilullah Ferozi of the Kandahar Supreme Court, an elderly, white-bearded man, stepped onto the bed of a truck to review the law and the circumstances of the crime. Abdullah had allegedly stolen medicine from a farmer, Abdul Wali, and when the farmer resisted, shot him dead.

Judge Ferozi concluded his speech by asking Wali's relatives if they would spare Abdullah's life in exchange for "blood money," a procedure prescribed under sharia law. They refused, and that sealed Abdullah's fate. Trembling with fear, his feet shackled and his arms tied behind his back, he was taken from another truck and escorted by armed Taliban guards to a spot between the goalposts at one end of the stadium where he was made to kneel and advised to say a final prayer. A guard handed a loaded Kalashnikov to one of Wali's relatives, who took the family's revenge with a short burst to Abdullah's back and another to the chest as the body lay twitching on the ground.[20]

Afghan civil law did not impose this penalty; sharia law did. People caught violating sharia law received no mercy. The sharia penalty for adultery by a woman was death by stoning; for theft, the severing of a hand or an arm, depending on the severity of the crime; for lesser penalties, perhaps a whipping. Under Taliban rule, half-literate, bearded young men educated in Pakistani madrassas roamed the streets of Afghan cities as a kind of morality police, seeing to it that citizens obeyed the call to prayers, that women covered their heads and faces when out of the home, and that shopkeepers sold no alcoholic beverages or other forbidden items such as television sets, radios, and tape recorders. Men who were clean shaven or had short beards might be whipped. At checkpoints, audio- and videotapes were confiscated and strung out on poles or frames the guards had erected. The government had no say in any of these matters; in fact, the government had no real power and little to do beyond routine functions. Government buildings were in various stages of decay, and the grounds, overgrown with weeds. Revenue to run the country came in the form of aid from Persian Gulf donors, toll collections on commercial traffic between Pakistan and Central Asia, and a percentage of the illicit drug trade generated by the abundant growth of opium on Afghan soil.[21]

BLOODBATH IN THE NORTH

Under Mullah Omar's leadership, the Taliban tried to bring all of Afghanistan under its rule. The Pakistani ISI lent significant tactical support. By 1997 provinces in the north inhabited predominantly by ethnic Tajiks, Uzbeks, and Hazaras remained outside the Taliban's grasp. Rashid Dostum, an Uzbek general known for his willingness to betray allies, controlled six provinces north of the Hindu Kush. That spring Dostum's second in command, Gen. Malik Pahlawan, believing that Dostum had murdered his brother, asked the Taliban to help him overthrow his leader. It was as if the fly had invited the spider to dinner. The Taliban agreed to help, and as they advanced, Dostum fled to Uzbekistan and then to Iran. Pahlawan tried to negotiate a power-sharing deal, but the Taliban now refused to share. Initially, however, this go-it-alone arrogance backfired. When they arrived in the liberal, ethnically mixed city of Mazar-e Sharif, they laid down sharia law and started to disarm the Uzbek and Hazara militias. These actions sparked Hazara resistance, followed by full-scale rioting. Thousands of Taliban, trapped in unfamiliar surroundings amid hostile people, were killed or captured—and most of those captured were tortured, killed, and buried in mass graves. In Afghanistan in those years, barbaric ethnic cleansing was an equal opportunity horror. But the Taliban would have its revenge.

Through the winter, as the Taliban waited in the wings, Uzbek and Hazara militias fought each other. In the summer of 1998, the Taliban, resupplied by Pakistan and Saudi Arabia, launched another attack on the north, overcoming the Uzbeks and Hazaras in turn, and went on an orgy of savage slaughter. An estimated six thousand to eight thousand Uzbek and Hazara people were killed in July and August. In September the Taliban turned its attention to the center of Hazara culture, Bamiyan, about a mile and a half above sea level in the Hindu Kush, eighty miles west-northwest of Kabul. Most of the Hazaras fled into the mountains, but the Taliban caught and summarily executed about fifty elderly people left behind. Then, motivated by their disdain of idols, they blew up two gigantic, world-famous statues of Buddha that had been carved out of the limestone cliffs and had stood for more than two thousand years as Afghanistan's most prized archeological treasures.

Life in the 90 percent of Afghanistan where the Taliban ruled was difficult for people accustomed to the twentieth century. State schools were closed, women confined to the home, and men required to wear beards of a certain prescribed length. The names of newborn babies had to be taken from an officially approved list. The Taliban's treatment of women was the object of international scorn. The UN and countries neighboring Afghanistan tried to mediate the continuing ethnic conflict, but the Taliban largely ignored them. Iran, Russia, and the Central Asian republics of the former Soviet Union strengthened their defenses, and Iran nearly invaded Afghanistan over the murder of eleven Iranian diplomats during the takeover of Mazar-e Sharif. Saudi Arabia cut off aid to the Taliban after Mullah Omar granted asylum to Osama bin Laden. Then, after bin Laden declared war on America and al Qaeda operatives bombed U.S. embassies in East Africa, the Taliban refused Washington's demand for his extradition. In the years leading up to 9/11, Afghanistan stood virtually alone in the world, a pariah nation, with only Pakistan to befriend it. Thus, the Taliban, acting in the name of Allah, seeking paradise on earth, and fortified with an ideology of destruction, took Afghanistan to the edge of hell.

ISLAMISTS RESURGENT

After 9/11, when al Qaeda's beaten warriors from Tora Bora arrived at the Pakistani border, young Pashtun tribesmen were waiting to lead them through the high mountain passes to their sanctuary in South Waziristan. Frontier troops who guarded the entrances to Pakistan at Khyber and Kurram were notably absent from the places where al Qaeda actually came across. South Waziristan was an ideal hiding place, easily defensible with steep ridges and patches of forest. Jalaluddin

Haqqani, a minister in Afghanistan's former Taliban government, arranged for the refugees to hire the young tribesmen as guides and to provide logistical services. For the Pashtun youth, it was an enriching experience in more ways than one. Not only were they well paid for their work, but they also learned the art of guerrilla warfare from veteran jihadists, who soon grew to a force of three to four thousand from Arab and Central Asian countries. With the help of their Pashtun guides, al Qaeda teams soon began to slip back across the Afghan border to conduct raids, plant roadside bombs, and ambush American and NATO troops. Before long the guides became the Pakistani Taliban and started to take over valley after valley in the tribal area.[22]

Al Qaeda fighters who escaped to the sanctuary in western Pakistan never really stopped fighting by unconventional means, as they easily crossed the border into Afghanistan and back with their new Pakistani Taliban allies. As early as 2002 there were two attempts on President Hamid Karzai's life, and in March 2003 a Red Cross worker was assassinated and two American GIs were killed in an ambush—all attributed to cross-border incursions by the new al Qaeda–Pakistani Taliban alliance. Two months later, in May 2003, Defense Secretary Donald Rumsfeld announced in Washington that most of Afghanistan was secure and that NATO forces had shifted from combat to reconstruction, even as the Taliban continued to infiltrate back into Afghanistan to attack Afghan, NATO, and nongovernment humanitarian personnel. From then on, the Pakistani Taliban steadily gained strength, while in the spring of 2006, the Afghan Taliban seized control in parts of the southern Afghan provinces of Uruzgan, Kandahar, and Helmand. Along the Helmand River are some of the richest poppy-growing areas in the world, netting the Taliban a substantial income to buy arms and facilitating the movement of opium products to the underground markets in Europe and North America.

Because NATO felt obliged to honor Pakistani sovereignty, the Western forces would not cross the border in force to attack the Islamists in their FATA and Baluchistan sanctuaries. The fact that Afghan Taliban retained close ties to elements of the Pakistani government, particularly the ISI, complicated this restraint. President Obama indicated in the 2008 campaign that he would attack the terrorist forces in their Pakistani sanctuary. But he reversed himself after taking office by saying he would not send American troops to fight in Pakistan. In a sense, he is keeping both promises, retaining the main forces on the Afghan side of the border while attacking the Islamists in Pakistan with pilotless drones and covert "snatch-and-grab" operations. America holds a huge advantage in technology but faces longer odds fighting against committed warriors on the enemy's home turf. The outcome remained in doubt after eight years of shilly-shally warfare.

4

INSIDE THE SURGE

The Obama administration reenergized the war in Afghanistan with a pragmatic approach that put protection of the community ahead of the death and destruction of the enemy. It is quite simple in theory: capture the hearts and minds of the people, isolate the enemy, establish political self-determination, and withdraw. But nothing about it is easy in practice. Unconventional war such as that being waged in Afghanistan poses unconventional challenges to powerful armies far from home. The enemy operates in the shadows to lay ambushes, plant roadside bombs, and send young men and women wearing bomb vests on suicide missions at crowded gathering places. A local leader who cooperates with the occupying authorities or opposes the rule of the insurgents becomes a target for assassination. When a powerful occupier like the United States takes over a village or district in insurgent-controlled territory, the enemy fades away. When the occupier moves on, the insurgents return with a vengeance. Fighting the elusive enemy with conventional sweeps and big bombs intended for a conventional foe can punish the innocent and throw noncombatants into the enemy's arms.

The new approach was put into effect in Iraq with unexpected success facilitated by special local circumstances and American troop reinforcements. Because it coincided with the infusion of fresh troops, it came to be called the surge. But the added troops are not integral to the procedure. David Kilcullen is an advocate. He lays it out analogously as the antidote to a viral disease in his book *The Accidental Guerrilla*. The infiltration of an extremist group such as the Taliban or al Qaeda into a village or district is the "infection." The spread of their influence is "contagion." Retaliation by government or international forces is an "intervention." If the retaliation is indiscriminate, the indigenous people will align themselves with the Islamist group in defense, what Kilcullen calls "rejection." Generations of these tribal people, who live isolated lives in mountain valleys, have always answered the call to defend their villages or join neighbors to fight against outsiders. Nowadays, they get mixed up in broader ideological struggles and become, in Kilcullen's term, "accidental guerrillas."

Kilcullen's prescription for combating the "accidental guerrilla syndrome" is to go easy on the intervention. Stanch the contagion by ousting the ideologues with superior military force. Sometimes it can be done without a fight, perhaps through negotiation with disgruntled non-Islamist leaders. Above all, the villagers must be carefully co-opted and not attacked recklessly as if the entire village were the enemy. Calling civilian deaths "collateral damage" does not save lives or win hearts and minds. Isolated from the village, the Islamists are in no position to enforce sharia law or otherwise influence the tribal culture, and they become more distinct targets, which lessens the chance that the attacking forces will take innocent lives. This approach by the interventionists requires an intimate knowledge of and respect for the locals' customs and tribal values, something the United States did not show in Iraq until the occupation was well along.[1] The Western forces will not necessarily avoid combat by using this approach. But they can hope, at least, to avoid alienating the villagers and, at best, to have the accidental guerrillas fighting on their side, as happened in Iraq during the Anbar Awakening (which is discussed later in the chapter).

As might be expected, this syndrome and its cure contain familiar elements of past terrorist wars. In Vietnam in the early 1960s, the infection (insurgent rule) was imposed with ruthless efficiency in rural villages. Communist-led Viet Cong guerrillas assassinated community and religious leaders sympathetic to the central South Vietnamese government and put the corpses on public display with notes explaining their "crimes." At the time U.S. special forces played an advisory role by employing a strategy that emphasized military defense against the enemy. In any case, American forces were not sufficient to cover more than a few rural villages, and the insurgents ultimately prevailed. "The assassination rate declined steadily from 1960 to 1965," said author Douglas Pike, "for the simple reason that there were only a finite number of persons to be assassinated."[2]

In and near the eastern Algerian seaport town of Philippeville in 1955, intervention was invited to provoke rejection. Two leaders of the National Liberation Front deliberately stirred Algerians to riot against French *colons* to incite French retaliation and gain support from the Algerian community for the revolution. The strategy worked in its perverse way with the reckless slaughter of Algerians by French security forces bent on revenge for the savage murder of a few Europeans. By official count 123 Europeans and pro-French Algerians died, some horribly mutilated, while the death toll for pro-revolution or uncommitted Algerians was 1,273. In the aftermath, anti-French feeling ran high among Algerian local residents.[3]

Kilcullen's strategy for curing the infection is also an echo from the past. In the wake of the communist victory in China in 1949, Chinese ethnics rebelled against the British colonial government in Malaya. The British promised self-determination to Malay ethnics (the governing class in Malaya) and launched a successful campaign to capture hearts and minds. Then a reinforced British army isolated the rebels in the Malayan jungles, cutting them off from their source of sustenance in the larger Chinese community, and gradually wore them down. By the time the British forces departed, the rebellion was well in hand with security left to the proud new noncommunist Malayan government.[4] The British performance in Malaya has been the gold standard of counterinsurgency ever since but has seldom been duplicated.

In the darkest days of the American adventure in Iraq, apologists for the war such as Defense Secretary Rumsfeld and even the much-admired General Petraeus spoke of insurgencies lasting many years with the implication that America would eventually win, but in fact, great powers such as the United States, Britain, France, the Soviet Union, and Israel have usually lost wars against determined local insurgents whose country they occupied. It might well be that the key to winning such a war is to declare victory and get out. America has finally done that in Iraq and hopes to do it in Afghanistan.

Of course Algeria, Vietnam, Malaya, Iraq, and Afghanistan/Pakistan were, or are, different wars with the common thread of foreign global powers engaging local insurgents. In the ongoing Islamist epidemic, following the Kilcullen prescription means that the Western forces need to know tribal customs before they can do an effective job of treating the Islamist infection. Western nation-building goes easier today in northern Afghanistan, where Tajik, Uzbek, and Hazara ethnics hold sway. In Pashtun zones in eastern and southern Afghanistan and the FATA in Pakistan, the Taliban are kin, so to speak, to the local villagers, and the accidental guerrillas are not always so accidental. Even al Qaeda fighters have been in the area since the 1980s, when they came to support the mujahideen against the Soviet occupation and stayed to live and breed with the local Pashtun. Even so, not all Pashtun tribes have the same values, and the Taliban cannot always count on their support. Whatever the degree of difficulty, it is most important for the interventionist nations of the West to show the tribes respect and to honor their customs. American forces learned that the hard way in Iraq.

THE SURGE IN IRAQ

The principles of the surge, as described in the previous paragraphs, were actually applied in two Iraqi cities before the surge officially began. In 2005, in the small northern city of Tal Afar near Syria, al Qaeda militants took advantage of reduced American troop levels in the region to infiltrate in greater numbers across the nearby border. They came as allies to Iraqi insurgents in the fight against the American occupiers and soon gained control of Tal Afar's 250,000 inhabitants with a terrorist campaign of intimidation. With their eyes on a bigger prize, they used the city as a base from which to send suicide bombers to disrupt life in Mosul, Iraq's third largest city forty miles to the east.

Col. H. R. McMaster, commander the Third Armored Cavalry Regiment stationed just outside Tal Afar, watched these developments with growing unease and decided to act. His troops closed off outlying al Qaeda safe houses and lines of retreat and then moved in on Tal Afar. McMaster knew that taking the city was the easy part. He needed to gain the confidence of tribal leaders who feared that if they cooperated with the Americans, the Islamists would mark them for assassination. He decided on a different approach. Instead of running patrols through city streets during the day and pulling them back to the main base at night, the standard operating procedure of American occupation forces, he established outposts throughout the city where troops were stationed day and night. He told his soldiers to concentrate on protecting the Iraqi residents. Gradually, the steady U.S.

presence inside the city gained the people's support. McMaster met with tribal sheikhs who had previously taken part in the insurgency, humbly apologized for past American mistakes, and told them that the time for honorable resistance had ended. He promised that his troops would help them protect the city from the Islamists. In 2005 Tal Afar was a major success story in the midst of an overall deterioration in the American situation in Iraq.[5]

The next city wrested from Islamist control was Ramadi, the capital of Anbar Province west of Baghdad. While Tal Afar was considered an isolated case, the struggle for Ramadi and nearby rural communities, which played out over several months, was the turning point of the Iraq War and became known as the Anbar Awakening.

When the time came for McMaster's unit in Tal Afar to redeploy, it was replaced by the First Brigade of the First Armored Division, known as the Ready First Combat Team—a mixed unit of Army and Marine combat troops and special operations task forces, including Army Delta and Navy SEALs, with air support from Air Force and Marine squadrons—and commanded by Army Col. Sean MacFarland. Ready First saw little combat in Tal Afar, and MacFarland was duly impressed with the security arrangement that McMaster had put in place. In June 2006 the team was assigned to Ramadi, then one of the most dangerous cities in Iraq, where al Qaeda terrorism had cowed the tribal Sunni government and its nearly 1 million people.

Initially, Ready First patrols into the city from its base outside were subjected to deadly enemy attacks. MacFarland quickly decided to apply the lessons he had learned in Tal Afar. He and his staff developed a plan to invade al Qaeda safe havens and establish company-size combat outposts like those in Tal Afar. Where feasible, some were to be manned by tank companies. They chose defensible buildings in contested urban neighborhoods. Eventually, Iraqi army units joined them.

The first outpost established in July 2006 triggered a large-scale assault by a multiplatoon al Qaeda force that was beaten back with heavy losses. After the first outpost was secure, Ready First wasted no time establishing another, and another, and another. MacFarland compared it to Pacific island-hopping during World War II. Patrols fanned out, and Iraqi police stations began to appear in the neighborhoods. The enemy's initial reaction to a new outpost was usually the strongest. As al Qaeda losses piled up and the strength of their responses diminished, people emerged from their homes and took to the streets for shopping and other daily activities. A big confidence builder was the establishment of an outpost just outside the general hospital. A unit of the Iraqi army patrolled the premises. What for the past year had been used almost exclusively for treating insurgents became available to all.

This patient offensive could not have succeeded without the people's support. Tribal leaders had tried in 2005, the year before Ready First arrived, to shake off the al Qaeda influence, but ended up losers, badly shaken by a series of assassinations. So the tribal chiefs were jittery about going along with the American plans. But MacFarland assured them that his brigade intended to be there until the job was done. The more Ready First secured neighborhoods, the more the community and its leaders came on board. Within about two and a half months after the first outpost was set up, a dynamic young sheikh named Sittar albu Risha organized a tribal council attended by more than fifty sheikhs who wholeheartedly voiced their support for the American effort by pledging to provide more badly needed police recruits. Secured neighborhoods turned promptly to repairing infrastructure even as fighting continued elsewhere in the city. MacFarland encouraged the tribal leaders to appoint a mayor or other political leader to coordinate the rebuilding. He had learned the importance of working through the tribes to accomplish mutual goals. Success in Ramadi turned out to be contagious. It ignited uprisings against al Qaeda in surrounding Anbar towns.[6] While the Anbar Awakening was reversing the direction of the war in Iraq, clueless Americans argued back home about whether to withdraw or stay the course.

Actually, the turnaround in Ramadi was easy to miss because media reporting focused that year on a vicious sectarian war in other parts of the country. One night early in 2006 several militant Sunni insurgents crept into one of the holiest sites in Shia Islam, the Askariya Shrine in Samara, sixty-five miles north of Baghdad; wired it with explosives; and blew off its golden dome, an act designed to incite civil war between Shia and Sunni factions—and it worked.[7] Previously in the course of the American occupation, Sunni insurgents had killed scores of Shia on several occasions, including during religious ceremonies, by setting off suicide bombs in crowded places, only for the Shia to ignore the provocations. In Samara no one was killed, but the sensitivity of the religious insult triggered an orgy of ethnic cleansing—apparently proving that reverence for religious symbolism is stronger than regard for human life. In the weeks that followed, Shia gangs roamed towns and city neighborhoods, killing Sunnis en masse and inflicting damage to Sunni mosques. Sunni gangs retaliated in kind. Fear and loathing gripped Baghdad, which descended into chaos. Some mixed Sunni-Shia neighborhoods were ethnically cleansed of Sunnis, who were driven from their homes—and less often other neighborhoods were cleared of Shia. Government security forces, far from playing a neutral role, joined in the slaughter of Sunnis because the security forces were heavily infiltrated by Shia militia. Ironically, the American strategy at the time was to train the Iraqi forces as fast as possible and turn the nation's security over to them. That had the effect, in reality, of building up the Shia side in the ethnic strife. At the same time, the Americans were training Sunni tribesmen to fight with them against al Qaeda. The situation went beyond insurgency to civil war. As casualties mounted, support for the American involvement in Iraq waned back home in the United States.

In America's 2006 legislative election, Iraq was the defining issue. Republicans lost control of Congress over it, and Rumsfeld lost his job as secretary of defense. Democrats, the newly minted majority in both the House and Senate, demanded that President Bush begin a drawdown of U.S. troops in Iraq. Bush refused, claiming that withdrawal would be tantamount to surrender. Instead, in a maneuver that became known as the surge, he sent in five additional combat brigades to stem the ethnic violence. He also realigned the occupation's American leadership, appointing General Petraeus as military commander in Iraq and career diplomat Ryan Crocker as ambassador to replace Zalmay Khalilzad, the able neoconservative who had been named ambassador to the United Nations.

Petraeus was totally in sync with the bold counterinsurgency steps taken by McMaster in Tal Afar and MacFarland in Ramadi. The new coalition commander had served previously in Iraq, taking part in the invasion as commander of the 101st Airborne Division. During the first year of the occupation, his division controlled the northernmost sector, which included the city of Mosul. In contrast to the other occupying generals, he took pains to put his troops in touch with the people, and it paid off when Mosul residents helped save American lives by pointing out where roadside bombs were buried.[8] After a second tour of duty in Iraq building and training Iraqi security forces, Petraeus spent 2006 as commanding general of the Combined Arms Center at Fort Leavenworth, Kansas, where he and Marine Corps Gen. James F. Amos oversaw the revision of an Army/Marine Corps field manual for counterinsurgency that formalized advice for carrying out small wars that had already been put into effect in Tal Afar and Ramadi. The staff that actually wrote the manual was a highly diversified collection of military officers, academics, human rights advocates, and journalists.

The lists of successful and unsuccessful practices in the final version of the new field manual were a stinging rebuke of then-current counterinsurgency policy. Call them the dos and don'ts of a new counterinsurgency doctrine. Here is a sample: Do emphasize intelligence and secure the populace; don't overemphasize killing and capturing the enemy. Do isolate the enemy from the populace; don't conduct large-scale operations as the norm or concentrate military forces in large bases for protection. Do expand the host-nation police force; don't build host-nation security forces in the U.S. military's image.[9]

When Petraeus arrived in Baghdad as commander of the coalition forces in February 2007, he was eager to implement these recommendations on a broad scale. He assembled a team of twenty-four military, diplomatic, and economic experts to develop an integrated civil-military campaign plan for Iraq. Colonel McMaster, the commander at Tal Afar in 2006, and David Pearce of the State Department led the team that included Kilcullen as an expert on counterinsurgency. The plan that emerged was, first and foremost, a political strategy to foster negotiations for power sharing among the warring factions and try to persuade disaffected insurgents—whether Sunni, Shia, or Islamist—to switch sides. With this firm political foundation, the team developed a military strategy that included joint operations of Iraqi and U.S. forces.[10] Some of the most dedicated Iraqi troops in the fight against al Qaeda were the former Sunni insurgents who once fought against the American occupiers.

Even before the fresh combat brigades showed up, and before Petraeus formally took command, Lt. Gen. Ray Odierno, who would be Petraeus's second in command, began implementing the essential strategy of protecting the populace. In January 2007 he deployed platoons (about 35 soldiers) and companies (about 100 soldiers) of the First Cavalry Division to outposts in the greater metropolitan area of Baghdad. In February the first surge unit, the Second Brigade of the Eighty-second Airborne Division, arrived and was similarly broken up and assigned to eastern Baghdad with the exhortation to get out of the tanks and armored vehicles and walk around.

As in Ramadi, fierce initial resistance from al Qaeda and certain rebellious Shia factions to the establishment of neighborhood outposts sorely tested the American resolve. One battle stood out. In Tarmiyah, a town of about forty thousand people just north of Baghdad, al Qaeda had gained control during the days of ethnic strife and in late 2006 ordered the Iraqi police to leave. The First Cavalry Division chose the abandoned police station for an outpost and installed a reinforced platoon. One morning soon afterward, al Qaeda attacked. A small truck crashed through the front gate, and before the driver died in a hail of small arms fire, he detonated fifteen hundred pounds of explosives that blew the facade off the building. Fighting raged for an hour before help arrived, and even then, with the outcome no longer in doubt, the battle continued a while longer. Of thirty-eight soldiers stationed at the outpost, two had been killed and twenty-nine wounded. With the police station in ruins, Lt. Col. Scott Efflandt, commander of the Second Battalion, Eighth Cavalry Regiment, moved the outpost to a school building two hundred meters north and ordered that patrols be resumed before sundown. He was telling the enemy that the Yanks were there to stay.[11]

In contrast to the insurgents, who reacted quickly, the people were slow to put their trust in American promises to protect them. It took weeks of steady and sometimes heroic efforts for them to accept the American presence in the troubled Baghdad neighborhoods and their surrounding suburbs. American credibility got an instant boost from Iraqis who witnessed a GI scoop up a wounded girl caught in a cross fire and carry her away for medical treatment.[12] Sometimes al Qaeda would overreact to the American penetration of neighborhoods they controlled, and they would take the damage to their egos out on local residents. "They'd kidnap children, kill women, threaten tribal leaders," Maj. Luke Calhoun, intelligence officer of the 1st Brigade of the 1st Cavalry Division, told author Thomas Ricks.[13] Often that would backfire and throw the locals into the arms of Americans. They became "accidental guerrillas" on the American side.

Once the buildup of new forces was complete in June 2007, the United States went on the offensive with division-level operations. They attacked Islamist strongholds pinpointed by improved intelligence, both high tech and human. Powerful air support with precision bombs and rockets helped weaken the insurgency. The goal was to clear several Islamist safe havens simultaneously and establish local security forces to keep the Islamists out permanently. For the long term, local police would have to be trained to register the population and develop effective counter-intelligence to root out Islamist sleeper cells trying to wait for the heavy military presence to disappear.[14] The key to success, as specified in the new counterinsurgency manual, was not necessarily to destroy the enemy, but to keep it isolated from the community on the theory that without the people, the insurgency would wither and die as an effective operation. Yet there was a certain amount of irony in the process: on the home front, the Bush administration spoke of Iraq as a bastion of democracy, but for Iraq to survive, it would have to learn invasive police tactics. Political rhetoric is so often contradicted by the reality on the ground.

Neighborhoods gradually came back to life. Markets opened, and people ventured out of their homes to shop and pick up their lives to where they had left off before the violence had made them prisoners in their own homes. But the improvement was not without its cost. In all of 2006, 822 American troops were killed, an average of 68.5 per month. In the first six months of 2007, while the surge was getting its legs, the death toll came to 576 or 96 per month on average, nearly 30 percent higher. May was the worst month with 120 American deaths. But after mid-2007 the casualty toll dropped significantly to 328 in the last six months of the year (55 per month) to a low of 23 in December. Iraqi civilian and security force casualties in the same time periods, conservatively estimated, were down by comparable proportions.[15] The Bush administration breathed easier. The president's neoconservative supporters claimed victory in Iraq. But the chief engineers of the surge, Petraeus and Crocker, were less assertive. They declared their gains "fragile and reversible," and indeed the violence continued, just at a lower rate.

Petraeus and Crocker also worked to shore up the elected central government in Baghdad. The United States stepped up the training of Iraqi security forces, both police and army. By 2008 Shiite prime minister Nouri al-Maliki felt strong enough to launch an attack against the Shia militia controlling the southern city of Basra. After early setbacks that included desertion, the government forces prevailed. Then they went after other militia strongholds, most critically the Baghdad slum called Sadr City, controlled by Muqtada al-Sadr, the Shia cleric whose support had elevated Maliki to the premiership. Again, the government forces emerged victorious, and Maliki used his accumulated political capital to negotiate an agreement with the Bush administration for the withdrawal of American combat troops by 2011.

The United States started reducing its surge-related reinforcements in 2008, and by July Reuters, citing a military spokesman, reported that the drawdown was complete.[16] The surge was considered a success, but the White House did not celebrate, nor did the president declare victory in front of a banner that read, "Mission Accomplished." The figures that measured success were rather grim in their own right, just not as grim as they had been. For the entire year 2008, 313 U.S. troops were killed, about 26 a month, while Iraqi civilians and security forces suffered 5,929 killed, or 494 per month. In the first five months of 2009, 86 U.S. troops died (17 per month) while 1,569 Iraqis were killed (314 per month).[17]

By treaty arrangement, on July 1, 2009, U.S. troops cleared out of Baghdad and other cities, leaving security entirely in Iraqi hands. The Iraqi casualty count declined significantly in July to 240 civilians killed. Prime Minister Maliki felt so good about it that he declared Baghdad safe and ordered the removal of concrete blast walls along major thoroughfares. Then on August 18, 2009, a series of explosions rocked the city, including car bombs that caused extensive damage to the Finance and Foreign ministries. On that one day about a hundred Iraqi people were killed, and more than five hundred were injured. Americans were safely ensconced in their bases outside the city. Investigators were initially uncertain about the who the perpetrators were. The episode had the earmarks of an al Qaeda operation. Maybe in the absence of the American forces, the Islamist sleeper cells had reawakened. Maliki blamed former Sunni in Saddam Hussein's regime who had teamed up with the Americans against al Qaeda but had never been reconciled with the new Shia government.[18] Either way it was bad news.

WILL IT WORK IN AFGHANISTAN?

That the Afghan Taliban should be America's enemy is unfortunate. Taliban rule is cruel, unfair to women, and disrespectful of international norms—conduct worthy of censure, but not worth fighting a war over. If they want to live in the seventh century, it's their business. If they are supported only by a minority and the rest of the people held in thrall out of fear, it is not a casus belli for the United States. America does not have to love them to accept the reality of their existence. But in practice, the Taliban's passionate theological relationship with the perpetrators of 9/11, al Qaeda, gets in the way. Both groups take inspiration from Wahhabism, the radical Sunni religion that sprang up on the Arabian Peninsula in the mid-eighteenth century. Al Qaeda leader Osama bin Laden grew up in a pious Wahhabi family and was further radicalized by the teachings of the Egyptian Muslim Brotherhood's militant wing. Later, Wahhabi ideas spread to the tribal areas of western Pakistan, where poor, illiterate Pashtun youth from Afghanistan and Pakistan soaked them up in hundreds of radical madrassas. So they—al Qaeda and the two Taliban—think alike theologically, if not always politically.

The seeds of both al Qaeda and the Afghan Taliban took root in the 1980s during the Soviet war in Afghanistan. Mohammad Zia-ul-Haq, a devout Islamist who had become the Pakistani president in a military coup, encouraged the growth of madrassas in the tribal areas. The ISI forwarded billions of dollars worth of U.S. and Saudi Arabian aid to the mujahideen fighting the Soviet occupiers of Afghanistan, favoring Pashtun warlords such as Hekmatyar and his Hezb-e-Islami.

Since 1947 Pakistan has lived in fear and loathing of India, and Afghanistan has been a bone of contention between them. Afghan presidents, for their part, have played each off against the other. In the 1990s, with the country locked in tribal warfare, the original Taliban became an instrument of Pakistani policy to install a government in Kabul responsive to Pakistan's interests and unfriendly to India, and the ISI guided the Taliban's conquest of most of Afghanistan. Osama bin Laden arrived in Taliban-ruled Afghanistan in 1996 with his internationalist, anti-U.S. agenda, and Mullah Omar, the Taliban ruler, gave him safe haven to plot and train agents for terrorist acts against American and other Western targets around the world. There is the crux of the problem. Mullah Omar could have put the issue to rest by denying sanctuary to bin Laden and his radical Egyptian partner, Ayman al-Zawahiri, and turning them over to an international tribunal to face justice for their terrorist atrocities. He might now refuse them safe haven, but he is not likely to betray them to the Americans or any Western institution. If he did, however, it would take the Americans and their NATO allies out of the picture and leave the Taliban to fight for power in Afghanistan. But that would be out of character. Mullah Omar is an ideologue, not a politician. He does not share power. He does not compromise. At least he did not when Presidents Clinton and Bush asked him to turn over bin Laden for his terrorist acts. The issue would probably be decided by civil war, which would favor the Taliban. America's interests would not be negatively affected unless the Taliban regime sponsored recruitment and training for global terrorists. The Taliban's natural enemies, India on the east, Iran on the west, and Russia beyond Central Asia to the north would make expansion very difficult.

For now, the West is left to fight the three forces of the Afghan and Pakistani Taliban and al Qaeda. The problem is as much political as military. The central Afghan government must extend its influence to forty thousand villages, many set apart naturally by the mountainous landscape and often alienated by the corruption, incompetence, and insensitivity in Kabul. Defeating the Taliban may be difficult, but overcoming corruption in the Karzai government makes the job of winning tribal loyalties vastly more complicated. On that score, the Taliban come out ahead of the Karzai government.

Despite the rout of the Taliban in 2001, the military effort in Afghanistan promises to be at least as tough and demanding for the United States as the war in Iraq. Afghanistan's rugged topography translates into strategic realities: the isolation that makes many villages harder for the central government to control; hiding places that improve the chances for ambush against Western forces; and contrasts in climate from snowcapped mountains to sunbaked deserts that try the resolve of Western soldiers. In these difficult conditions, U.S. and NATO troops plunge ahead to fight the kind of unconventional war at which great powers have been notably unsuccessful in the past six and a half decades. When you factor in the sanctuaries to heal wounds and replenish supplies without fear of attack from Western ground forces that the Islamists enjoy in western Pakistan, the odds for winning grow shorter. That's why the emergence of pilotless drone technology is so important. It tends to tip the scales back to the American side.

Only in the fight against the Afghan Taliban can the principles of the surge be implemented. The modest goal of the international forces, as defined by Kilcullen, is "less about directly defeating the Taliban and more about building an Afghan state that can handle the Taliban . . . without permanent large-scale international assistance." That means building trust between villagers and the central government, which must grow infrastructure and provide services that the villages can depend on. Kilcullen's method of going about it is to curry favor with tribal leaders. Although the Pashtun heritage may work somewhat in the Taliban's favor politi-

cally, their strict interpretation of sharia law is a downer. Kilcullen, who has made
field trips in Afghanistan and Pakistan, estimates that a certain low percentage of
tribal people are dedicated Islamists, a roughly similar amount pro-government,
and the remaining majority simply want peace and stability. This silent majority
tends to go with the winning side so they can continue with their lives. They may
become accidental guerrillas unless the international and government forces can
win their loyalty.[19] That fits with the part of the strategy that seeks to drive a wedge
between the Taliban and tribal leaders. It does not help that some Taliban fighters,
who are well paid for their service, flip to the other side on the promise of jobs and
land for their families, only to find after switching sides that neither jobs nor land
are available. Empty promises are another reason why people in Afghanistan don't
trust their government.[20]

Kilcullen offers a road-building project in Kunar Province as exhibit A, not
because the road per se was the solution to the problem, but because of the way
the road builders had to organize and implement a strategy that would improve
local conditions. He describes it as "a full-spectrum strategy . . . to separate insurgents from the people, win local allies, connect the population to the government,
build local governance capacity, modify and improve government behavior, swing
tribes that had supported the insurgency onto the government side," and thereby
take positives strides in counterinsurgency.[21] The reader can readily perceive the
contrast in this approach to the military's search-and-destroy sweep, which takes
innocent lives and leaves destruction in its wake.

The Kunar Valley lies north of Jalalabad along the border with Pakistan. The
Kunar River runs south and empties into the Kabul River, which flows to the
Indus River in Pakistan. About 400,000 people live in Kunar, most of them along
the valley floor. Ninety-five percent of the inhabitants are Pashtun, with some
tribes and subtribes set apart by high ridges that rise up between tributaries that
descend from the mountains on either side of the river. (In 2005 one of these
isolated valleys, Korengal, was the scene of a special operations disaster that cost
nineteen American deaths, America's worst single-mission loss of life in the first
seven years of the war. The episode is described in chapter 5.)

A paved road, of course, is an asset to any lagging economy. To build the
road through Kunar, local people, many of them disenchanted youth otherwise
vulnerable to Taliban recruitment, were hired in 2006 for the construction work.

To secure the construction site, American and Afghan government troops cleared the Taliban from the road's path and from the commanding high ground, and then newly recruited Kunar police helped to keep the Taliban away. Planning and implementation required the participation of tribal leaders, who thus became active in the project with the Kabul government.

For Kilcullen at least, Kunar Province can be counted as a success in that the road project separated the people from the Taliban and connected them to the national government. But the fact remains that in 2009 the Korengal Valley in Kunar was still teeming with Pakistani Taliban, al Qaeda, and other Islamist groups, such as the followers of former Taliban minister Jalaluddin Haqqani and Gulbuddin Hekmatyar. *Vanity Fair* magazine christened Korengal the "Valley of Death," where American patrols were under constant vigil and frequent attack from the surrounding ridges.[22] On July 13, 2009, nine American troops were killed and fifteen wounded in an all-day battle with Islamist fighters. Four more were killed a month later by a roadside bomb.[23] Pakistan's interior minister, Rehman Malik, in denial about al Qaeda sanctuaries in Pakistan, even suggested rather flippantly to London *Sunday Times* reporter Christina Lamb that Osama bin Laden himself might be hiding there.[24]

The West should be building infrastructure like the Kunar Valley road in Afghanistan, if the Afghans agree to it. But the way is not always paved with good intentions. Projects are often stifled by corruption, which feeds on too much money pumped into a community. Contractors might win a bid and then sell the contract, taking their 10 percent off the top. If this happens often enough, the contractor that eventually builds the road, schoolhouse, or municipal building will have to cut corners to make a profit—with the end result of shoddy construction and a disappointed, cynical community. Then the Taliban might sweep down from their mountain hideaway one dark night and blow up a shiny new structure or plant a roadside bomb.

It is that way in much of Afghanistan, where Western troop strength is too thin to keep the Islamists at bay, but conditions improve with enhanced deployments. In the late fall of 2009 ABC News correspondent Martha Raddatz donned her Sunday best flak jacket and took a helicopter ride to a dusty village in Logar Province south of Kabul. She found conditions much improved since her last visit, ten months earlier. Where there had been a small U.S. forward base for three hundred soldiers and a largely deserted village, there was now a larger base to house three thousand additional troops and a lively village filled with busy people shopping at open markets. The larger U.S. force made the difference. Troops engaged the people and patrolled the newly paved main road illuminated by solar street lights that encouraged after-dark shopping. They fought the enemy, too, suffering 28 killed and about 260 wounded. This was clearly the army's showcase made for prime time of how things should go. But the large American base included rows of military buildings and a small airfield. One must ask what will happen to the village when the Americans depart.[25]

Southern Afghanistan prior to 2010 was more of a painful example of slow-footed progress with inadequate force. Even in defeat in 2002, when most of the Taliban fighters in southern Afghanistan retreated in disorder across the border to Baluchistan Province, many Taliban remained behind and simply went underground. The Afghan Taliban, including Mullah Omar, set up headquarters in the Baluchi city of Quetta, while Islamabad denied their existence and the ISI refitted them with new arms and equipment. By the end of that year small Taliban units were being infiltrated back into southern Afghanistan.

Meanwhile, American troops occupied the Pashtun south, including Helmand, Kandahar, Uruzgan, and Zabul provinces, but the troops were spread too thin for effective control. They could not cover such vast territory where the Afghan Taliban retained a presence in many remote areas in greater numbers than the Americans imagined. In December 2005 Secretary of Defense Rumsfeld, preoccupied with Iraq, made matters worse in Afghanistan by ordering the withdrawal of three thousand troops, reducing the American force to sixteen thousand, half of which were put under NATO command.

The timing of the American troop reduction was particularly unfortunate because in the spring of 2006, the Afghan Taliban launched its heaviest offensive yet into Afghanistan, targeting Kandahar and Helmand provinces in particular. They came in bunches from sanctuaries in Baluchistan and deployed in units up to battalion size of four hundred soldiers. That summer a Taliban force prepared for an attack on Kandahar city, until September when ten thousand American, British, Canadian, and Afghan government troops attacked them in the nearby district of Panjwai. After a fierce two-week battle, sometimes fighting house to house or hand to hand, the Taliban were finally subdued. When the victors swept the battlefield, they discovered more than a million rounds of unused ammunition, training facilities for suicide bombers, and a surgical field hospital.[26]

While the Western forces barely held onto Kandahar, the fighting was even less decisive in Helmand Province. The Helmand River rises out of the Hindu Kush and flows southwest through most of the province into the Margow Desert and then turns north to the Seistan marshes and the lake region near Zabol, Iran. Its waters are used to irrigate the thirsty semiarid land for agriculture and in recent years have made it the richest poppy-growing region in the world. The poppies provide an excellent cash crop for local farmers, and the Taliban have taken their cut from the underworld business that turns the sap from the poppy plant into heroin for distribution to Western black markets. Revenues from the drug trade are a major source of funding for arming and equipping the Afghan Taliban.

A British force deployed to Helmand to shore up the NATO defense, but it was not enough. Next to the capture of Kandahar, continued control of Helmand was the Taliban's major objective. They came from Quetta in droves. One convoy of more than a hundred Toyota Land Cruisers, packed with soldiers and supplies, arrived in Helmand in June.[27] Once in Helmand, they meant to stay. A British brigade counterattacked and captured a few towns, but the Taliban fought them to a standstill in fierce combat.

Stalemate was also the operational word in 2008 in the abandoned, mud-brick town of Now Zad, in a sparsely populated district where a U.S. Marine company faced off against a line of Taliban defenders stationed five hundred yards away under cover of pomegranate orchards. Neither side had the strength to dislodge the other or the desire to withdraw and accept defeat. The situation left no chance for the American forces to implement their new strategy of protecting the people and isolating the Taliban. In fact, Now Zad was a ghost town with few if any residents to protect. The American high command was willing to tolerate the stalemate there until reinforcements arrived.

The next year, President Obama, following the lead his predecessor had taken in Iraq, dispatched 21,000 additional troops to Afghanistan. In July 2009, in the first major offensive action of the "Afghanistan surge," 4,000 U.S. Marines and 650 Afghan national troops were airlifted into a seventy-five-mile stretch of the Helmand River valley. The brigade split up into smaller units and deployed around the area. In some situations, early contact with the enemy created more stalemate.

The rules of engagement reflected the new strategy as the Marines took care to avoid civilian casualties. Initially, according to reports, they refrained from calling in air strikes or using artillery. When met with small arms and rocket fire, they would hold their own fire until they could determine that no civilians would be hurt. Before entering one town they first asked permission of village elders to bed down for the night in abandoned homes rather than setting up camp behind sandbags and barbed wire on the outskirts.

One Marine company landed by helicopter at the town of Mianposhteh only to see the townspeople flee en masse into the surrounding desert amid the Taliban, who remained in control of nearby villages. The Marines and a smattering of Afghan government troops did not have enough force to clear them out. A few residents drifted back to their homes, but the marketplace in Mianposhteh was still vacant when *Washington Post* reporter Ann Scott Tyson visited a month later. People feared the Taliban would punish them if they shopped there; instead, they patronized a market down the road in Taliban territory. In Mianposhteh, at least, the new American strategy was not working. The people spurned their American protectors and seemed to go out of their way to stick with the Taliban, probably out of fear that they would be punished for consorting with the Americans. One elderly resident put the issue in plain language to a Marine patrol: "What are you doing in Afghanistan?" he asked. "You should go back to your country."[28]

Despite the stalemate at Now Zad, four hundred Marines and a hundred Afghan troops used the town on August 12 as a base from which to assault Dahaneh, five miles down the road. Dahaneh is a hot, dusty little town of about two thousand residents in normal times and serves as a hub for the transport of narcotics. The Marines hoped to secure it ahead of an August 20 national election that the Taliban had threatened to disrupt. The Taliban had controlled Dahaneh for the past four years and were not about to give it up without a fight. As the Marines pushed into town in midday temperatures that rose above 120 degrees Fahrenheit, the militants responded with mortar, rocket, and heavy machine-gun fire and bombarded Marine positions from the nearby mountains. One Marine was killed by a rocket-propelled grenade. After three days of heavy fighting, Taliban resistance ended on the fourth day. There was no formal surrender. The fighters just faded out of sight. Voting booths were set up in a nearby village, and a few residents of Dahaneh actually voted on August 20.

Encounters with both the Afghan and Pakistani Taliban have taught the U.S. command to respect the enemy's improved military tactics. The Taliban have generally abandoned large-unit attacks and have learned to fight effectively in small groups the way American soldiers are taught in advanced Ranger training. They use mortars to force U.S. troops into defensive positions, and then open up with grenade and small arms fire. When on the move they maintain radio silence. When in fixed positions they sprinkle the ground behind them with water so that dust from the recoil of their weapons does not give away their location.[29] Kilcullen noted "excellent" Taliban marksmanship and fire discipline in describing the ambush in 2006 of an American patrol in an Uruzgan Province valley. "Taliban snipers [firing down from concealed positions] were achieving first-round hits, focusing on communications specialists, heavy weapons operators, and commanders," he wrote. One U.S. soldier was killed and seven others wounded before the patrol could extricate itself under cover of darkness.[30] The tiny village of Wanat, nestled in the narrow Waygal Valley of the Hindu Kush in northeast Afghanistan, witnessed an even bloodier battle. Shortly before dawn on July 13, 2008, two hundred Taliban troops opened up from the surrounding hills on a small, newly established forward outpost occupied by a platoon of about forty soldiers. The enemy knew what it was doing. The opening fusillade of rocket-propelled grenades destroyed the base's antitank missile system and mortar tubes, and then poured down a murderous fire on the outpost. Nine U.S. soldiers were killed and twenty-seven wounded. It seems that the days of easy U.S. victories as in 2001 are over.

THE INTOLERABLE SANCTUARIES

Pakistan's role in this war is as twisted as a jungle vine. A Muslim nation growing increasingly Islamist, Pakistan was America's cold war ally and received billions of U.S. dollars in military aid. When President George W. Bush exhorted nations in 2001 to choose sides in the "war on terror"—"Either you are with us or you are with the terrorists"—then–Pakistani prime minister Pervez Musharraf, his eyes fastened on continued military aid, fell in line. His decision paid off handsomely. In fiscal year 2001 U.S. aid to Pakistan totaled $91 million, and only $3.5 million of that was military and/or security aid. From 2002 to 2007 the aid totaled $3.17 billion of which $1.57 billion was security related.[31]

But the ISI had already guided the Taliban to the conquest of most of Afghanistan. So enmeshed was Pakistan with the Taliban that in late 2001 hundreds of ISI officers and soldiers of its paramilitary Frontier Corps fought against the Northern Alliance and, by proxy, against America. These Pakistani fighters were trapped with several thousand Taliban troops at Kunduz after the fall of Mazar-e Sharif and Taloqan in northeastern Afghanistan, and American planes pounded them with laser-guided bombs. Musharraf called President Bush to ask for a pause in bombing so Pakistan could extricate them. Anxious to keep Musharraf in the fold, Bush granted the request on the advice of his then-mentor, Vice President Dick Cheney. The Pakistanis were airlifted out of Kunduz over several dark nights, and it is reported that a number of Taliban and al Qaeda leaders squeezed onto the rescue planes with them.[32] These militants would live to fight American troops in future battles.

When the bulk of the Islamist fighters retreated from Afghanistan in the winter of 2001–2, the welcome mat was out on the Pakistani side. Mullah Omar established his command at Quetta in Baluchistan, where most of the original Taliban from southern Afghanistan gathered. Al Qaeda was excluded from Quetta in order not to draw the attention of the Americans focused singularly on bin Laden and his followers, who settled initially in the high mountains and deep ravines of South Waziristan. The tribal area became the chosen training ground not only for Arab Islamists and the Pakistani Taliban but also for terrorist candidates from around the world, including Central Asia, Africa, China, Kashmir, and Chechnya. In effect, the Taliban (speaking generically) were now fighting a three-front war. Those taking safe haven in Baluchistan, the original Afghan Taliban, infiltrated across the border into southern Afghanistan. The new crop, the Pakistani Taliban, spread out within the mountain valleys of FATA and NWFP while helping al Qaeda soldiers move across the border they had never recognized to attack Western and Afghan government targets in northeastern Afghanistan.

Because NATO and American forces were primarily interested in crushing al Qaeda, they initially ignored the resurgence of the Taliban in Quetta and pressured Islamabad to act against the Islamist mix in the tribal area. The Musharraf government played a double game, placating the Americans and denying the presence of foreign militants, while the ISI and the Pakistani army continued their outreach to the Islamists, especially the Afghan Taliban, with the open political backing of the powerful Islamist party, JUI. After the Arab television network Al Jazeera ran a video clip on the second anniversary of 9/11 of bin Laden and Zawahiri out for a stroll in a mountainous landscape, Musharraf finally decided that the hills were rife with Islamist fighters and that he should do something about it.

In March 2004 a small, lightly armed unit of the paramilitary Frontier Corps surrounded the Wazir village of Wana, where militants were thought to be hiding. Musharraf suggested disingenuously that a high-value target, possibly Zawahiri, might be among them. But the militants were actually set up in the hills for an ambush. They rained down a deadly fire that riddled the corpsmen and broke up the government attack. Eight thousand regular army troops were rushed to the scene and took two weeks, using heavy artillery, helicopter gunships, and fighter bombers, to subdue the militants. Fifty thousand civilians, their homes destroyed, fled the scene. The militants came out of the fray thinking they had won the battle despite losing more than two hundred fighters killed and captured. The army, which had shown a lack of discipline within the ranks and reluctance to fire on Islamist civilians, negotiated a feeble agreement forgiving Taliban leaders and requiring that foreign militants register, but the agreement quickly broke down.[33]

The army then deployed more troops in South Waziristan in what amounted to an occupation. The militants moved to North Waziristan. More fighting broke out later in 2004 and then ended in another capitulation by the Islamabad government. The army agreed to pay compensation to the militants, then sealed off the entire tribal area to outsiders, barring nongovernment aid agencies and journalists from entering while the Pakistani Taliban tightened their grip on the people by imposing their version of sharia law. In 2007 the Pakistani army launched a new offensive against the Taliban in the tribal area. It brought pitched battles, but no decisive gain for either side.[34]

The Taliban turned its attention to the scenic Swat Valley in the NWFP, only a hundred miles from Islamabad, where Islamist militancy had been on the rise since 2003. Local police fled, and militants gained control of a district in the upper valley. The regular army was called in, and after two weeks of heavy fighting, the Taliban took to the hills. From there they resorted to systematic violence. They might swoop down to kidnap or assassinate prominent Swat leaders, or conduct middle-of-the-night raids to burn down a girls' school, or decapitate police officers and put the headless bodies on public display, or punish someone who violated their sharia law. In 2008 a suicide bomber drove a truck loaded with explosives into a local police station, killing twenty people. By the end of the year the Taliban had regained control in most of the valley. In April 2009 the Pakistani government, now headed by Asif Ali Zardari, the widower of the assassinated Benazir Bhutto, agreed to let the Taliban enforce sharia law in exchange for a cease-fire. But the agreement broke down almost immediately as the Taliban infiltrated Buner, a neighboring valley only seventy miles from Islamabad. Although the capital was not in imminent peril, the army became fully cognizant of the monster it had helped to create. With a renewed sense of commitment on the part of the Zardari government, it opened a full-scale counterattack against the Taliban, retook Buner, and attacked the militants in Swat. Despite the flight of more than 2 million residents who took refuge outside the valley, the army claimed by the end of summer that it had essentially defeated the Taliban in the Swat Valley, although pockets of resistance remained. The success of the Pakistani army has resulted in the capture of several Taliban leaders, which in turn has blocked any further Taliban advance beyond Swat.[35]

American and NATO forces, officially barred from crossing the border into Pakistan, have relied heavily on superior weapons technology and intelligence. In particular, pilotless, remote-controlled American drones capable of conducting both reconnaissance and missile attacks fly across the border over Islamist billets and training camps. Their missiles, fired by CIA technicians (by the military in Afghanistan) amid electronic equipment in a secure communications room from as far away as the United States, have killed a large but undetermined number of militants, including Taliban and al Qaeda leaders. Among the notables reported killed were fourteen of twenty top al Qaeda leaders, and Baitullah Mehsud, the leader of the Pakistani Taliban and the alleged mastermind behind Benazir Bhutto's assassination. These high-tech measures (sigint) have been effectively combined with low-tech intelligence (humint) to impede al Qaeda and Taliban performance. Western intelligence, including the CIA, the British MI6, other NATO agencies, and military SOF, also recruit local spies the old-fashioned way—by paying them for snooping.

Al Qaeda has let its pain be known in a book by one of its field commanders, Abu Yahya al-Libi, who complained that Western spies have "spread over the lands like locusts." Al-Libi wrote in July 2009 that the spies are everywhere in all walks of life in Muslim societies and are ultimately responsible for most of the Islamist soldiers killed or captured by the occupation forces.[36] Two months later a former British intelligence officer confirmed al-Libi's dire plaints without mentioning him by name. Richard Barrett, currently chief of the United Nations' al Qaeda and Taliban monitoring group, gave a speech before the Washington Institute for Near East Policy, citing improved intelligence against al Qaeda: a "much better" technical collection, such as intercepts and overhead surveillance, and "better" human intelligence.[37] As he spoke, top civilian and military strategists were preparing for a White House review of U.S. policy in Afghanistan, specifically how many additional troops to send in.

After the Pakistani Taliban recovered from the loss of their leader, Baitullah Mehsud, they went on the offensive to avenge his death. Attacks included a car bomb in Peshawar that left forty-eight people dead and another car bomb in the Shangla District of Swat Valley that killed forty-one people and injured many more. Residents returned to Shangla after the Pakistani army declared it cleared of militants. The most daring attack was a commando raid against army headquarters in Rawalpindi that killed nineteen and set off a twenty-hour siege before the army regained control.[38] These attacks proved that victories in Pakistan are dearly bought and that the people pay a hefty price.[39] They came as the Pakistani army, under pressure from the United States to do something about the sanctuary problem, prepared in the onset of winter to launch an offensive against Islamist strongholds in South Waziristan.

———

Taking everything into account—the nature of unconventional warfare, the enemy's fanaticism and fighting skill, the topography that in some places limits U.S. mobility and firepower, and especially the sanctuary that allows the enemy to rest veterans and train recruits—the prospects for an American victory in Afghanistan seem poor. The people-first strategy that asks soldiers to hold their fire when fired upon to avoid civilian casualties can only increase the risk to Western troops.

It is unfair to put soldiers in the line of fire wearing handcuffs, figuratively speaking. The president knows all this, but he is under the pressure that goes with the rampant militarism in the American society. Getting in was the easy part; getting out is very difficult.

The hearts and minds strategy itself is both sensible and sensitive, but not entirely effective. It succeeded in Iraq because the Sunni tribesmen were fed up with the extremists grasping for power by killing tribal elders under cover of sharia law. The Islamists were as much outsiders as the occupying Americans, and the tribesmen chose to side with the Americans, the lesser of two evils in their mind. It worked well enough to allow America to declare victory and promise to leave. Not so pretty in Afghanistan, where the indigenous fighters, the Taliban, are on an ideological par with al Qaeda. The Taliban are almost entirely Pashtun, so it is no accident that that they are most successful in the Pashtun belt in southern and eastern Afghanistan. While not all Pashtun are Taliban, many tribesmen might side with the Taliban out of ethnic solidarity. What they really want is to be left alone to pursue their tribal ways and fight their own battles. Taliban rule in the Pashtun belt is really for the Pashtun to decide. It becomes an American, and more generally a Western, problem only when the Taliban allow al Qaeda and other militant organizations to train for international terrorism. Based on their unyielding adherence to the Salafist belief system and the history of Taliban rule, there is every reason to believe that they would do exactly that if the Taliban were to regain power in Afghanistan.

The problem is clear, but the solution is not. The existence of sanctuaries in FATA or elsewhere that allow al Qaeda to plot terrorist acts in America and around the world is intolerable. But U.S. and NATO ground troops cannot attack them without violating Pakistani sovereignty. So they skirt the issue by employing human and high-tech intelligence and precision rocket attacks sending pilotless drones against al Qaeda and Taliban targets in Pakistan, as well as al Qaeda targets in Afghanistan. These tactics have produced positive results for Western forces but stimulated anti-American feelings in both countries over civilian casualties. The United States has pressured Pakistan to send its army against the sanctuaries. A lot depends on if, and how well, the Pakistani army carries out that mission.

5

SHADES OF RAMBO

The modern era in special operations began with the tragic death of eight Americans in the Iranian desert on April 24, 1980. They were on a mission called Operation Eagle Claw to rescue fifty-three hostages seized in the American embassy in Tehran the previous November by young Iranian ideologues. Out of the wreckage and death in the Iranian desert, a more organized form of small-war fighters was established under the Joint Special Operations Command (JSOC) in December 1980. It draws the cream of the armed forces—originally and still prominently Army Delta and Navy SEALs with high aptitude and advanced training in the skills of warfare—to fill the ranks of covert-action teams for counterterrorism missions, including intelligence, reconnaissance, air strikes, raids, rescues, protection, and small ground assaults. Over the years these teams have operated at home and abroad in places such as Central Asia, Latin America, the Philippines, the Middle East, Grenada, Panama, Somalia, and the chaotic Balkans.

Even if the 1980 hostage rescue mission in Iran had not been aborted during the stopover in the desert, the odds for total success were limited by a lack of human intelligence on the ground in Tehran. It later surfaced that the CIA had assets with useful information about precisely where the hostages were located and exactly how to get them out. But reportedly unwilling to risk a perceived failure that would reflect negatively on the agency, the CIA withheld the information.[1] The bane of government bureaucracy had apparently doomed the mission before it got off the desert.

The problem was bigger than just the CIA. Every branch of military service had to be involved whether or not they knew what they were doing. Consequently, the mission was ill coordinated, and the participants were poorly trained. Helicopters stowed aboard ship in the Persian Gulf were badly maintained, and when three of the eight broke down by the time the rescue team reached the desert staging area, the mission had to be aborted because a minimum of six were deemed necessary for success. Then the air collision that killed eight men turned what could have been a quiet failure into a public fiasco.

Preparations began immediately for a second rescue attempt code-named Honey Badger. This operation had an intelligence unit attached to it called the Foreign Operating Group (coincidentally called FOG), which had been established the year before to secretly survey U.S. embassies abroad for security weaknesses. FOG was put to use for Honey Badger to check out the embassy in Tehran. The intelligence team learned a great deal about the guards, their weapons, and the kinds of locks on the doors—information that would have been useful for the first attempt. Most importantly, it learned that the hostages had been widely dispersed, making a second attempt unfeasible.

The success of the FOG experience was an eye-opener. Military intelligence became an indispensable element of the renewed covert organization, which would combine personnel from the various services into an integrated special unit. FOG was drawn in and renamed the Intelligence Support Activity (ISA). Where a crisis arose, the ISA could enter a country under cover with pockets full of cash and run agents to turn up vital information that the rescue mission for the Iranian hostage situation did not have. And for new missions, the ISA could go along to keep track of the enemy by monitoring cell phone conversations and to harvest any intelligence the mission uncovered.

In short, the ISA would perform the sort of information gathering the CIA and National Security Agency (NSA) did routinely on a larger scale, only it would zero in on a particular situation and be under military control. Not wanting to set up a rivalry with the CIA, Gen. Edward C. Meyer, who led the push to revamp special ops in 1981, decided to run the intelligence plan by CIA Director William Casey, who was close to President Ronald Reagan. Casey heard him out and told him to keep the ISA under military control.[2] Subsequently, JSOC and the CIA cooperated on many special missions, along with their British and other NATO counterparts who often participated in joint operations.

THE BASICS

Only the crème de la crème need apply to the special operations forces, and the chances of making it are slim. To enter the Navy SEAL program for basic underwater demolition, the applicant must be able to swim five hundred yards breast- or sidestroke in twelve and a half minutes, run a mile and a half wearing boots and long pants in eleven and a half minutes, do forty-two push-ups and fifty sit-ups in two minutes each, and do six pull-ups (no time limit). Before they take the test, recruits are offered a thirteen to twenty-six week regimen of running, swimming, calisthenics, and weight-lifting to get in shape. Even so, most applicants do not qualify. The basic program takes twenty-five weeks for physical conditioning, diving, and land warfare. Then it's on to army jump school and six to twelve months of training for real situations.

The Army qualifications are no less demanding. Delta Force, the highest rung on the ladder, recruits primarily from the elite Army Special Forces and Rangers. (Special Forces, or Green Berets, a lower level of elite than Delta, should not be confused with SOF, the generic term for the combined special services.) Those wishing to enter Special Forces must first undergo basic military training and then try out for the program. If they make it, the program takes from twenty-four to fifty-seven weeks, and the applicant might spend up to another year learning a language.

Rangers must go through jump school and pass a Ranger fitness program that requires completion of a five-mile run in forty minutes, fifteen meters of combat water survival in full combat dress, and two long road marches (including one of ten miles). For those aspiring to lead a Ranger unit, a tough two-month course in Ranger School awaits.

Then the very best in these units ranking sergeant or above can apply for Delta Force.[3] The Delta training course is classified, but Eric L. Haney gave an account of his personal experience as a candidate for Delta in 1978 in his fascinating book, *Inside Delta Force*. Selection started with push-ups, sit-ups, a "run-dodge-jump," an "inverted crawl" (crawling face up), a two-mile run, and a swim test wearing fatigues and combat boots. Except for the swim test, the exercises were timed. That evening, there was an eighteen-mile walk carrying a forty-pound rucksack. Then for a week, the recruits (all ranked sergeant or higher) were put out alone in the woods with maps, compass, and survival equipment to test their ability to find their way from point A to point B. Then they spent ten days bivouacking, hiking uphill and downhill, and orienting themselves in rugged mountain terrain, all of it topped off with a forty-mile hike starting at 3 a.m. that became a fifty-mile-plus hike for Haney because he turned onto the wrong path in the dark. The entire hike took him eighteen hours. Psychiatric tests were in the mix, and a final review from a team headed by the top honcho, Col. Charles Beckwith. Haney was one of 12 selected out of 163 who started.[4]

Steven Emerson gave his readers a sense of advanced Delta training in his 1988 book, *Secret Warriors*, about covert operations during the Reagan era. "Its members jumped blindfolded from planes," he wrote, "stormed buildings and planes in mock rescue missions and often practiced their shooting techniques with live ammunition. They could drive trains, refuel aircraft, pacify hysterical hostages, and perform whatever other tasks were necessary under a myriad of adverse conditions."[5]

According to insider Haney, the smallest unit of Delta is the team, consisting of four members. Each team has its own special set of skills. Four or five teams come together as a troop. Two or three troops make up a squadron, and squadrons can be broken down into smaller units for missions. Other highly trained individuals with particular skills might also be assigned to a mission as needed.[6]

In *Black Hawk Down* Mark Bowden personified Delta in the image of Sgt. Paul Howe during the Mogadishu disaster of 1993. Howe had "the massive frame of a serious bodybuilder, and a fine, if impatient analytical mind," wrote Bowden. Having entered Delta selection and training in a class of 120 highly motivated soldiers, Howe was one of only thirteen to finish. Howe and his Delta buddies disdained the spit and polish of regular army and paid scant attention to the protocols of rank. They often tried to hide their Delta identity by growing beards, keeping their hair long and dressing in civilian clothes. Howe looked down on the Rangers who fought with him in Mogadishu as poorly trained and unprepared for battle, and they looked up to him in fear and awe, but followed him when their lives were on the line.[7]

The elite SOF—Delta, SEALs, etc.—are few in number. Their activities are necessarily limited to small but important missions that most soldiers could not be expected to carry out. Where a mission requires greater numbers, the call would go first to the lesser elites—Green Berets, Rangers, etc.—and then, on still bigger missions, to regular army. In Mogadishu, Delta successfully completed the most important part of the ill-fated operation of October 3, 1993: the snatch of top aides to militia leader Mohamed Farrah Aidid while Rangers provided cover. Then all hell broke loose. The reader should keep in mind that Deltas are human. They can die too, and five Deltas did die in Mogadishu that day.[8]

British special ops are trusted partners in this dangerous pastime. *Jane's World Armies* reports that a UK soldier must serve at least three years to be considered for the Special Air Service (SAS), that only 15 percent of applicants are accepted, and about a third of those accepted don't make it through the rigorous training course. The Special Boat Service (SBS), the British navy's version of the U.S. SEALs, lays down similar training requirements for membership.[9] Often American and British special teams carry out missions together, just as the CIA cooperates closely with MI6, British foreign intelligence. Sometimes, as in Operation Enduring Freedom in Afghanistan, the separate elite national forces became international teams. In fact, several NATO countries contributed specialists to the Afghanistan operations that helped the Northern Alliance rout the Taliban in 2001–2.[10]

The training program for the American ISA puts added stress on the brain. Trainees, who might come from any number of special operations programs, are conditioned to expect the unexpected. They might be inserted in the middle of a desert without food, water, or communications equipment and given the task of completing a difficult intelligence assignment. Or they might be forced to go without sleep for days and then dropped off in an unfamiliar city to carry out a mission with "enemy" agents on their trail. Then they would be taught tricks of the trade: survival skills, parachuting, weapons training, and agent running.

Once in action, ISA personnel might be called on to enter a hostile country to gather intelligence by observation or running agents. They might be asked to set up a landing zone for a covert raiding or rescue mission. When assigned to accompany a special ops raiding party, one of an ISA soldier's primary tasks is tuning into enemy cell phone conversations.[11] When the raiding party has completed its job, the intelligence team will sweep the premises for useful short- or long-term information that might extend the operation.

PRE-9/11

During the Gulf War (1990–91) American and British special operations forces provided important targeting information for air attacks on Scud missile sites.

At least eighty-eight Scud missiles were fired at Israel and the Arabian Peninsula, sometimes, if not always causing death and damage.[12] But because they were not very accurate their main effect was psychological. For this reason, Scud-hunting had a low priority, and air strikes against fixed and mobile launch sites in the western Iraqi desert had minimal impact. Special ops also conducted reconnaissance operations deep into enemy territory and trained Kuwaiti and other Arab recruits.

The American and British partners carried out a particularly sensitive and dangerous Gulf War mission in January 1991. The air war to soften up Iraqi defensive positions in occupied Kuwait had already begun. In the dark of a moonless night, two Royal Air Force Chinook helicopters carried thirty-six British commandoes and three American specialists from ISA to Iraq's Amariya communications center thirty miles from Baghdad. As the helicopters descended at Amariya, the team could see a pulsating glow on the horizon from a diversionary bombing raid on Baghdad. Once on the ground, twenty commandoes, armed with machine guns and antitank weapons, split off to form a defensive cordon to parry any Iraqi response to their presence. The other sixteen prepared explosive charges while the Americans dug for a length of fiber-optic cable that they had the particular training to identify. The cable had been requested by the NSA to help the eavesdroppers more than six thousand miles away intercept messages to the Iraqi front lines in Kuwait. After an hour and a half of locating and digging, the Americans found and retrieved the sought-after cable, and the British demolition crew dropped their charges into the hole and blew the leftover wiring to shreds, an action that covered evidence of a missing cable. Then the defenders pulled back from their perimeter, and the lot of them piled into the helicopters for the return trip to Saudi Arabia, just minutes before an Iraqi military force arrived to learn that they were late for the party.[13]

ISA also spearheaded intelligence gathering in the former Yugoslavia a few years later by tracking mobile telephone intercepts for a NATO operation to kidnap accused Bosnian Serb war criminals for trial at the Hague, Netherlands. The Bosnian Serbs were accused of murdering thousands of Muslims in an orgy of ethnic cleansing. Most of the actual NATO abductions were carried out by Dutch and especially British commandoes working in Bosnia. One British team penetrated fifty miles inside Serbia on September 27, 1998, to snatch Stevan Todorović at a remote hideaway. He went to trial at the International Criminal Tribunal for the former Yugoslavia and negotiated a plea of guilty to a single count of a crime against humanity and received a ten-year sentence.[14]

Later, U.S. Navy SEALs joined the action with the capture of Radislav Krstić, the so-called butcher of Srebrenica, where more than seven thousand Muslim men and boys were massacred at a United Nations camp that was supposed to be a safe haven. Krstić surrendered quietly to the heavily armed SEALs who stopped his chauffeur-driven car in northeastern Bosnia. The charges against Krstić were far more serious than the one against Todorović. Krstić's act was considered the worst case of genocide since the Holocaust. He was tried, convicted, and sentenced to forty-six years in prison. The sentence was reduced to thirty-five years on appeal. If he serves out his full term, he will be eighty-eight when released in 2036.

THE EARLY HUNT FOR BIN LADEN

Osama bin Laden was on the American hit list well before 9/11, having twice declared war on America: in 1996, soon after moving from Sudan to Afghanistan, and in 1998, when he joined with Zawahiri to form the IIF. In the first he called terrorism against America "a legitimate and morally demanded duty."[15] In the second he repeated his bellicose preachment with greater emphasis: "We call on every Muslim . . . to abide by Allah's order by killing Americans and stealing their money anywhere, anytime, and whenever possible."[16]

Just the big talk was enough to arouse the Clinton White House. On May 22, 1998, President Clinton appointed Richard A. Clarke to head the newly created White House Counterterrorism Security Group, an office that Clarke himself had proposed to advise the president on terrorist activities around the world and coordinate U.S. covert operations. The White House pressed Gen. Hugh Shelton, chairman of the Joint Chiefs of Staff, to come up with a plan to snatch bin Laden, but Shelton, haunted by the ghost of failure in the Iranian desert, was reluctant to commit to any special ops plan that carried the risk of a similar fate. That left the president's civilian security staff in a bind. The CIA kept proposing ways to get bin Laden but lacked the necessary muscle to carry them through. Special ops had the muscle, but the Pentagon brass shied away from creating ideas for using it.

One of the first operations Clarke considered was a plan to capture bin Laden offered by Gary Schroen, chief of the CIA station in Islamabad, Pakistan. It focused on a former agricultural cooperative near Kandahar Airport called Tarnak

Farm, which the Taliban regime had made available to bin Laden. The facility contained about eighty living units for bin Laden's family and followers and a six-story office building, about a hundred acres in all surrounded by a ten-foot mud-brick wall. Bin Laden was in and out and often slept there with one or another of his four wives. The plan called for a raiding party of about thirty Afghan tribesmen in the CIA's employ to slip into Tarnak one dark night; search the separate wives' living quarters until they found the tall, bearded leader; bundle him off to a mountain hideout about thirty miles distant; and hold him until the CIA took him away. The White House wanted to avoid killing anyone, including bin Laden. It was a flawed plan, and doubts about its chances for success surfaced at higher levels of the CIA and within the White House. The proposal died before it ever reached the Oval Office for the president's signature.[17]

Then bin Laden struck. At mid-morning on August 7, 1998, two truck bombs exploded within less than ten minutes at the American embassies in Nairobi, Kenya, and Dar-es-Salaam, Tanzania, about 450 miles apart. The eighteen-hundred-pound Nairobi bomb went off in the rear of the embassy in a U-shaped courtyard flanked by two commercial buildings. The embassy and a bank building were severely damaged. The third building was completely destroyed. Two hundred and thirteen people, including twelve Americans, were killed. In Dar-es-Salaam, a refrigerator truck carrying a bomb of lesser strength failed to gain entry through the embassy's front gate, and the explosion was less devastating than Nairobi's. Eleven people died, all Africans. More than five thousand suffered injuries in the two bombings. Al Qaeda operatives from the inner core managed both attacks.[18]

This was al Qaeda's first major strike in its newly declared war on America, and it called for a serious response from Washington. At the strong urging of CIA chief George Tenet and Clarke, President Clinton ordered missile attacks against the Zawhar Kili training camp in eastern Afghanistan and an alleged chemical weapons plant in Khartoum, which actually made pharmaceuticals. About twenty terrorists were killed in the Afghanistan raid. The Americans hoped bin Laden would be among them, but he was not.[19] In all, eighty-eight missiles were fired at the two targets at a cost of $750,000 each, a total of $66 million, or about $3.3 million per kill.

After the embassy bombings, bin Laden's capture gained a high-priority status, and if he should be killed in the effort, that would be acceptable. Sandy Berger,

President Clinton's national security adviser, ordered the Pentagon to station two cruise-missile submarines off the coast of Pakistan, ready to fire on short notice in case bin Laden's location should ever be fixed with a high degree of certainty. Once the president signed the order, the missiles could be launched in about four hours. Soon, the CIA reported that the al Qaeda chief would be sleeping one night in the governor's house in Kandahar, but because Clinton feared that a missile might miss the target and hit a nearby mosque, killing innocent civilians, the missiles were never launched.[20]

In February 1999 the CIA's Gary Schroen located bin Laden falcon hunting with sheikhs from the United Arab Emirates in the western desert of Afghanistan. Based on human and signal intelligence and satellite photography, the agency had full confidence in its information. But higher-ups worried that members of the UAE's royal family might be in the hunting party. The United States had close economic, military, and intelligence ties to the UAE government. Clarke had actually worked in its employ and knew the royal family. Both Clarke and Tenet recommended against a missile launch, and the Pentagon was very reluctant to go through with it. The opportunity arose just as President Clinton was facing an impeachment vote in the Senate over the Monica Lewinsky affair. Clinton told his staff not to take the Lewinsky affair into account in their deliberations over bin Laden, and still no missiles were fired at the hunting camp.[21]

POST-9/11, AFGHANISTAN

In the aftermath of 9/11 SOF have been in the thick of the action in Afghanistan and Iraq, going after "high-value targets" as part of America's counterterrorism effort. Designated as task forces (TFs) and usually working in small groups, they are in constant flux. Shaped according to the mission and equipped with the best available high-tech weaponry for the job at hand, they have become a basic unit of counterterrorism and counterinsurgency. Different task forces are created for different tasks.[22]

The CIA, together with MI6, took the lead in Afghanistan immediately after 9/11. In late September the tenacious Gary Schroen, who put off retirement in this time of crisis, flew into the Panjshir Valley and across northern Afghanistan at the head of a ten-man team to make contact with the Northern Alliance, whose ethnic tribes had little in common except hatred for the Taliban. He brought with him a metal suitcase filled with $3 million in $100 bills to rent, not buy, the loyalty of tribal leaders (their loyalty was ensured only as long as the money held out).[23] The air campaign beginning in early October initially focused on training camps near major cities and then on command, control, and communication targets, the classic strategy for air operations to soften up the enemy.

The battle plan, as drawn up by Gen. Tommy Franks, commander of U.S. Central Command, initially targeted Mazar-e Sharif near the Uzbekistan border to secure a land route for supplies. Next it called for the capture of Taloqan in the far northeast of Afghanistan near Tajikistan to clear the NA's rear. Finally, the main attack southward would come against the Taliban forces on the Shomali Plains fronting Kabul. As the Tajik ethnics emerged from their stronghold in the Panjshir Valley to face off against the Taliban on the Shomali Plains, the Uzbeks and Hazaras attacked Mazar-e Sharif from opposite directions.

Before they advanced, American airpower asserted itself with unimaginable force. Special ops teams assigned to the NA militias were armed with laser designators to "paint" targets and satellite radios in order to coordinate the variety of warplanes that flew up to a hundred combat sorties a day. The ground teams would aim their lasers and call for a nearby plane to lay its eggs. The bombs would lock onto the laser beams and hit their targets with uncanny accuracy. Less frequently, precision targeting was accomplished using global positioning satellites. One type of bomb, the BLU-82, nicknamed the "daisy cutter," was so big it had to be carried by an MC-130 transport plane and rolled out the rear cargo door. Originally designed to clear helicopter landing zones in Vietnam, it was used in Afghanistan for its antipersonnel and psychological effects. It explodes just before it hits the ground, leaves no crater, and has a lethal radius variously reported to be somewhere between three hundred and nine hundred feet.[24]

At the Tangi Pass outside Mazar-e Sharif, where Taliban forces were dug in to protect the city, one day of intense precision bombing was enough to benumb the defenders who survived. NA militia on foot, on horseback, and in pickup trucks rushed in to capture the city. Taloqan fell as the militia charged without waiting for the bombs to prepare the way. Kunduz, where Islamist forces had gathered between Mazar-e Sharif and Taloqan, held out for eleven days of aerial bombardment before the two sides negotiated the Taliban's surrender. The Taliban, fearing they would die at the hands of the Northern Alliance, preferred to surrender to

American troops, but the United States refused. The Taliban's fears were justified. Thousands died in captivity. About 250 were killed in a six-day prison revolt at Qala Jangi outside Mazar-e Sharif that also took the lives of about a hundred Uzbek militiaman under the command of Rashid Dostum sent in to quell the rioting. One casualty at Qala Jangi was a CIA officer, Johnny "Mike" Spann, who became the first American to die in the Afghan war. After the prisoners were subdued, about 7,500 of them were packed into the containers of about thirty trucks, 250 or more to a truck, stuffed in like sardines with little air to breathe, for transport to a jail at Shiberghan, Dostum's hometown. Only a few in each truck survived the journey. The thousands of Taliban who suffocated were buried in mass graves dug by bulldozers.[25]

In the meantime, Kabul, the Afghan capital, fell in only three days as the U.S. Air Force decimated the Taliban defenses on the Shomali Plain. The attack on the southern city of Kandahar came from two directions. Hamid Karzai, a Pashtun and future leader of Afghanistan, approached from the north with a special ops team. He picked up anti-Taliban fighters as he went. At Tarin Kot in the rugged foothills of the Hindu Kush, Karzai halted to negotiate with the Taliban. The Taliban responded by sending a force of a thousand men in pickup trucks to attack him. But special ops spotters zeroed in on the convoy, and American planes turned it back with precision bombs. Another Pashtun force loyal to former provincial governor Gul Agha Sherzai accompanied by a special ops team moved up from the southeast. Kandahar fell on December 7.[26]

The Northern Alliance conquest of Afghanistan had taken only forty-nine days, thanks to U.S. airpower. About fifteen thousand NA troops, aided by about 350 SOF and a hundred CIA officers routed fifty to sixty thousand Taliban, several thousand al Qaeda, and several hundred Pakistani Frontier Corps troops.[27]

To backtrack somewhat, the CIA played a critical role as the battle for Kabul shaped up, highlighting the curious ways that war can be fought in that part of the world. A few days before the bombing began, Schroen, finally on his way to retirement, departed the scene. In his place, Gary Berntsen, a veteran of the clandestine service, took over as field commander with a money chest of $8 million, more than twice as large as Schroen's. Berntsen bought a few trucks and jeeps and spent $500,000 to induce a Taliban chieftain to defect. Seven hundred and thirty men walked with their leader to the winning side with hands up and weapons down.

Before crossing over, they killed twenty diehard al Qaeda fighters attached to their unit.[28] That and other defections coincided with the start of the air campaign against the dug-in Taliban, and the combination put the defenders in a panicky flight.

With the fall of Kabul, Berntsen shifted his command center to the Afghan capital and sent teams east to Jalalabad and south to Logar Province, two areas teeming with Taliban and al Qaeda, in search of bin Laden. They became TF 11. Bin Laden was pinpointed first in Jalalabad, and his trail led south and uphill to the mountain hideaway of Tora Bora, near the border with Pakistan. The American team followed with an assortment of CIA, SOF, and language specialists. Afghan tribal forces were enlisted to engage the enemy in combat, but these men were of dubious reliability. They were happy to earn a paycheck from Uncle Sam, but some of them still harbored sympathies for al Qaeda. Four men from the U.S. special ops team, armed with a laser designator, split off from the rest and climbed out of sight of the enemy to a height overlooking an al Qaeda camp. They discovered hundreds of bin Laden's soldiers well armed with guns, trucks, and tanks, milling around amid living quarters and command posts. The U.S. team set up the designator, trained it on the targets below, and called in air strikes. Soon the encampment was turned to rubble, and the valley floor was littered with bodies and wreckage. Survivors moved deeper into Tora Bora, where caves and tunnels dotted the mountainside, and the spotter team followed, reinforced by another special ops team that climbed to a different location overlooking the enemy. Two laser beams trained on the camp meant more death and destruction for al Qaeda. Bin Laden and his forces were thoroughly defeated at Tora Bora, and the death toll of militants would have been much worse had not one of the Afghan tribal leaders on the U.S. side, Hazrat Ali, agreed to a temporary cease-fire that allowed several hundred al Qaeda fighters to escape into Pakistan.[29] At this point in the war, when bin Laden strolled into Pakistan, the American high command has been faulted for its failure to put U.S. troops in place to block the exit.

Back in Kabul, Berntsen asked more than once that American ground troops be airlifted behind the surviving al Qaeda fighters to block their retreat into Pakistan. But it never happened. Instead, Franks sent twelve hundred Marines to the Kandahar region, where they saw little action. After taking a terrible pounding at Tora Bora, the battered al Qaeda forces escaped. General Franks, in after-battle testimony on Capitol Hill, suggested that he had not put U.S. troops in a blocking position because he was concerned about American casualties and defended his reliance on the unreliable Afghans who actually aided al Qaeda. General Frank's errors, unusual for a soldier, seemed to reflect a desire by the Bush administration to win big without paying a high price in American casualties. The capture or killing of the al Qaeda leader would have evened the score for the 9/11 atrocity and put a serious crimp in (but probably not stopped) the forward march of global terrorism.[30]

During this period, U.S. and British SOF launched a modestly successful commandolike offensive in southern Afghanistan, deep inside Taliban territory. The Taliban may have been surprised by the Allies' operation, but the Allies were equally surprised by the fast response and fierce resistance of the Taliban fighters. Special ops soldiers complained that they were being used as infantry in numbers too small against an enemy too strong in a manner inconsistent with their training.[31] Several soldiers who had endured expensive training were wounded for an objective of little practical value, and their comrades accused Pentagon brass of staging the operation and taping it with grainy video to counter public criticism of their failure to commit sufficient American troops to battle.

IRAQ

TF 20 appeared in Iraq soon after the invasion in 2003 to go after the missing Saddam Hussein; his notorious sons, Uday and Qusay; and other Baath Party loyalists—fifty-five individuals in all, pictured on gimmicky playing cards. TFs 5 and 20 were merged to form TF 121, focused primarily on Iraq. In a matter of months Saddam and most of his followers were in custody, and his sons were killed in a shootout.

TF 20 caught up with Uday and Qusay in Mosul on a hot July day in 2003. An Iraqi who had once served three years in prison for impersonating a relative of Saddam Hussein provided the tip-off that they were hiding in his villa. His incentive for turning them in was probably the $15 million price tag on each of the brothers' heads. Delta men stormed through the front gate while elements of the 101st Airborne Division provided cover. Inside the exterior wall, they separated into two groups. One broke down the front door while the other entered from the back through a basement garage. They quickly cleared the ground floor and learned that the brothers, ready to fight to the death along with Qusay's fourteen-year-old son, Mustafa, and a bodyguard, had barricaded themselves upstairs. Other bodyguards had been quartered in a nearby house and cordoned off by the U.S. support troops. The assault team pulled out of the villa to allow automatic fire and heavy armor that included antitank missiles to be trained on the building. The exchange of fire lasted four hours. Mustafa, the brave teenager, was the last of the four to die.[32]

TF 121 spent the next five months chasing the fugitive Saddam around Iraq. He never stayed put for more than a few days. Sometimes it was a matter of hours. Once or twice his pursuers found warm slippers he had hastily left behind. The reward for fingering him was $25 million. In December the tip came from one of Saddam's bodyguards that he was hiding on a farm ten miles south of his home-town, Tikrit. From satellite imagery, special ops developed a plan to cut off elec-tricity and surround the farm with six hundred troops from the Fourth Infantry Division. At 10:00 p.m. on the thirteenth, forty Delta soldiers and ISA specialists moved in to conduct a search. Inside a mud-brick, two-room building one of the soldiers spotted a crack in the floor next to a dirty rug. They pulled back the rug, lifted a slab of Styrofoam, uncovered a hole in the ground, and found the fugitive president of Iraq, who meekly surrendered after trying to negotiate with his cap-tors with $750,000 found in his possession. Saddam Hussein was taken into cus-tody and later turned over to an Iraqi court. He was tried, convicted, and hanged for crimes against his own people.

Then TF 121 went after the Islamist infiltrator, Abu Musab al-Zarqawi, whom bin Laden designated as his man in Iraq. Bin Laden had also dubbed Zar-qawi's organization al Qaeda in Mesopotamia. During the three years that the elite SOF troops chased Zarqawi around the countryside, TF 121 evolved into TF 145 with several subgroups. They came close to capturing the man several times, but he managed each time to slip away, as if he had nine lives. On one occasion at night, they knew his itinerary and set up a roadblock, but Zarqawi zipped through it. The blocking group jumped into a military vehicle and took off after him. Zarqawi's driver turned a corner out of sight of the pursuers and let Zarqawi off into a dark field. The Americans caught the driver and confiscated a wealth of documents but lost Zarqawi. Another time, TF 145 raided a house while Zarqawi was meeting with three top lieutenants. In a firefight, the three aides were killed and Zarqawi was wounded but escaped through a tunnel. One U.S. soldier also died in the exchange of fire. As time passed, most if not all of Zarqawi's top Arab lieutenants who had trained in al Qaeda camps were killed or captured, leaving Zarqawi to lean on green Iraqi volunteers.[33]

Finally, in June 2006 the American unit zeroed in on him at a safe house north of Baghdad and called in an F-16 fighter jet to lay two five-hundred-pound precision bombs on the target. The bombs leveled the house, killing six people, including Zarqawi. Both the execution and aftermath of that exercise tell a lot about the growing sophistication and dynamics of the ISA unit that went along with the muscle men and was on the spot to search the premises. From documents, computer hard drives, and other digital equipment ISA found at the scene, and without waiting for analysis from the experts back at headquarters, TF 145 carried out seventeen other raids that night, killing one other person and capturing twenty-five militants. More raids followed in subsequent nights as TF 145 made optimal use of their newfound intelligence.

BACK TO AFGHANISTAN

If Iraq became the major focus of SOF in 2003, Afghanistan and the Islamists' sanctuaries in Pakistan were not entirely forgotten. The principal goal was always to kill or capture the Islamists' Big Three: Osama bin Laden and Ayman al-Zawahiri, numbers one and two of al Qaeda, and Mohammad Omar, leader of the original Taliban. The sovereignty of Pakistan, America's ally by virtual shotgun wedding, remained a sensitive issue. It kept U.S. and NATO ground troops from crossing the border in large numbers to attack the Islamists in their sanctuaries. Frustrated on the ground, the CIA began using Predator remote-controlled, pilotless drones armed with Hellfire missiles over the tribal areas of Pakistan to bombard Islamist forces. In June 2004 the U.S. military reported that a Hellfire missile knocked off Nek Muhammad Wazir, a Taliban chieftain.[34] The following year the drones dispatched an explosives expert and a high-ranking al Qaeda leader, Abu Hamza Rabia.[35] While the remote attacks may have been aimed at al Qaeda and Taliban militants, they often killed innocent civilians. In January 2006 the United States attacked the village of Damadola, where Zawahiri was thought to be meeting with other al Qaeda leaders. If he was there, the bombs missed him, but at least eighteen other people were killed.[36]

In 2009 a drone attack killed Baitullah Mehsud, the aggressive leader of the Pakistani Taliban.[37] Later that year Saleh al-Somali, al Qaeda's number three man, was killed in a drone attack. Somali was responsible for planning terrorist operations in Africa and Europe.[38] The process of decapitating militant leaders is a tried and true method of quelling terrorism. Russia and Israel did it in their respective ways in Chechnya and Gaza and achieved the results they were looking for. In Pakistan the drone bombings are more like full-scale aerial warfare aimed at followers and leaders alike, which probably explains why so many civilians are caught in the carnage.

It is always hard to know from a distance with such incidents how many victims were jihadists and how many, innocent people. Reports out of Pakistan suggested that the missiles were killing mostly civilians and very few militants. Even David Kilcullen, who is invested in the principle of protecting civilians while isolating Islamists, has harshly criticized the drone killings. In an article published on the *New York Times* op-ed page, he cited news reports over three years of seven hundred civilians killed in drone attacks compared with only fourteen militant leaders who died the same way during the same time period, thus causing victimized civilians to cast their lot with the militants. These figures seem wildly misleading.[39] Peter Bergen and Katherine Tiedemann of the New American Foundation have made a valiant effort to sort out fact from fiction. Combing news sources they considered reliable, they estimated that in the eighty-three drone attacks from 2006 to October 2009 a total of about 760 to 1,050 people have been killed. Of those numbers, they judged that 500 to 720 were militants, including about twenty al Qaeda and Taliban leaders, and 260 to 320 were civilians. In other words, about two-thirds of those killed were militants and about a third, civilians. From January through October 2009, with President Obama taking a hard line against the terrorists, at least forty-two drone missile strikes were launched, exceeding the number fired during the entire Bush term.[40] The achievements of the air campaign, together with Pakistani army gains against the Taliban in the Swat Valley, gave American strategists a boost of confidence.[41]

In November 2009 the *Nation* magazine revealed that JSOC had covertly outsourced drone operations in Pakistan to a private civilian company known formerly as Blackwater USA and subsequently as Xe Services and U.S. Training Center. Blackwater had made an ugly name for itself in Iraq by killing innocent people with random gunfire, including an incident on October 4, 2007, when Blackwater guards escorting U.S. State Department personnel killed seventeen

Iraqi civilians with unprovoked gunfire in Baghdad's Nisour Square. For the Pakistan drone operation, the company hired U.S. special ops veterans and paid them handsomely to man a nondescript control room in Karachi to guide the pilotless drones and recommend missile strikes against likely Taliban or al Qaeda targets in a program that roughly paralleled the CIA operation. Official sources within the Obama administration and the Pentagon either declined comment or denied that such an operation existed.[42] Such denials or "no comments" are standard operating procedure for covert operations. If the report is true, it is a major new development in the latest growth industry of outsourcing military operations to civilian contractors. The *New York Times* later reported that Blackwater personnel hired in Iraq and Afghanistan to protect government agents and transport detainees were actually participating in snatch-and-grab activities conducted by the CIA. Both the CIA and Blackwater denied the allegation.[43]

After the battle at Tora Bora in late 2001, most of American SOF were redirected to Iraq, and what was left of them in Afghanistan fell under NATO command. One duty left to them was the training of Afghan forces. They also carried out missions for reconnaissance and in search of so-called al Qaeda persons of interest. One mission backfired. In June 2005 four Navy SEALs were flown by helicopter into Kunar Province in northeast Afghanistan to reconnoiter a Taliban force that had been inflicting casualties by attacking Marines in the area. Three Afghan goatherds stumbled on them in the midday sun, and the SEALs, alone in enemy territory, made the fateful decision to set them free. Before long the SEALs were under attack by a larger militant force. They radioed base for help and put up a tough fight against impossible odds, taking a heavy toll of the enemy before three of the four were killed. The fourth, Petty Officer Marcus Luttrell, was wounded and knocked unconscious by a grenade blast. Sixteen other special ops personnel were sent out to rescue the missing SEALs, but they were killed when their MH-47 Chinook helicopter was shot down. A grenade round entered through the open rear door, and the explosion blew several men out of the helicopter. The chopper, crippled, crashed into a mountainside and exploded.[44] Meanwhile, Petty Officer Luttrell was discovered by local villagers who took him in and refused to give him up to the Taliban.[45] Eventually, a helicopter came to take him back to his outfit.

Late in 2005 intelligence revealed that Zawahiri was attending a meeting just across the border in Pakistan. Task Force 88 hatched a plan to parachute a platoon of SEALs in for a kill/capture operation, with plenty of support force on hand in case anything went wrong. Back in Washington, political leaders fretted about the possible damage a major sovereignty violation would do to the Pakistani government of America's ally, Pervez Musharraf. With the plane already in the air carrying the SEALs to their drop zone, Washington aborted the operation.[46]

Three years after the tragedy in Kunar, the SEALs undertook another dangerous mission outside their normal range of activities with a much better outcome. Neither al Qaeda nor the Taliban were involved in what for Afghan tribes might be called a normal business enterprise. A tribal militia was holding an American businessman captive in a mud hut about eight thousand feet high and thirty miles east of Kabul. Negotiations over ransom money had gone on for several weeks without resolution. Two young captors who belonged to a militia led by Gulbuddin Hekmatyar stood guard, one inside and the other outside the shack. Earlier the captors had been moving him around, but here in this remote, rugged location, they felt safe to stay put. That was a fatal mistake. They allowed their captive, whose name was withheld for security reasons, four calls to his wife in Kabul. The last call after he was moved to the mountainside hut, together with solid human intelligence from local sources, gave special ops a fix on the American's location. After dark on October 14, 2003, three Chinook helicopters flew two dozen or more SEALs and other SOF to a location out of sight and sound of the kidnappers. The soldiers, wearing night-vision goggles, hiked about three miles up and down the steep terrain to a spot about 275 yards from the hideout, and then seven of them, most or all of them SEALs, quietly made the final approach in the early morning darkness. Both Afghan guards were asleep, but their American captive was not. One of the SEALs threw a pebble against the door to signal their arrival. He undid the latch and walked in, followed by two or three others. They bid the American be silent and dispatched the sleeping guards using a gun equipped with a silencer. They wanted to keep the guards from firing their weapons and alerting militia forces nearby. Soon the American captive, happy to be alive and well, was out of harm's way, and SOF had pulled off perhaps the smoothest rescue operation of the first decade of the twenty-first century.[47]

In unconventional wars, unconventional troops are needed to play unconventional roles. Special ops fits the bill. All signs point to a larger role for SOF in Afghanistan/Pakistan. In addition to the 21,000 regular troops he dispatched to the war zone early in his administration, President Obama quietly deployed another thousand elite SOF to Afghanistan. At the same time he appointed the man who led the manhunts in Iraq, Gen. Stanley A. McChrystal, to overall command in Afghanistan and gave the three-star general a fourth star. It remains to be seen whether SOF, with its special intelligence and finely tuned training, can finally succeed in the Obama administration at the kind of warfare that President John F. Kennedy called for nearly a half century ago.

Based on their new experience in counterterrorism, the Army and Marines updated the field manual for special operations, the first such revision in two decades. It promises to expand the options available to the president in fighting the war against terrorists. After surviving a "competitive selection process, coupled with technological training and education," said the report, the special operations soldiers will be "adaptable, mature, innovative, culturally aware, self-assured, and self-reliant."[48] They will need to have all of those attributes to meet the challenge at hand.

6

GLOBAL TERRORISM

The American presence in Afghanistan is justified by a very practical need: self-defense. Afghanistan/Pakistan is only the venue; al Qaeda anywhere is the target. Pressuring al Qaeda in places where it plots global terrorism and trains terrorists is one important tactic in this strange war. "It was from [FATA]," wrote Pakistani journalist Ahmed Rashid, "that the bomb plots in London, Madrid, Bali, Islamabad, [and others] were planned. . . . FATA became the world's 'terrorism central.'"[1] It is hard to imagine a more powerful argument for engaging al Qaeda in Af/Pak.

However, since Rashid published his book *Descent into Chaos* in 2008, al Qaeda has established a new outpost in the barren hills of Yemen where the terrorists plot attacks against the United States and European countries, so far with limited success. The terrorists, who go by the designation al Qaeda on the Arabian Peninsula (AQAP), are concentrated in remote, rugged terrain ideal for defense, and they benefit from the added protection of a weak Yemeni government that must walk a narrow path between Western and terrorist intruders in a society where Islamists have considerable support among the people. Yemen is bin Laden's ancestral home. His father, Mohammed bin Laden, migrated from there to Saudi Arabia and founded a successful construction conglomerate, Bin Laden Brothers for Contracting and Industry, which enjoyed the patronage of the royal Saudi family. No evidence has turned up that Osama has moved to the al Qaeda camp in Yemen, but the fact is that nobody in the West seems to know exactly where he is located, or even whether he is still alive.

Anti-West terrorist activities in the modern era go back to the 1960s and the Palestine Liberation Organization's struggle with Israel. While Yasir Arafat's Fatah initially concentrated on cross-border raids on Israel, the Popular Front for the Liberation of Palestine staged spectacular airliner hijackings in what were essentially public relations stunts—dangerous stunts, to be sure—to publicize the Palestinian cause. As the years wore on, other PLO factions joined in the struggle, and the terrorist attacks became bloodier and more diverse.

The Iranian Revolution in 1979 was a watershed event. In an affront to international norms, Iranian youth stormed the U.S. embassy and held fifty-two American diplomats and embassy personnel hostage for fourteen and a half months. Of more lasting effect, Shia Iran sought to export its revolution by sponsoring terrorist attacks in Europe, in Saudi Arabia, and against Jewish facilities in Argentina and elsewhere. Al Qaeda later joined in the terrorist assault on American assets. It directed attacks against two U.S. embassies in East Africa in 1998 and the assault on the USS *Cole* in Aden harbor, Yemen, in 2000. When al Qaeda struck the Pentagon and World Trade Center in 2001, America began to understand what it was up against. But America is not alone; the entire world is up against it. Since 9/11, terrorism has literally exploded in many parts of the world.

THE ISLAMIST CRUSADE

Osama bin Laden, a Sunni Muslim, took inspiration from the Shiite Iranian Revolution, and he welcomed all comers to the fight against America. So powerful was his image after the attack on America that he was sometimes credited for terrorist acts in which he had no part. While it is true that he gained stature during the Soviet war in Afghanistan, he was only one among several "Arab Afghan" leaders. The Islamist crusade that followed the Soviet-Afghan war began with him on the sidelines.

The first postwar Islamist involvement came about in the Balkans during bin Laden's time in Sudan. In March 1992, the same month that the mujahideen stamped out Communist rule in Afghanistan, Bosnia-Herzegovina broke away from Yugoslavia and almost immediately descended into ethnic and sectarian fighting. Bosnian Serbs launched a campaign of ethnic cleansing against Muslims, expelling them from communities where they had lived for centuries and committing atrocities that bear a resemblance to the Holocaust, if on a smaller scale.

For several months Serb fighters dug themselves in on the high ground above the capital city of Sarajevo and relentlessly trained their artillery and sniper fire on the Muslim quarter below. In three years of war 150,000 people were killed, and 2 million Muslims were made homeless.[2]

About four thousand Arab Islamist veterans of Afghanistan infiltrated to fight alongside the Bosnian Muslims. Volunteers came from throughout the Muslim world. Some may have come from bin Laden's training camps in Sudan, and he may have contributed financially or otherwise. But he was not in control. In 1993 the Arabs formed their own regiment, called el-Muzhahidun, under the command of Abu Abdul Aziz, better known by his nom de guerre, Barbarossa. Like bin Laden, he was a former student of Abdullah Azzam in Jeddah, whom he followed to Afghanistan. The regiment's contribution to the Bosnian conflict was minimal, but they stood out for barbarous acts, which included beheadings and mutilations of Orthodox Christian Serbs—tit for tat.

The conflict ended with an American-brokered agreement, the Dayton Peace Accords, after which el-Muzhahidun disbanded. The Arabs' stay in the Balkans had not been a happy one. They did not get along well with the native Muslims, who retained their Muslim identity but were European in appearance and outlook and paid less attention to their religion. Like their Serb and Croat neighbors, the Bosnian Muslims drank, smoked, ate pork, and after fifty years of Communist rule, hardly knew how to pray. The Wahhabi tried to stiffen their spiritual resolve, urging women to wear veils and men to grow beards, and they demolished cafés that sold liquor and tobacco. Even the Bosnian mosques, with their ornate Ottoman architecture, offended the rigid Wahhabi sensibilities, and in the war's aftermath, where the Saudi charity funds were used for reconstruction, they plastered over fine centuries-old ceramic tiles and frescoes to give the mosques more of the drab Arabian look, the better for the faithful to concentrate their thoughts on God.[3]

Even before bin Laden returned to Afghanistan in 1996, Islamist fighters began showing up in Russia's Muslim province of Chechnya. As in Afghanistan, the native rebels in Chechnya fought the Russians simply for their freedom, while the Arabs entered prepared for jihad and eager for martyrdom. But unlike the raw Arab recruits of the Afghan campaign, the jihadists in Chechnya were veteran fighters.

Most of the former Muslim republics along Russia's southern tier gained their freedom with the breakup of the Soviet Union in 1991. Chechnya was not among them. There, a former Soviet air force major general, Dzhokhar Dudayev, overthrew the Chechen-Ingush government and declared Chechen independence in 1991. Under Dudayev, Chechnya was hardly a model democracy. His followers thrived on arms and drug smuggling while he flouted Moscow control. The frustrated Russian president, Boris Yeltsin, finally resorted to armed intervention. In December 1994 forty thousand Russian troops retook the capital, Grozny, after turning the city into rubble with ground and air bombardments. The forces loyal to Dudayev retreated to the wilds of the northern Caucasus Mountains.

At this point Shamil Basayev emerged as leader of the Chechen guerrillas. Basayev had stood with Yeltsin at the Moscow barricades in 1991 and then returned to the Caucasus. In the fight for Chechen independence, the First Chechen War, he proved to be a formidable military leader. Basayev's guerrilla forces inflicted one humiliating defeat after another on the Russian army, and the Russian people began to lose faith in the war. In April 1996 Dudayev was killed in a Russian rocket attack. Basayev, promoted to command of the Chechen armed forces, led a campaign to retake Grozny. With the collapse of the Russian army, the discredited Yeltsin government sued for peace, and Chechnya gained de facto independence.

Chechnya took on an increasingly Wahhabi cast as Islamist legions filtered in to join the struggle. Many of the Chechen field commanders formed cells, or *jamaats*, that required the adoption of Islam, including a commitment to jihad, as a way of life. Basayev was already in the fold. In 1994 he visited camps in Afghanistan before bin Laden arrived from Sudan. In 1997 Dudayev's successor as the political leader, Aslan Maskhadov, declared Chechnya to be an Islamic state, the Chechen Republic of Ichkeria, which, significantly, was recognized internationally only by the Taliban regime in Afghanistan.

From 1997 to 1999 several hundred radical Arab Islamists turned up in Chechnya, among them the Ansar Al-Mujahideen (supporters of Muhammad) and its militant leader, Samir ibn al-Suwaylim, known by his nom de guerre, Khattab (probably after Muhammad's successor as caliph, Umar ibn al-Khattab). Khattab's trademark perversion, according to one author, was to videotape the torture of captive Russian soldiers. Such torture sessions could be seen in cassettes that turned up for sale in radical mosques.[4]

Khattab joined forces with Basayev as chief of military operations. They invaded neighboring Dagestan in 1999, but startled by opposition from Dagestan Muslims, they were beaten back. Their brazen initiative combined with their campaign of terrorism prompted a second Russian invasion of Chechnya later that year. Vladimir Putin, the new Russian prime minister, vowed to crack down hard on the Chechen separatists. Russian troops reoccupied Grozny early in 2000, and the Second Chechen War lapsed into a continuous bloody stalemate. Khattab died in March 2002 from a poisoned letter delivered by a messenger working undercover for the Russian secret service.[5]

Chechen/Islamist terrorist acts have been laced with as much bloodlust as any in the world, and heavy-handed Russian responses have often made matters worse. For example, on October 23, 2002, forty-one Chechen terrorists, including women who said they were Chechen War widows, stormed the Dubrovka Theater Center in Moscow during the performance of a musical, *Nord-Ost* (Northeast), and took about six hundred hostages. The terrorists demanded the withdrawal of Russian troops from Chechnya and set a deadline of dawn on October 26. If the deadline were not met, they threatened, they would start killing hostages. As it happened, Russian troops stormed the theater before the deadline arrived. They began by pumping in clouds of incapacitating gas and wore gas masks in the assault. The gas proved to be more lethal than the rescuers expected. It killed a few terrorists and 113 hostages. In contrast to the large number of deaths caused by army errors, the hostage takers killed only six people, including one policeman and five hostages.[6]

Thirty-two Chechen and Arab terrorists seemed bent on testing the limits of cruelty at the start of the school year on September 1, 2004. Only one unarmed policewoman stood guard outside School Number One in the town of Beslan. The terrorists swept past her and took hostage nearly twelve hundred children, teachers, parents, and relatives—plus the guard.[7] They crowded their captives into the school gymnasium, placed schoolchildren at windows as human shields, booby-trapped the room with explosives previously stored under the floor, and threatened to blow the building up if the troops and police who gathered outside attacked. In the days that followed they denied the hostages food and water. Many captives shed clothing in the stifling heat and drank their own urine. On the third day pandemonium broke loose. At midday, a bomb went off inexplicably. Some hostages tried to flee in the confusion, and the terrorists reportedly opened fire on them. The troops fired back and then stormed the building, blowing a hole in its side to facilitate evacuation. Fighting continued the rest of the day and into the night. The final toll was 366 dead, including 156 children and 31 of the 32 fighters, and another 747 people injured.[8]

Since then, the Chechen rebellion has been in decline. In March 2005 the president of their shadow government, Aslan Maskhadov, was killed when Russian security forces tracked his cell phone and zeroed in on him with artillery. His successor, Abdul-Khalim Saydullayev, was killed the following year. The biggest blow to the rebel movement came in July 2006 when Basayev was killed as he rode in a car near a truck filled with munitions that mysteriously exploded. Russian and Chechen sources have disputed the cause of the explosion. The movement did not die with him, but for boldness, imagination, and brutality, Basayev's shoes will be hard to fill. The Russian security service has benefited from improved intelligence as declining morale in the rebel ranks has induced many to desert and inform on their erstwhile comrades.[9]

THE VIRUS SPREADS

Despite the isolation of al Qaeda leaders since late 2001, major terrorist attacks have continued throughout the Muslim world and into Europe. Terrorist bombs that have killed or injured thousands of innocent people have gone off in Indonesia, India, Turkey, Saudi Arabia, Egypt, Morocco, Spain, and England—all consistent with al Qaeda's global jihad, even if al Qaeda was not directly responsible for the attacks. Although no single incident rises to the level of death and destruction of the 9/11 attack on America, the cumulative effect of global terrorism in the first decade of the twenty-first century—beyond the horrors inflicted in hot spots such as Palestine, Iraq, Afghanistan, and Pakistan—is no less shocking to contemplate, like the news of cancer spreading throughout the body.

On October 12, 2002, more than a year after 9/11, Jemaah Islamiyah (Islamic Group) struck Bali, the exotic Indonesian island of literature and song that has morphed into a popular tourist destination. Two bombs went off shortly after 11:00 p.m., one inside a bar and the other outside a nightclub, in the resort town of Kuta, killing 202 people and injuring 209. The dead from twenty-two nations, most of them young revelers in their twenties and thirties, included eighty-eight Australians and seven Americans.

An Indonesian named Riduan bin Isomuddin, better known as Hambali, was the military leader of Jemaah Islamiyah, which was dedicated to establishing an Islamist state in Southeast Asia that would include Indonesia, the world's largest Muslim nation; Malaysia; Singapore; Brunei; and southern parts of Thailand and the Philippines, with a combined population of 420 million people. Hambali had gone to Afghanistan in 1983 as a teenager and fought with the mujahideen. There, he met bin Laden and became close friends with Khalid Sheikh Mohammed. His connection with al Qaeda made him a key player in the Islamist terrorist network in Southeast Asia.

More terrorist incidents followed the Bali attack. On August 5, 2003, a powerful car bomb that exploded outside the Marriott Hotel in Jakarta killed thirteen and injured more than a hundred. On September 8, 2004, terrorists planted another car bomb outside the Australian embassy in Jakarta. This one killed eleven people, all Indonesians, and injured about 160. After Hambali was captured and imprisoned, Islamist terrorists revisited Bali on October 1, 2005. Three suicide bombers in three resort restaurants killed themselves and nineteen other people, fourteen Balinese and five foreigners. Suspicion fell on Jemaah Islamiyah, but police could not confirm the identities of the suicide bombers, whose heads were blown off.[10]

India has also borne the brunt of terrorist attacks from al Qaeda affiliates, while radical elements of its Hindu majority have made their own significant contributions to the nation's legacy of blood and death. The major flashpoint for terrorist activity has been the scenic Kashmir Valley, where the Indian army sustains Indian rule over a predominantly Muslim population. Kashmiri Islamist groups sprang up beginning in 1989 in the aftermath of the Soviet withdrawal from Afghanistan, undoubtedly an outgrowth of the movement that fostered al Qaeda. Two to three dozen Kashmiri militant groups were still active after 9/11, and some are affiliated with al Qaeda in the International Islamic Front.

At ground level, these groups have virtually made terrorism a way of life in that beautiful land. They launched attacks large and small against civilian and military targets, killing women and children, teachers, journalists, clergy, politicians, and security personnel. In the week before assembly elections in October 2002, terrorists attacked multiple election targets—including candidates, polling officials, and voting facilities—on an almost daily basis. Incidents have reflected radical Islamist beliefs: a woman was beheaded for not covering her head with a burqa, a wine dealer was shot for selling alcohol, a shopkeeper—and his shop— were set on fire for selling cigarettes. Some incidents are simply depraved. In one case, militants carved their names on a captive's body before shooting him dead. Security forces struck back, killing hundreds of militants, but the attacks continued relentlessly. Events like these on a small scale tend to fly under the radar of the world press, but they have occurred in such volume since 1989 that the cumulative death toll has reached the tens of thousands.

Occasionally, a bold terrorist attack captures a wider audience, as on October 1, 2001, when a suicide car bomber blew a hole in the gate of the state assembly building in Srinagar, creating a breach that militants poured through to turn the legislative compound into a killing field. Thirty or more people died in the attack, according to the U.S. State Department.[11] Blame was laid at the foot of Lashkar-e-Toiba (LET), possibly in conjunction with Jaish-e-Mohammad, two groups representing al Qaeda's most powerful allies in Kashmir.

LET struck directly at India's proud democracy on December 13, 2001, with a brazen assault on the parliament building in New Delhi. Twelve people died in the shootout, including five militant gunmen, and twenty-two were injured. Again on August 25, 2003, the Kashmir terrorists took their argument inside India when two car bombs were touched off minutes apart at lunchtime in the city of Mumbai (formerly Bombay). One exploded at the Gateway of India outside the Taj Mahal Hotel, both prominent tourist attractions; the other went off in the jewelry market in central Mumbai. The two blasts killed fifty-two people and injured 150.

Mumbai, one of the world's largest cities with 18 million inhabitants, is a favorite terrorist target. At least seven attacks, large and small, have been carried out there since September 11, 2001. In the evening of November 26, 2008, ten Islamists, sent by LET and heavily armed with bombs, grenades, and automatic rifles, arrived by sea and spread out over the city. In a three-day frenzy of murder and destruction they attacked tourist hotels, restaurants, train stations, a cinema, a hospital, and a center for Orthodox Jews, leaving at least 170 dead and more than 300 wounded. Nine of the ten assailants were killed, and the tenth was captured.

An incident beginning with a train fire that killed fifty-nine Hindu pilgrims showed that terrorism in India is not a one-sided affair. The fire spread through two cars of the Sabarmati Express to Ahmadabad as it pulled out of the Godhra station in the western state of Gujarat on the morning of February 27, 2002. Initially, blame for the fire fell on Muslim terrorists said to have attacked the train and set it afire. Three days of Hindu rioting followed. As many as two thousand Muslims died. Human Rights Watch, the international organization based in New York, charged in a report two months later that the riots were preplanned and led by Gujarat state officials and men belonging to Hindu nationalist organizations such as the Vishwa Hindu Parishad (World Hindu Council, VHP) and the Bharatiya Janata Party (BJP), the ruling party in Gujarat. Using information obtained from municipal records that identified Muslim properties, they looted and burned homes, businesses, and mosques. They raped and murdered Muslim women and left thousands of families homeless.[12] Evidence from the police investigation ultimately proved that the fire started on the inside of the train and could not have been ignited by terrorists from the outside. An official investigation led by Indian Supreme Court judge Umesh Chandra Banerjee concluded that the fire was accidental, but the BJP dismissed that conclusion as "politically motivated."

India lives with tensions left over from centuries of conquest and internal conflict. Out of a population of 1.17 million people, 80 percent are Hindu and 13.4 percent, Muslim, based on the 2001 census.[13] The underpinning to the tragic Godhra incident dates back five hundred years, when the ruling Moguls built a mosque in Ayodhya, in the northern state of Uttar Pradesh, on a site that Hindus revere as the birthplace of their god Ram. The mosque was destroyed in Hindu rioting in 1992.[14] Hindus now want to put a temple on the site, and the men, women, and children killed in the train fire on February 27, 2002, were returning from a pilgrimage to Ayodhya. The issue remained in abeyance in Gujarat court until October 25, 2010, when the Indian supreme court gave Gujarat the green light to finally rule on it.[15] One location holy to two religions—at Ayodhya as at the Temple Mount in Jerusalem—is a volcano that can lie dormant for centuries and then erupt.

Turkey, once a great empire blanketing parts of the Middle East, North Africa, and Eastern Europe, was a stand-up American ally during the cold war. It is still a member of NATO and currently (in 2010) an applicant to the European Union. It became the first Muslim nation to officially embrace Western culture, and then from its grassroots it turned back to Islam. Now suspended between two worlds, it can claim no immunity from Islamist terrorism. In November 2003 the first native Turkish suicide bombers hit Western targets in the principal city of Istanbul. On the fifteenth, two bomb-laden trucks crashed into two Jewish synagogues, Beth Israel and Neve Shalom. Five days later two more truck bombs exploded outside the British-based HSBC Bank and the British consulate. The four terrorists and fifty-seven other people, most of them Turkish Muslims, died in the four explosions. Up to seven hundred others were wounded. Roger Short, the British consul in Istanbul, was among the dead. The Islamic Great Eastern Raiders Front (IBDA-C) claimed responsibility for the synagogue bombings. Another militant group, the Abu Hafz al-Masri Brigades, said it carried out the attacks on the British buildings. Both groups associated themselves with al Qaeda, although they are homegrown and address specific local issues.[16]

In Saudi Arabia, Islamic militants allegedly tied to al Qaeda directed their anger at the ruling monarchy and Western influence. On May 12, 2003, they carried out three suicide car bombings in upscale Riyadh neighborhoods that were home to Westerners and wealthy Saudis. Those attacks killed forty-one people, including eight Americans, and injured two hundred.[17] The following November terrorists struck Riyadh again, this time at a housing complex for foreign Arab workers, a seemingly counterproductive exercise unless they meant to undermine the Saudi economy by discouraging the influx of low-wage workers. Seventeen people were killed; five were children.[18] The following April, a car bomb exploded outside a former police building, killing five and injuring 148.[19] On May 29, 2004, terrorists scaled the fence of a Khobar housing complex, took hostages, killed nineteen foreign oil workers, and then escaped.[20] In the late spring and summer that year, several Westerners were killed in a series of isolated attacks, among them the American Paul Marshall Johnson Jr., an employee of Lockheed Martin who was kidnapped at a fake police checkpoint in Riyadh. Like *Wall Street Journal* reporter Daniel Pearl, Johnson was beheaded; unlike Pearl, the media paid scant attention to Johnson's equally hideous plight.[21] Starting in January 2005, the terrorist campaign died down, at least temporarily. It took a heavy toll of the perpetrators, partly because successful suicide bombers don't live to stage another attack. Police claimed that in the two-year period beginning in the spring of 2003, more than a hundred militants were killed or captured, including twenty of twenty-six on their most-wanted list.[22]

On the far side of the African continent in May 2003, five bombs exploded within thirty minutes and tore into Western targets in Casablanca, Morocco. Two European-style restaurants, the Belgian consulate, a Jewish center, and a five-star international hotel were hit on the night of May 16, 2003. Forty-one people died. Among the dead were ten suicide bombers said to have been members of Salafia Jihadia, an offshoot of the Moroccan Islamic Combatant Group (GICM), an al Qaeda ally made up of jihadist veterans who trained or fought in Afghanistan and seek to establish an Islamist regime in Morocco.[23]

EUROPE DEFILED

GICM was implicated in the bombing of four commuter trains in Madrid on March 11, 2004. Ten bombs ripped through the trains in a five-minute period during the morning rush hour, killing 191 people and injuring about fifteen hundred. The casualty toll could have been worse. Three other bombs had been planted but failed to go off. In a nation that had long experienced Basque terrorism, this was the bloodiest single terrorist attack in Spanish history. Spanish authorities initially blamed the Basque terrorist group Euskadi Ta Askatasuna (Basque Fatherland and Liberty, ETA), but the evidence soon pointed to Islamic terrorists. That evening after the attack, a stolen van that contained detonators and an Arabic-language audiocassette with verses from the Koran was found in the town of Alcalá de Henares, the point of origin for three of the targeted trains and a station stop for the fourth. Two days later investigators traced a phone card found inside a bag of unexploded bombs to a cell phone shop in the Moroccan quarter of Madrid. The shop owner, Jamal Zougam, along with his half-brother and a friend who worked there, was arrested. Before the month was out, the authorities had rounded up a dozen prime suspects, most of them Moroccans, and sought another dozen or so. On April 2 Spain averted another potential catastrophe when an unexploded bomb was found on the high-speed intercity train tracks between Madrid and Seville. Tests later showed it to be the same type as those used on March 11. The next day police surrounded an apartment in Leganés, south of Madrid, a base of operations for the terrorist ring. A bomb went off during the assault, killing four men, including a Tunisian named Sherhane ben Abdelmajid Fakhet, the alleged ringleader.

The Madrid attacks, more than most terrorist incidents since September 11, 2001, bore the earmarks of an al Qaeda international operation. For one thing, Zougam, the cell phone shopkeeper, was said to have associated with Imad Eddin Barakat Yarkas, aka Abu Dahdah, the head of an al Qaeda cell in Madrid later convicted of giving logistical support to the 9/11 bomber Mohammed Atta. Although not directly involved in the March 11, 2004, Madrid bombings, Zougam was a central suspect in the plot because of his technical know-how. He was born in the Moroccan city of Tangier on the Strait of Gibraltar, later a hotbed of Islamist intrigue. At the age of ten, he moved with his family to the rundown Lavapiés district of Madrid. Growing up, he discovered a gift for understanding electronics, and in his shop he tinkered with stolen cell phones and credit cards. During the year prior to the Madrid bombings, Zougam became less sociable with his neighbors along the Calle de Tribulete. He spent more of his time secluded in his cluttered basement workshop, and the neighbors noticed a different crowd of young immigrants, more aggressive and secretive, hanging out at the store. Occasionally, Zougam went on out-of-town trips, but he never talked about them.

According to Spanish authorities, he spent at least one of these trips, on April 20, 2003, in Tangier, where he met with another Tangier native, Abdelaziz Benyaich, an alleged al Qaeda operative who may have given him the design for the cell phones used to trigger the Madrid bombs. Benyaich, a naturalized French citizen married to a French woman, used his French passport to travel freely in Europe and the Middle East, allegedly on al Qaeda business. Moroccan authorities said Benyaich met several times with Abu Musab Zarqawi in 2002 to plan and coordinate terrorist activities in North Africa. Whether Zarqawi ordered the Madrid bombings was uncertain, but they were clearly on al Qaeda's agenda. In October 2003 bin Laden had threatened to retaliate against countries involved in the U.S.-led invasion of Iraq and singled out Britain, Spain, Australia, Poland, Japan, and Italy.[24]

In political terms, the Madrid bombings paid off handsomely for al Qaeda. National elections followed three days later, on March 14. The incumbent People's Party, led by Prime Minister José María Aznar, was favored in the polls. Aznar supported the American invasion of Iraq and had contributed a token force of about thirteen hundred Spanish troops to the occupation. His chief opponent, José Luis Rodrígues Zapatero, leader of the Spanish Socialist Workers' Party, ran on an anti–

Iraq War platform, promising to withdraw from Iraq if he became prime minister. The terrorist attack turned into a political windfall for Zapatero, partly because of his opponent's inept public stance. By strongly insisting initially on blaming the Basque ETA, Aznar seemed to be shifting the onus away from his now-discredited Iraq policy. The voters made him pay by giving the Socialists a firm plurality in the Congress of Deputies, the 350-seat lower house. With the support of minor parties, Zapatero formed a government and made good on his promise to pull out of Iraq. At the same time, he vowed to continue the fight against international terrorism, essentially aligning himself with the positions of France, Germany, and Turkey, key NATO allies that had fully supported the invasion of Afghanistan in pursuit of al Qaeda but refused to follow the American lead on Iraq.

London's turn came the following year. On July 7, 2005, three bombs exploded within fifty seconds on three London Underground trains, and a fourth bomb blew the roof off a double-decker bus fifty-seven minutes later. The first bomb went off on an eastbound Circle Line train between the Liverpool Street and Aldgate stations; the second on a westbound Circle Line train at Edgware Road; the third on the southbound Piccadilly Line deep underground between King's Cross St. Pancras and Russell Square. The bus exploded in Tavistock Square after picking up passengers evacuated from the stricken Underground. Fifty-six people were killed in the four explosions, including the four suicide bombers, and more than seven hundred were injured. Except for the 1988 bombing of Pan Am Flight 103 over Lockerbie, Scotland, which killed 270 people, the July 7 bombings in London were the deadliest terrorist event ever in the United Kingdom.

Three of the four suspected bombers were British citizens of Pakistani descent. The fourth was Jamaican. None of them was previously known to police, who learned from their investigation that they were part of an Islamist cell from Leeds in the north of England. They had traveled by car to Luton outside London, taken a train to King's Cross Station, and then spread out to their respective destinations. Police later discovered a bomb factory in Leeds and found bomb materials in the car the bombers left at Luton Station.

Terrorism experts, noting the sophistication of the bombs and the synchronization of the attacks, ventured that only Islamists with advanced training in Afghanistan could have planned the bombings. Indeed, al Qaeda claimed responsibility, relating the attacks to British involvement in Iraq. But unlike the immediate electoral impact of the Madrid bombings, those in London had no short-term effect on British politics.[25]

A deadly bombing aftershock was averted two weeks later, on July 21, when four men on a copycat mission aboard three Underground trains and a bus tried to take innocent lives by blowing themselves up, but the bombs failed to detonate. All four would-be bombers, young Muslim men and British citizens, were tracked down and arrested. One of them, Hussain Osman, was born in Ethiopia and raised in Italy, where he fled after the failed bombing attempt. He was arrested there and returned to Britain. He told Italian police that his group was trying to avenge the British role in Iraq.[26]

NO END IN SIGHT

On July 22, the day after the failed London bombing, terrorists struck in the small hours of the morning in the Egyptian Red Sea resort town of Sharm el-Sheikh, near the southern tip of the Sinai Peninsula. A suicide bomber driving a pickup truck crashed into the lobby of a luxury hotel, the Ghazala Gardens, and triggered a huge explosion. A second terrorist, also driving a pickup, blew himself up at the city's Old Market. A police official speculated that he may have been trying to attack another hotel but couldn't break through security. A third terrorist left a bomb hidden in a knapsack at a beachfront parking lot two miles from the hotel and made his escape. The death toll for the three bombings was initially put at eighty-eight, later revised downward to sixty-four, making it in either case the deadliest terrorist episode in Egyptian history.

Egyptian police dismissed any suggestion of an al Qaeda connection, although a group calling itself the Abdullah Azzam Brigades (al Qaeda in Syria and Egypt) claimed responsibility. The authorities noted a similarity in methods between the Sharm el-Sheikh bombings and an attack the previous year, on October 7, 2004, at Taba, up the Aqaba coast, near the Israeli border. There, bombers struck the Taba Hilton, which catered to Israeli tourists, and at nearby seaside campgrounds, killing thirty-four people. The same group, the Abdullah Azzam Brigades, claimed responsibility. The Taba bombers also used pickup trucks and the same type of explosives, but at Sharm el-Sheikh they packed the bombs with nails to maximize casualties. The trail in the Taba investigation led to an Islamist cell in the northern Sinai town of el-Arish on the Mediterranean Sea. Ten months and two terrorist attacks later, Egyptian police, acting on a tip from local informants, reported that they killed the gang leader, Nasser Khamis el-Mallahi, during a shootout in an olive grove south of el-Arish in May 2006. A police spokesman insisted that the gang, Monotheism and Jihad, had no connection to al Qaeda.[27]

The Radisson Hotel in Amman, Jordan, which had survived the millennium plot in 2000, ran out of luck in 2005. It was one of three American-owned Amman hotels, also including the Grand Hyatt and the Days Inn, targeted by suicide bombers on November 10. The simultaneous attacks killed at least fifty-six people, including family and friends gathering for a wedding reception at the Radisson. In this case, Abu Musab al-Zarqawi, the Islamist who made his mark in Iraq, claimed credit. Zarqawi had been trying for years to hit targets in his native Jordan, and this was his most successful effort. Seven months later he was killed when American bombs destroyed his safe house north of Baghdad where he was meeting with coconspirators.[28]

THE AMERICAN CONNECTION

The next terrorist strike might well be aimed at America. Ever since 9/11 al Qaeda has been trying for an encore, and there have been a number of near misses. Khalid Sheikh Mohammed, in fact, had plans beyond 9/11 to wreak havoc on several American cities and destroy special targets.[29] In 2006 British law enforcement broke up an Islamist plot to sabotage seven commercial jets flying from London Heathrow Airport to North America, including two Air Canada flights to Toronto and Montreal; three United Airlines flights to San Francisco, Chicago, and Washington; and two American Airlines flights to Chicago and New York. The plotters allegedly planned to smuggle liquid explosives disguised as soft drinks on board the seven airliners and blow a hole in the side of each plane at high altitude. They hoped to kill up to fifteen hundred people. Eight British men of Pakistani origin were brought to trial in 2009 on charges related to the airline bombing plot. Three were convicted of conspiring to bomb airliners, one was found guilty of conspiracy to murder, and one was acquitted on all counts. The remaining three cases were unresolved because of a hung jury. The alleged mastermind of the plot, British-born Rashid Rauf, never faced trial. He was arrested in Pakistan, later escaped, and later still was killed in an American bomb attack.[30]

From September 2009 to November 2010, six plots against homeland America surfaced. One in September 2009 against New York City subways was nipped in the bud. A second in November, a shooting spree at Fort Hood, Texas, was carried out and killed thirteen people. In this case the connection to al Qaeda is somewhat tenuous. Two other plans—one for a Christmas Day airliner bombing on approach to Detroit from Amsterdam and another for a May 2010 car bombing in New York City's Times Square—failed to materialize because of the perpetrators' inexperience and/or incompetence—dumb luck for America. A fifth scheme in October 2010 involved bomb-laden packages sent on UPS and Fed-Ex cargo planes to American destinations. (A sixth plan, to set off a car bomb at a crowded Christmas tree lighting ceremony in Portland, Oregon, was thwarted by an FBI sting.)

U.S. officials have confirmed that the New York subway plot was an al Qaeda operation. Najibullah Zazi, the twenty-four-year-old man arrested in New York, was born in Afghanistan and came to America legally at the age of fourteen. He worked on Wall Street as a sidewalk vendor, and then moved to Denver where he drove an airport shuttle limousine. He admitted to authorities that he had attended an al Qaeda training camp while on a trip to Pakistan in 2007–8 with two friends, Zarein Ahmedzay and Adis Medunjanin, to join in the fight to overthrow the Afghan government. According to Zazi, the three met in FATA with two al Qaeda operatives, Saleh al-Somali and Rashid Rauf, who told them they would be more useful to the jihad if they carried out operations in the United States. Zazi, the only one of the three with explosives training, said targeting New York subways instead of landmark buildings was his idea based on his supply of materials. Zazi, who is reportedly cooperating with authorities, and Ahmedzay pleaded guilty in a Brooklyn federal court to charges of conspiracy to commit murder and use weapons of mass destruction. Medunjanin pleaded not guilty and denies participating in the plot. Somali and Rauf allegedly died later in U.S. drone missile strikes.[31]

The killer at Fort Hood and the young Nigerian involved in the Christmas Day airliner incident had both corresponded with Anwar al-Aulaqi, an American-born Islamic cleric who had migrated to Yemen to join AQAP as a high-level operative and now talked radical chic. Major Nidal Malik Hasan was a psychiatrist who counseled soldiers back from the war zone with posttraumatic stress disorder. On November 5, 2009, at Fort Hood, Texas, he opened fire on soldiers preparing to ship out to the war zone in Iraq. Hasan killed twelve soldiers and one civilian and wounded another forty-two soldiers before he was shot and severely wounded by two civilian police officers. Hasan's connection to Aulaqi traces back to a Falls Church, Virginia, mosque where Aulaqi preached and Hasan worshipped. The FBI intercepted several e-mails that passed between them after Aulaqi moved to Yemen, but characterized them as too innocuous to trigger an investigation prior to the shooting. Aulaqi called Hasan's shooting spree "a heroic act" and the only way for a Muslim to justify serving in the U.S. Army. Eleven months after the shooting spree, Hasan attended a military pre-trial hearing in a wheel chair, paralyzed from his mid-chest down.[32]

Umar Farouk Abdulmutallab, a twenty-three-year-old Nigerian, became known as the underwear bomber for trying to ignite explosive material that he carried in his shorts. On Christmas Day 2009, as Northwest Airlines flight 253 from Amsterdam was approaching Detroit, passengers heard popping noises that sounded like firecrackers. Then smoke rose from Abdulmutallab's window seat and fire torched his pants and the plane's side panel. A hero passenger, Jasper Schuringa of the Netherlands, jumped across the aisle and subdued Abdulmutallab. Crew members and other passengers doused the flames with fire extinguishers and blankets. Abdulmutallab suffered first- and second-degree burns on his inner thighs and genitals. Schuringa was treated for burns on his hands.

The near-fatal Christmas incident was viewed in Washington as a chilling lapse in U.S. intelligence. Vague clues about Abdulmutallab turned up in the bloated U.S. intelligence bureaucracy, but, as in the 9/11 plot, officials failed to connect the dots. Abdulmutallab had been to an AQAP training camp in Yemen and had conversed with Aulaqi. His father had expressed concern to authorities about the radical turn in his son's life.[33] The Senate Select Committee on Intelligence cited the failure of the CIA to disseminate information it had on Abdulmutallab, a failure of watch-listing, and a State Department failure to revoke Abdulmutallab's visa. The Directorate of National Intelligence, established during the Bush administration to address such problems, remained plagued with bureaucratic turf wars. Three days after the Senate report was released in May 2010, President Obama demanded Director Dennis C. Blair's resignation. AQAP has claimed credit for the so-called Christmas bombing plot, and the CIA has marked Aulaqi for assassination on a hit list approved by the White House. Aulaqi is the first United States citizen to make the list.[34]

A fourth terrorist plot against America, the second in New York, unraveled on May 1, 2010, a pleasant spring Saturday evening in Times Square brimming with fun-seeking tourists. A sidewalk vendor noticed smoke coming out of a Nissan Pathfinder SUV parked on 45th Street near Broadway. He notified a mounted patrolman, who then notified headquarters. The area was cleared of tourists, and the bomb squad was called in to investigate. They found that the car was packed with gasoline, propane, fertilizer, firecrackers, and alarm clocks. New York City police commissioner Raymond Kelly said the timing devices were wired to the firecrackers, which were meant to ignite the gasoline, causing the propane to explode along with the fertilizer. Had it worked, there would have been a large fireball and significant casualties. Fertilizer was used in the devastating 1995 bombing of the federal building in Oklahoma City, but the fertilizer found in Times Square was nonexplosive.

Because the SUV remained intact, police and federal investigators harvested an abundance of evidence. They identified the perpetrator as Faisal Shahzad, a U.S. citizen of Pakistani descent, and traced him to his home in Shelton, Connecticut, about fifty miles from Times Square. But he managed to slip their surveillance until he turned up at Kennedy International Airport on an Emirate Airlines jet preparing for departure to Dubai. Customs agents discovered his name on the passenger manifest and arrested him after he had boarded the plane. Shahzad readily admitted his role in the attempted bombing and cooperated with authorities in their investigation.[35]

Here the plot took a surprising twist. Shahzad said his Islamist backers were not al Qaeda but the Pakistani Taliban, who first claimed and then denied that they were behind the bombing attempt. Soon thereafter, their role was confirmed by U.S. attorney general Eric H. Holder Jr. This was a major expansion of the conflict. The Pakistani Taliban had been concentrating on targets in Pakistan until the United States, at the behest of the Pakistani government, killed the Taliban leader, Baitullah Mehsud, with a drone missile. On June 21, 2010, Faisal Shahzad entered a guilty plea in federal district court to a ten-count indictment for terrorism and warned that Islamist attacks against America would continue as long as the United States waged war in Muslim countries. He will be able to follow the conflict from his prison cell; he received a life sentence.[36]

The terrorists do not give up. Failure is followed by a new effort, more creative than the last. In December 2009 a man carried the explosive PETN to America in his underwear; ten months later the terrorists tried to deliver it via FedEx and UPS, so cleverly hidden that British experts, who knew what to look for, took twenty hours to find it. PETN is a white, odorless, nitrogen-based crystal, low in weight but highly explosive, that can be touched off by heat or an electric impulse. Al Qaeda bomb-makers favor it because it is difficult to detect, even for bomb-sniffing dogs.

In late October 2010 a young woman walked into a UPS office in Sana, the capital city of Yemen, with an innocuous-looking package addressed to a synagogue in the Chicago area. Inside the package was an electronic printer, and inside the printer was PETN. She paid for the shipment with a stolen credit card. A similar scene played out at FedEx a few blocks away. The packages went on their way, from city to city, from plane to plane, with cargo handlers unaware of their deadly content. Most of the time, the packages sat in storage at airports. Since 9/11, airline passengers have been thoroughly screened before boarding; less attention has been paid to cargo, especially on planes like those of UPS and FedEx that don't take passengers. Two days after the shipments in Sana, Saudi intelligence sounded a general alarm. A frantic search followed. Police in several nations were looking for packages from Yemen destined for America. They did not know which, or how many had bombs inside. Just the two were found, one in Dubai, the other in Nottingham, England, the PETN packed inside the printer. After a careful analysis, British authorities revealed that the bomb was probably timed to explode while the plane flew over the densely populated northeastern corridor of the United States. But that conclusion was later retracted, reportedly because the cargo planes often fly different routes to the same destination. The plane was scheduled to land in Philadelphia.[37]

So disaster was averted, thanks to the Saudi tip. Momentum would build for tighter cargo security. The search was intensified for al Qaeda's top explosives expert, Ibriham Hassan al-Asiri, also suspected in the Christmas Day plot. The young woman whose stolen credit card was used, a medical student, was picked up by Sana police and then released when a shipping clerk said she was not the right person.[38]

THE ROUNDUP

A recurring issue in this strange terrorist conflict is whether the West should respond to threats militarily or by police enforcement, and as it happens in the real world, the answer is both. As the months sped by after 9/11, the broad fight against terrorism that began in Afghanistan against al Qaeda became something less than war but more than a simple police action against a wider collection of Islamists. In the unremitting global search, human and signal intelligence and the cooperation of other governments were key pieces of the struggle. To a large extent the achievements of civilian law enforcement passed under the radar and perhaps got less credit than they deserved.

One early morning in March 2002, Pakistani police and the FBI raided a two-story house near Faisalabad in western Pakistan. Inside on the second floor, a dozen or so Arabs, Afghans, and Pakistanis awoke to shouting and the earsplitting booms of exploding stun grenades as the police swarmed over an outer wall and broke down the doors to the house. While the defenders tried to hold off the invaders with kitchen knives, their leader tried to escape. Zayn al-Abidin Muhammad Husayn, a thirty-one year-old Palestinian, better known as Abu Zubaydah, was wounded. In the immediate aftermath of his capture, he was depicted as al Qaeda's chief of operations, a brilliant young man fluent in English, expert in computers, and trained in terrorist arms, logistics, and tactics. He had allegedly run the al Qaeda training camps in Afghanistan, singling out the most promising recruits for advanced training and assignment to terrorist operations, many of which he helped plan.[39] Abu Zubaydah was turned over to the CIA and taken under the "extraordinary rendition" program to a secret prison, where, as will be detailed in the next section, he was reportedly tortured.

Pakistan's ISI, once the mother lode of Hekmatyar and then the Taliban, has since 9/11 also worked with American agents tracking al Qaeda, while protecting its Taliban protégés. The Pakistani police rounded up hundreds of al Qaeda suspects and transferred many to American custody. The police nabbed an important al Qaeda figure in a six-hour shootout in Karachi on September 11, 2002, the first anniversary of the Pentagon/World Trade Center attacks. Karachi, a sprawling Indian Ocean port city of 14 million people, has long been a hotbed of Islamist fervor. Police there were on the lookout for Arab terrorists after a series of sophisticated attacks against Western targets. Acting on a tip, they staked out a building in a recently constructed housing and commercial complex for middle-class families. The shooting started shortly after 7:00 a.m., and by the end of the morning, more than two thousand police and paramilitary rangers were pitted against a handful of heavily armed, well-entrenched defenders who had taken up positions in their fifth-floor apartment and on the roof above. Police fanned out onto surrounding rooftops, and their snipers killed the gunmen in the apartment and pinned down those on the roof. A contingent then rushed up the stairs and captured the surviving Arabs. The most important of these was Ramzi Binalshibh, the youthful Yemeni who helped coordinate the 9/11 attack. Originally chosen to fly an airliner into one of the American targets, he had to be scratched because Yemenis were not allowed to enter the United States after the USS *Cole* bombing. Under the CIA's extraordinary rendition program he was whisked away to a secret hiding place, possibly for a time to a prison run by Jordan's General Intelligence Department on the outskirts of Amman where torture is allegedly used on inmates.[40]

Not long after the gunfight in Karachi, a report surfaced that a much bigger fish, Khalid Sheikh Mohammed, had died in the apartment.[41] The report may have been a screen to cover Mohammed's tracks. Several months later, on March 1, 2003, Pakistani police, working in cooperation with the FBI and CIA, captured him in Rawalpindi, seized a computer, cell phones, and documents, and turned him over to American authorities.[42] He, too, was swallowed up in the CIA's extraordinary rendition program and eventually wound up at the Guantánamo Bay Detention Center in Cuba, where the Pentagon held so-called enemy combatants. The next year Pakistani militants murdered Raja Saqlain, the police officer who arrested Mohammed.[43]

The computer and subsequent interrogations yielded many secrets. But Mohammed told a military tribunal created to determine prisoners' status as enemy combatants that while under CIA control, he was sometimes tortured and did not always tell his interrogators the truth. When the presiding officer asked him if he was under duress at the time of the hearing in March 2007, he answered no. Then he freely admitted to directing or taking part in more than thirty terrorist plots. First and foremost, he was al Qaeda's operational director "for the organizing, planning, follow-up, and execution of the 9/11 operation." He boasted of killing Daniel Pearl, the *Wall Street Journal* reporter who had gone to Pakistan in 2002 to research a story on the shoe bomber, Richard Reid. "I decapitated with my blessed right hand the head of the American Jew, Daniel Pearl," said Mohammed with obvious satisfaction. "For those who would like to confirm, there are pictures of me on the Internet holding his head."[44]

He also claimed to have directed for al Qaeda Reid's December 2001 attempted shoe bombing of an American Airlines passenger jet over the Atlantic Ocean and the 2002 Bali nightclub bombing carried out by his friend Hambali. Prior to joining al Qaeda, he said he directed, as a freelance terrorist, the 1993 World Trade Center bombing executed by his nephew Ramzi Yousef, as well as the aborted Bojinka plot, also involving Yousef, to blow up as many as twelve airliners over the Pacific Ocean. He put in the record a long list of unfulfilled al Qaeda or freelance missions that he claimed to have championed, including attacks against the Library Tower in Los Angeles; the Sears Tower in Chicago; the Empire State Building in New York; the New York Stock Exchange; the Panama Canal; U.S. suspension bridges; Heathrow Airport, Canary Wharf Tower, and Big Ben in London; American and Israeli embassies; nuclear power plants in the United States; American military bases in South Korea; NATO headquarters in Europe; and other targets in the United States, Turkey, and Israel; and assassination attempts against Pope John Paul II, President Clinton, former president Jimmy Carter, and former president Musharraf of Pakistan.[45]

If Mohammed did all that he said he did, he made a convincing case for his importance to al Qaeda and America's good fortune at his capture. Senators Carl M. Levin, Democrat of Michigan, and Lindsay O. Graham, Republican of South Carolina, witnessed the tribunal and afterward issued a statement affirming that the tribunal was professionally conducted and that KSM was respectful of his interrogators. They stated, "It was apparent to us that KSM wanted to use the tribunal process to detail his role in 9/11 and many other terror plots. . . . " His allegations of torture, they said, must be taken seriously and properly investigated. The part of his testimony about torture was redacted from the official transcript.[46]

About two months after Mohammed's arrest in 2003, Karachi police nabbed another high-ranking al Qaeda operative, Walid Muhammad bin Attash, aka Tawfiq bin Attash and Walid Ba'Attash. Attash was turned over to American authorities, held in extraordinary rendition for two and a half years, and then transferred to Guantánamo Bay. At a separate enemy-combatant-status hearing, he admitted to heavy involvement in the 2000 bombing of the USS *Cole*.[47]

Another high-profile terrorist figure, Hambali, who led bombing attacks in Bali and Jakarta, Indonesia, turned up in computers the CIA had confiscated that had once belonged to Ramzi Yousef and Khalid Sheikh Mohammed. Hambali's trail grew hot in the summer of 2003. Thai police arrested two of his associates, who led the police to Hambali. He was caught in August at Ayutthaya, Thailand, about fifty miles north of Bangkok. At the time he and his followers were preparing to plant bombs at an upcoming economic summit conference of Asian and Pacific leaders, including President Bush, in Bangkok. Reportedly proud of his exploits, he readily admitted to coordinating bombings in Bali, Jakarta, and elsewhere with funding from al Qaeda.[48]

EXTRAORDINARY RENDITION

The cases of Abu Zubaydah, Ramzi Binalshibh, Khalid Sheikh Mohammed, Walid Muhammad bin Attash, and Hambali are only five of many extraordinary renditions carried out by the CIA since September 11, 2001, under the approving eye of the Bush administration. It is important to distinguish between "rendition" and "extraordinary rendition," which are easily confused and often used interchangeably by the media in error. Here I rely on definitions provided by Scott Horton, who helped prepare a report on renditions issued jointly by New York University Law School and the New York City Bar Association and who was an expert witness in hearings leading to a report on renditions for the European Parliament.

Renditions date back at least to the Reagan presidency. They were kept in place by succeeding presidents up to and including Bill Clinton. Only George W. Bush used extraordinary renditions. Ordinary renditions were restored by President Obama. They refer to the transfer of foreign nationals from one jurisdiction to another for delivery to a criminal justice system. An example would be the capture of Bosnian Serbs for transfer to the Hague for trial. Extraordinary renditions, on the other hand, were authorized in a classified finding signed by President Bush after the 9/11 attacks on America. Their overriding purpose was to isolate prisoners from civil society and deny them due process. In other words, extraordinary renditions under George W. Bush were qualitatively different from the renditions practiced by other presidents. Bush's extraordinary renditions famously involved long-term detention and rough handling that arguably amounted to torture.[49] Foreign intelligence agencies cooperated in extraordinary renditions in various ways, including turning over terrorist suspects to U.S. intelligence, facilitating the transportation of prisoners with landing and refueling rights and permission for overflights, and, less frequently, providing secret detention sites in which prisoners could be kept out of sight and possibly tortured.

CIA rendition groups were not your friendly neighborhood welcoming committees. They broke laws and often treated their prisoners indignantly. Dressed entirely in bullyboy black and wearing face masks, members of a rendition group would follow a standard procedure for extraordinary abductions. After the snatch or handoff from local intelligence, they would blindfold the prisoner and cut off his clothes, inject an enema to clean out his bowels, administer drugs to help him sleep, and outfit him with diapers and a jumpsuit for the long and often circuitous trip to the "black site," or secret prison.[50]

In prisons controlled by the CIA, interrogators were authorized to use certain procedures formalized by the Bush Justice Department in 2002, including such practices as waterboarding, or simulated drowning; sleep deprivation; dousing the prisoner with cold water; stripping him naked; making him stand for hours on end; or slamming him against a flexible wall that might frighten but not seriously hurt him. These were enhanced interrogation techniques, to be sure: America prosecuted Japanese soldiers for waterboarding (calling it a war crime) after World War II.[51] The *New York Times* reported in April 2009, based on an Obama Justice Department memorandum, that after their capture Khalid Sheikh Mohammed was waterboarded 183 times in March 2003 and Abu Zubaydah, 83 times in August 2002.[52] That waterboarding had to be used so frequently seems to indicate that the technique was not very effective. However, the Justice memo, citing the CIA, indicated that it "yielded critical information."[53] Mohammed, who apparently talked when he thought he was going to drown, said later outside the CIA's control that he hoped to be executed so he could become a shahid. In the case of Abu Zubaydah, the CIA sought to play on his fear of insects by placing a harmless caterpillar inside a box where Zubaydah was held and informing him that the caterpillar could inflict a poisonous sting. That and the waterboarding appear to have loosened Zubaydah's tongue. The Obama administration released the Justice Department memos spelling out these techniques in 2009 as a court was preparing to rule on a petition by the American Civil Liberties Union asking that they be made public.[54]

In August that year the Justice Department released more details of a CIA report on interrogation techniques that may have gone beyond what Justice had approved in the aftermath of 9/11. In one case, an interrogator told Khalid Sheikh Mohammed his children would be killed if there were another attack on the United States. In another, an agent threatened Abd al-Rahim al-Nashiri, the alleged mastermind of the *Cole* bombing, with a gun and a power drill pointed at his head. The agent also suggested that his family would be sexually abused in his presence.[55]

What goes on at prisons controlled by friendly foreign countries is left somewhat to the imagination. Muhammad Saad Iqbal endured six years in captivity and came out of it lame from lower back problems, an ear infection, and dependence on antibiotics and antidepressants. He was arrested in Jakarta, and at the airport he was punched, stripped, and thrown against a wall. Then he was flown to Cairo, where he spent three months in a small basement prison. There, he said, he was subjected to interrogations lasting up to fifteen hours. His jailers wanted to know about his ties to Osama bin Laden, which he denied having. He said they gave him electric shock treatment and made him drink liquids laced with drugs. He was then flown to Afghanistan, later moved to Guantánamo Bay, and finally, after six years, released without being charged with a crime.[56]

Too often, as in the case of Iqbal, extraordinary rendition turned into the erroneous rendition of innocent suspects. Maher Arar, born in Syria, was brought by his parents to Canada as a teenager. He passed through Canadian schools and went on to graduate from McGill University in Montreal. At the age of thirty-four, on September 26, 2002, American intelligence agents arrested him as he changed planes at Kennedy Airport in New York. He was returning home from vacation in Tunisia with his family. One of hundreds of thousands of individuals on an FBI terrorist watch list,[57] he was held in New York for nearly two weeks for questioning about his alleged association with suspected terrorists. Then he was flown to Jordan by way of Washington; Portland, Maine; Rome; and Amman in a Gulfstream executive jet and driven to Syria, where he spent a year in prison. Arar said in Syria he was beaten with two-inch-thick cables and kept in a small windowless cell without light that was "like a grave." Eventually, he confessed to being trained by al Qaeda in Afghanistan because, he said, that was what his jailers wanted him to say. After he had served a year in prison, the Canadian government applied pressure for the United States to release him. Later, a Canadian board of inquiry found no evidence to link Arar with terrorism, but he remained on the FBI watch list.[58]

Khalid el-Masri's experience stands out as a case of mistaken identity. His name resembled that of Abu Ayyub al-Masri, erstwhile aide to the late Abu Musab al-Zarqawi. Khalid was born of Lebanese parents in Kuwait in 1963, moved to Germany in 1985, became a German citizen in 1995, married a year later, and fathered six children. He was a carpenter by trade and had also worked as a car salesman in Ulm, Germany. In December 2003, he said, he had a spat with his wife and took off through the Balkans for a vacation. At the Macedonian border he was detained, held incommunicado for more than three weeks, and questioned about his associates, his mosque, and his activities in Ulm. He denied all accusations against him and then went on a hunger strike. On January 23 he was turned over to a CIA extraordinary rendition team. The men in black took him to an airport in Skopje and performed their usual routine. In addition, according to Masri, they beat him with fists "and what felt like a thick stick." He was flown to Afghanistan; beaten some more on his head, the soles of his feet, and the small of his back; and left "in a small, dirty, cold concrete cell." Back at CIA headquarters in Langley, Virginia, analysts carefully examined his passport and found it to be genuine. They had the wrong man. From that point on, the CIA engaged in damage control, trying to keep a lid on their mistake. But, alas, the story came to light with a lengthy article in the *Washington Post*. Masri was returned to Macedonia and then flown to Germany, only to find that his wife, thinking that he had abandoned them, had gone back to Lebanon with their children. They were reunited back in Germany, but he has since had trouble finding work and pursuing a normal life.[59]

In carrying out extraordinary rendition, American intelligence might initially take a suspect into custody by kidnapping or entrapment, often with the cooperation of local intelligence. Hassan Mustafa Osama Nasr, the Imam of Milan, aka Abu Omar, was snatched off a Milan street in broad daylight on February 17, 2003, on the way to his mosque for noon prayers. In Italy the operation became known as the *Imam Rapito* (Kidnapped Imam) affair. The CIA team drove Nasr to NATO's Aviano Air Base and flew him on to Ramstein, Germany, and Egypt. Nasr had fled from Egypt in 2001, when Egyptian intelligence was investigating his radical group, al-Gamaa al-Islamiyya. Italy had granted him political asylum, but by the spring of 2002 Italian and American intelligence agencies and local Italian prosecutors had put him under surveillance for suspected links to al Qaeda and the recruitment of terrorists.

Nasr claims that he was tortured by the Americans at Aviano and by the Egyptians during his prison time in the Cairo area. He was locked up for four years, with a brief break in 2004, when his sentence was reduced to house arrest. While in limbo he told family and friends of his treatment during his incarceration and so was soon back in prison for his temerity. In 2007 he was released after an Egyptian court ruled that the evidence against him was unfounded

The Imam Rapito case blew the cover off the CIA's extraordinary rendition program. It created big headlines in Italy and pitted federal prosecutors against the Italian intelligence agency, formally the Military Intelligence and Security Service (SISMI), which was accused of conspiring with the CIA to break Italian law. Prime Minister Silvio Berlusconi, harboring worries about his political future, fervently wished that the issue would go away. At the time of the abduction, federal prosecutors were dumfounded by the disappearance of their suspect, Imam Nasr, but it did not take long for them to pick up the CIA trail. They traced cell phone calls in the vicinity of the disappearance and a few hours later at Aviano. Some calls went to the American consulate in Milan and some to Northern Virginia, where CIA headquarters is located. The CIA agents also used easily traceable credit cards in their own names, which revealed their movements. At the very least, they should have encrypted their calls and paid the bills in cash—basic spy craft—but apparently they did not because they thought they would be covered by their alliance with SISMI.[60]

Eventually, federal prosecutors indicted twenty-six Americans, twenty-five of them from the CIA, including the head of the Milan station, Robert Seldon Lady, who had argued internally against the abduction. Nine Italians, including numbers one and two of the Italian spy agency, were also indicted, and two of them turned state's evidence. The case has been delayed by legal maneuvering, as can be expected in a proceeding of this magnitude. But in November 2009 the Italian court returned convictions for twenty-three CIA officers, including Lady, and two Italian agents. Lady received an eight-year sentence; the other twenty-two, five years; and the two Italians, three years. None of the Americans showed up for the trial and will probably never serve a day in prison as long as they don't venture outside the United States.[61]

As the story of extraordinary renditions circulated, President Bush went on record denying that the United States practiced torture at detention sites it controlled or delivered prisoners to other countries for torture. His denial was based on the Justice Department's narrow definition of torture, a matter hotly contended in legal circles. Eventually, the United States closed down all of its so-called black sites and transferred its terrorist suspects to Guantánamo Bay, Cuba. Soon after President Obama took office, he made good on campaign promises by banning the use of extraordinary rendition and announcing his intention to close Guantánamo Bay within a year. He did not ban rendition altogether, only the extraordinary form. Left over was the form of rendition that remands the prisoner to a criminal justice system. As for closing Guantánamo, he did not make good on the timeline he had initially set.

———

The extraordinary rendition program offers an example of overzealous management of the war on terrorism. The Italian prosecutors who brought the case against twenty-five CIA employees had already been gathering evidence against Imam Nasr, whom they suspected of recruiting terrorists. If the Americans had let the investigation run its course, it might well have ended in jail time for Nasr. Instead, they broke Italian law and left their fingerprints, so to speak, at the scene of the crime and then took Nasr on a ride to torture and imprisonment without formal charges.

Extraordinary rendition was a misguided policy from the beginning. The argument against it does not even have to rely on the "rights" of the terrorist suspect. Ramzi Yousef, for example, went through ordinary rendition. He was captured in Pakistan and turned over to American authorities. He stood trial in federal court in New York, was convicted, and now rots in prison. His docket is clean; he faced the American criminal justice system.

Yousef's uncle, Khalid Sheikh Mohammed, experienced extraordinary rendition. He, too, was captured in Pakistan and turned over to CIA officers who whisked him out of sight to an unknown prison and later took him to Guantánamo Bay. There is undoubtedly enough evidence coming from his own mouth to convict him for planning the 9/11 attacks. To say he confessed would be putting it mildly; he has boasted of this and other misdeeds. He is proud of his iniquity. Designated as an enemy combatant, he, too, rots in prison. But his docket was not clean under the Bush administration; he did not face the criminal justice system. Not until November 2009 did Attorney General Eric Holder announce that Mohammed would be tried in federal court in New York. But the announcement met with such a storm of protest that he put the decision on hold while the issue was publicly debated.

"Enhanced interrogation techniques," the euphemistic term for torture, raise a separate issue. The main problem with such techniques is that they violate the golden rule, "do unto others as you would have them do unto you." This rule may seem like an ethical command coming straight from God, but it is also practical advice. If we practice torture on enemy combatants, we are hardly in a position to lecture the enemy about torturing Americans who might fall into their hands. So the higher-ups in the Bush administration who approved those techniques were, in effect, smoothing the way for the torture of the enemy's American prisoners.

An exception to the rule can be cogently argued. If there is reason to believe that the prisoner possesses information of major consequence, such as details of an imminent attack on an American city, the interrogator might be forgiven for using torture. Possibly, that fear of imminent danger motivated our use of torture and saved an American city from disaster. But the waterboarding of Abu Zubaydah apparently did not meet that threshold. According to the Justice Department memo, it led merely to the subsequent arrest of Ramzi Binalshibh, a relatively minor al Qaeda figure. If that is all we gained from violating the standards of civilized society, then we paid too high a price for the capture of Binalshibh.

Not to be overlooked after this diverting tour of extraordinary rendition is the importance of police enforcement in global counterterrorism. The Pakistani police, in particular, although they surely have skeletons in their closet, have earned America's gratitude and respect. Police activity is one good option for fighting terrorists in Pakistan, where American influence is tenuous. But that option has worn thin. The imperative remains for America to hold off the terrorist threat. To that end, perhaps the most powerful nation in history, with its array of remotely controlled precision weapons, covers the tribal areas with pilotless drones that fire precision missiles and sends in elite fighting men armed with state-of-the-art weapons on special missions. Will that bring about the desired solution? Or is it counterproductive? Will it do more harm than good? The jury is out. Only time will tell. If America can learn just one thing from this entanglement that President Bush has called the "war on terror," it should be respect for the principle of self-determination.

7

NUCLEAR JIHADISM

Of all the negatives associated with the terrorist wars, the worst possible scenario for America would be the explosion of an atomic bomb in a large U.S. city. Most Americans banish the very idea, yet it is, perhaps not inevitable, but a real possibility. A ten-kiloton fission bomb detonated on any workday at noon in New York's Times Square would make that famous American tourist mecca "vanish in the twinkling of an eye," wrote Harvard professor and former Defense Department official Graham Allison. Every building within a third of a mile would be turned to dust and rubble. The firestorm would engulf Rockefeller Center and Carnegie Hall to the north, Grand Central Station and possibly United Nations headquarters to the east, the Empire State Building and the Penn Station–Madison Square Garden complex to the south, and most everything west to the Hudson River. Half a million people would die instantly, and hundreds of thousands more would die in the following days and months.[1] The nuclear age would have come full circle. The United States, the creator of nuclear weapons and the only nation to use them in war, would finally feel the catastrophic effects of its invention.

Professor Allison's numbers, while only best estimates, are not speculative. The Hiroshima and Nagasaki bombs that ended World War II had the force of about 15,000 and 22,000 tons of TNT, respectively. Hiroshima, with a population of about a quarter of a million, was flattened while Nagasaki, about 190,000 people, was spared the full impact of its more powerful blast by the topography between ground zero and the city center. Together, the two bombs killed about

135,000 people instantly. Another 230,000 died within five years from injuries and radiation sickness. The grand total of deaths from the two A-bombs is about 83 percent of the two cities' cumulative population. In any ranking of weapons of mass destruction, the nuclear bomb is right at the top. There seems little doubt that if bin Laden had the wherewithal, so crazed is he with hatred for America that he would detonate one in a major American city.

During the cold war between the United States and the Soviet Union, the world was spared nuclear holocaust by the knowledge that each possessed enough bombs to destroy civilization. It was called the principle of mutually assured destruction (MAD). MADness hardly survives in the twenty-first century and likely will not keep the advanced industrialized world free from nuclear destruction. In the wake of the would-be bomb in Times Square or in some other city, what comparable target could America demolish? A mountain village in South Waziristan? An al Qaeda training camp? America would be much the worse for the exchange and probably no closer to victory over the Islamists.

After the Soviet Union broke up into its constituent parts, Russia remained a major power and retained much of the Soviet Union's nuclear arsenal, but loosely guarded nuclear warheads and materials were left over in Russia and many of the other former Soviet states. Western intelligence is uncertain how much weapons-grade uranium or plutonium remains in unsafe depositories or how much of it has leaked into the global black market. Russia no longer threatens imminent disaster. The threat now is nuclear proliferation, especially the real possibility that terrorists might acquire a nuclear bomb or enough enriched uranium-235 to build their own.

After the American bombs were dropped in 1945, the Soviet Union tested its own bomb in 1949 with the help of spies from inside the American nuclear laboratory in Los Alamos, a factor in the acceleration by an estimated two years of the Soviet nuclear program. Nuclear tests by Britain, France, and China followed, and these three nations plus the United States and the Soviet Union negotiated the Treaty on the Non-Proliferation of Nuclear Weapons, which went into effect in 1970. India and Pakistan have tested nuclear weapons but have never belonged to the non-proliferation club. India's first test came in 1974. Pakistan's came much later, in 1998, but according to Dr. Abdul Qadeer Khan, the so-called father of the Islamic bomb, Pakistan could have built an enriched uranium bomb in 1984.[2]

North Korea, which withdrew from the non-proliferation treaty in 2003, has also conducted nuclear tests. South Africa and Libya have started nuclear programs and then voluntarily discontinued them. Start-up nuclear facilities in Iraq and Syria were destroyed in Israeli air attacks. In 2010 the Federation of American Scientists listed nine nuclear powers: United States, Russia, Britain, France, China, India, Pakistan, Israel and North Korea.[3]

Iran has built uranium enrichment plants, which it claims are for the peaceful production of nuclear power, but many experts and political leaders in the West suspect the country wants to make nuclear bombs. In the 1970s Washington debated whether to sell nuclear technology to the shah of Iran for allegedly peaceful uses, but the sale never materialized on the grand scale proposed.[4] Israel possesses an underground nuclear weapons facility at Dimona in the Negev Desert but has never admitted its existence or tested a nuclear bomb. In 1969 President Richard Nixon made a deal with Israeli prime minister Golda Meir to allow Israel to build its nuclear arsenal as long as Israel remained quiet about it. Israel has kept its end of the bargain, but in 2008 the U.S. Joint Forces Command broke official American silence on the subject by publishing a document that referred to Israel as "a nuclear power."[5] The Israeli case demonstrates American hypocrisy on nuclear proliferation.

The good news, as far as the West knows, is that al Qaeda and its Islamist allies do not have a nuclear program or the large capital resources and the technical know-how to build one. But possessing one or two bombs or a sufficient quantity of enriched uranium to build their own from publicly available documents is an entirely different proposition. Sneaking a bomb past busy ports or porous borders and into an American city would be the easy part. Building a bomb from scratch might take up to a year, but it is entirely possible. It would probably have to be a uranium bomb. A simple gunlike mechanism, invented by European scientists Rudolf Peierls and Otto Frisch at England's Birmingham University early in World War II, ignited the Hiroshima bomb. The gun trigger propels a small amount of uranium-235 at high speed into a larger chamber of uranium and creates a critical mass to cause the explosion. Any bright individual with the ability to read publicly available technical literature could easily duplicate this setup. Creating another Nagasaki bomb, however, would require an implosion mechanism to create critical mass in its plutonium core. This is a much more elaborate undertaking and demands precise measurements that would be very difficult to achieve—and probably not worth the effort for the likes of al Qaeda.

It is highly possible—even probable—that al Qaeda has acquired a "dirty bomb," a weapon of mass destruction that is not nearly so massive. A dirty bomb is nothing more than a conventional explosive mixed with radioactive material. It is not fissionable like a plutonium or uranium bomb, and it ranks well down the scale as a weapon of mass destruction. To put an exclamation mark on it, one of the twentieth century's experts on evil, Saddam Hussein, had a one-ton dirty bomb built in 1987, only to decide that the bomb was not sufficiently lethal for his purpose. Besides, its radioactive effects are partly dependent on which way the wind is blowing, and it would not do to have the wind blowing back on his own forces. Of course, a dirty bomb has more punch than a Fourth of July fireworks display. A powerful conventional bomb could kill scores of people, and a radioactive cloud could in time infect thousands more with cancer. The greatest immediate impact in a large city might be from panic, which could put hundreds of thousands of people trying to flee out on the streets in cars and on foot.

Dirty bombs are easy to make and have a brief known history of use for purposes of terrorism. Chechen rebels planted one packed with radioactive cesium-137 in Moscow's Izmailovsky Park in 1995. But instead of setting it off, they reportedly used it as a calling card by notifying authorities of its whereabouts. Jose Padilla, an American citizen and an alleged al Qaeda operative, was arrested in 2002 and charged with plotting to build a dirty bomb to detonate in a U.S. city. The next year in Afghanistan, British intelligence discovered al Qaeda documents that included diagrams of a dirty bomb.[6]

THE ISLAMIC BOMB

Other than the former Soviet states, where in recent years nuclear security has been tightened but not sealed, the terrorists' most promising market for a nuclear bomb or enriched uranium-235 would be some of the more recently arrived nuclear states. Pakistan tops a short list despite assurances from the Islamabad government that its nuclear arsenal is secure. The threat is not so much from official Pakistan as it is from individual Pakistanis. A. Q. Khan directed Pakistan's nuclear program, and then he built a nuclear black market in which he sold nuclear secrets to other Muslim countries and set the stage for trading uranium enrichment machinery to

North Korea in exchange for missile technology. Members of Khan's team of Pakistani nuclear scientists are known to have met with al Qaeda's leaders, bin Laden and Ayman al-Zawahiri.

Khan began his career in 1972 at the Physics Dynamic Research Laboratory in Amsterdam, part of a British–Dutch–West German consortium called Urenco, formed to develop centrifuges for uranium enrichment. He arrived with a doctorate in metallurgy from the Catholic University of Leuven, Belgium, after studies at German and Dutch universities and had recently been married to an ethnic Dutch woman born in South Africa and raised in Rhodesia. Khan took the job at the Dutch research laboratory as a last resort. He had applied unsuccessfully for work in Pakistan, a country for which he had developed a nationalist's fervor because of his hatred of India, where he had spent the first sixteen years of his life and endured the insults of the Hindu majority. As he became absorbed in his work at the lab, he began to realize its significance. Impelled by an inner desire to do something significant for Pakistan and without any assurance that the opportunity would come his way, he began to copy plans and photograph designs of European centrifuge machinery. He passed freely between the lab in Amsterdam and the enrichment plant being built near the rural Dutch village of Almelo and contributed to specifications for metals in new centrifuges. Because he was fluent in both German and Dutch, he was given the assignment of translating the latest German centrifuge plans into Dutch, and he exploited the opportunity to take his own notes and smuggle them out of the secure room where the documents were stored. In the three years he spent at the Dutch lab, Khan accumulated a large dossier of atomic secrets, which, if Dutch authorities had brought down the hammer, would have landed him in prison. But the Dutch, out of embarrassment over their security lapses, covered up his treachery until too late.[7]

When India tested its first nuclear bomb in 1974, a collective chill went up the spine of the Pakistani nation. Khan wrote to Prime Minister Zulfikar Ali Bhutto explaining his situation and offering his services. Bhutto was intrigued and, after checking him out, invited the scientist to a meeting, which took place a few months later when Khan was on an annual family visit to Pakistan. At the time Pakistan was trying to buy plutonium technology from France but meeting American resistance. Khan told the prime minister that Pakistan could build a uranium bomb much faster than a plutonium bomb and in secret, and Bhutto decided to go both ways. This decision worked to Pakistan's great advantage because Western intelligence knew of the plutonium program, but when orders for centrifuge parts indicated a uranium program also, the spymasters of the West were slow to catch on.

Bhutto sent Khan back to Holland with a code name and the confidential phone number of an undercover contact at the Pakistani embassy, Siddique Butt, who, working through front companies, would order centrifuge components specified by Khan for shipment back to Pakistan. This was the beginning of what became known to insiders as "the Pakistani pipeline." Because the components the Pakistanis ordered were often identical to those required for the European centrifuge, Khan again came under the suspicion of Dutch intelligence officers, and this time they notified the CIA. But no arrest was made. The CIA, still focused on the plutonium program, asked that he simply be put under close watch in order to uncover more about the Pakistani uranium operation. For the CIA, exposing secrets came first and law enforcement second, so the request was perfectly reasonable. But Khan slipped out of the West's grasp. In December 1975 he went on his regular family visit to Pakistan and never looked back.

Ali Bhutto put Khan in charge of the uranium enrichment program and, at Khan's insistence, gave him an unlimited budget and complete freedom from bureaucratic oversight. Khan built an empire for himself totally separate from the plutonium program. He made every decision in his own bailiwick, down to the smallest detail. The people he hired answered to him, and he answered only to the prime minister. He shortened the timeline for completion of individual phases leading up to a full enrichment program by launching projects simultaneously that should have run consecutively. He oversaw the construction of a processing plant in a wooded area outside Islamabad called Kahuta. The parts that had been shipped ahead of him were inadequate, and he added to the inventory with acquisitions in the pipeline. Khan also renewed old school and work friendships in Germany and Holland and made new connections elsewhere to obtain the machinery he needed. By 1979 U.S. intelligence finally recognized from Khan's shopping spree in Europe and North America for centrifuge parts that Pakistan was building a uranium enrichment facility. Satellite photos of the huge construction site at Kahuta confirmed it. In 1981 Prime Minister Zia-ul-Haq, who had ousted Ali Bhutto in a military coup and had him hanged for alleged corruption, dedicated the plant and named it the Dr. A. Q. Khan Research Laboratories. In 1983 the Netherlands put Khan on trial in absentia for his theft of the centrifuge secrets, found him guilty, and sentenced him to four years in prison, but the verdict was overturned two years later. By the mid-1980s thousands of centrifuges were running smoothly in the cavernous rooms in the Kahuta complex, and Khan boasted in the Urdu press that Pakistan was enriching uranium. Asked if Pakistan could build an atomic bomb, he said the job "is not beyond our reach."[8]

THE NUCLEAR BLACK MARKET

Some called it the Pakistani pipeline. Others described it as "Khan's network." Both terms are apt descriptions of the nuclear black market that parallels the illicit drug market as an underground supply-and-demand mechanism. It started with Khan's resolute effort to obtain centrifuges for Pakistan. That firmly established an infrastructure for nuclear proliferation. But when Pakistan's immediate needs were satisfied by the late 1980s, the market began to dry up, and suppliers looked for ways to keep the business going. One eager customer at the time was the apartheid regime in South Africa. But once it became clear that the days of white South African power were numbered, Prime Minister F. W. de Klerk dismantled six nuclear bombs and scuttled the program, ending one fruitful black market channel. Iran and Iraq were potential customers, but they were engaged in an internecine war that ate up most of their resources.

Gotthard Lerch, a German working for the firm Leybold-Heraeus, a heavy-duty player in the nuclear market, had sold Khan vacuum valves, vacuum pumps, and a gas purification plant, all used in Pakistan's enrichment program. Although he broke no laws, Lerch attracted the interest of German intelligence, and Leybold pushed him out the door. He moved to Switzerland with his special knowledge (including Leybold secrets) and started his own company, which kept him in the pipeline. South Africa was one of his early customers.

When the nuclear proliferation market softened, Lerch reached out to Iran. To an Iranian scientist who had approached him in 1987 about buying conventional weapons, he offered a blueprint for a complete enrichment plant and designs for nuclear weapons components. Intrigued, the agent passed the proposal up the chain of command to the senior clerics at the top, and they approved the initiative. Lerch and the Iranians set up a meeting in Dubai, an unregulated tax-free zone in the Persian Gulf. The German brought other black marketers into the deal, notably Mohammed Farooq, an Indian with an export business in Dubai; Friedrich Tinner, a Swiss engineer who made vacuum valves for Kahuta; and Khan, who supplied the centrifuges. Farooq's young nephew, Buhary Sayed Abu Tahir, who would later become Khan's business manager, served tea and ran the copying machine at the meeting. The meeting came off to the satisfaction of both sides. Iran received its specifications and two sample centrifuges, for which it paid $10 million on the spot. Khan's cut was $2 million, even though he did not attend the meeting.[9]

The easy money may have whetted his appetite. Khan had already lined his pockets with kickbacks as he built up the Pakistani enrichment program, but he now saw opportunities that even Midas might envy. In 1990, after Iraq had overrun Kuwait and threatened to invade Saudi Arabia, Khan sent intermediaries to Baghdad with an offer to sell nuclear technology similar to what had been passed to Iran three years earlier. Saddam Hussein, ever eager for nuclear power, was of course interested, but with his utter defeat in Kuwait early in 1991, the deal fell through. Inspections subsequently carried out by the International Atomic Energy Agency (IAEA) revealed an advanced Iraqi atomic weapons program built independently from Khan's network. Between 1979 and 1984 Iraq imported low-grade uranium from Italy, highly enriched uranium from the Soviet Union and France, yellowcake (uranium oxide) from Portugal and Niger, and uranium dioxide from Brazil, and through the 1980s it processed the low-grade material for electromagnetic separation, gaseous diffusion, and centrifuge enrichment in its own plants. The results, however, were less than satisfactory. The IAEA concluded that Iraq had produced no more than a few grams of bomb-grade material and had failed to build nuclear weapons.[10] It seems reasonable to surmise, therefore, that the technology Khan offered in 1990 would have given a tremendous boost to Saddam's dream of joining the nuclear club.

If the deal had been consummated and if the IAEA inspectors had traced centrifuges back to Khan, the nuclear black market might well have been discovered sooner than it actually was. But Khan moved on. He cooperated with Iranian scientists on their uranium enrichment program. The obsolescent centrifuges he originally sold to Iran (known in the industry as P1) often broke down, and he worked hard to make good on his business deals. In 1994, working through young

Tahir in Dubai, he sold Iran a limited number of Pakistan's next generation (P2) centrifuges. Iranian diplomat Ali Akbar Omid Mehr, who had been in charge of Iran's Pakistan desk and eventually defected to the West, told of Khan's close cooperation with Iranian scientists, cooperation that so pleased the Iranians that they paid him tens of millions of dollars and gave him a villa near the Caspian Sea.[11]

During the early 1990s Khan visited many Islamic countries, such as Syria, Turkey, the United Arab Emirates, Saudi Arabia, and Libya, to urge them to buy his nuclear wares and know-how as protection against U.S. power. In general, these states cautiously turned him down, but Libya came around to the idea. At the time Khan was making frequent trips to Iran to give advice and technical aid as needed. Efforts to trade Pakistan's uranium enrichment technology to North Korea for its No-dong missile, a nuclear delivery vehicle coveted by the Pakistani army, also impinged on his time. But the demands placed on him by the Libyan project dwarfed anything he had undertaken since Pakistan's initial buildup. The finished package proposed by Khan envisioned a plant for Libya that would turn out three or four nuclear weapons a year, and he would supply all the parts. It would require a major expansion of his black market network. First, he would need a plant to make centrifuges. He converted a large warehouse in Dubai and hired Urs Tinner, son of his old vacuum valve supplier, Friedrich Tinner, to run it. As noted, Tahir became the general manager of the enterprise. He needed someone to build a complicated centrifuge control system. Lerch recommended Gerhard Wisser, a German who had moved to South Africa. Wisser said his small shop could not handle the job, but for a $1 million finder's fee, he enlisted a South African engineer, Johan Meyer, who owned a business called Tradefin, to put all the tubing and other parts together for a two-story, $33 million machine. Tahir told Meyer the machinery was for oil production, but Meyer knew better. Both he and Wisser were veterans of the South African A-bomb project and had participated in the nuclear black market.[12]

Khan must have thought he was invincible. His black market empire stretched from Europe to the Far East and from Turkey to South Africa. But he had reached too far. The growth of his enterprise paved the way for his downfall. The CIA greased the skids for him with some nifty undercover work. A tip that Khan's suppliers had a big new, unidentified customer came from German intelligence in 2000. The investigation focused on the Tinner family, which was already known to international intelligence. Urs was in trouble with the law in France, and with the help of French intelligence, the CIA used Urs's legal problem as leverage to obtain his cooperation. An agent tracked him down in a Dubai bar and offered to help him beat the rap in France. Urs took the bait. After many conversations the agent was able to report a detailed insider's picture of Khan's dealings with Iran and Libya. Owing to a lack of skilled labor, the Dubai plant ran into trouble meeting its orders, so Tahir moved the operation to Malaysia, where skilled labor was plentiful and the business atmosphere was relaxed. Urs Tinner moved with it and continued his cooperation with the CIA agent, who followed him east. Urs let his father, Friedrich, and brother, Marco, know that he was working with the CIA, and they, too, began telling the agency about their ties to Khan for payouts in the millions of dollars. When it comes to buying inside information, the CIA is no piker. Marco signed a contract with the agency for $1 million payable to Traco Group, his front company in the British Virgin Islands, for the sale of proprietary information held by the Tinners about the manufacture of vacuum devices. The information made it possible for American nuclear engineers to sabotage black market centrifuge parts. For example, vacuum pumps made for Iran and Libya that looked exactly like a product from the Tinners were manipulated at the Los Alamos National Laboratory in New Mexico to make sure they would not work.[13]

Scomi Precision Engineering owned the new plant in Malaysia. One of its investors was Tahir's wife, Nazimah Syed Majid. Another investor was Kamaluddin Abdullah, the son of Malaysian prime minister Abdullah Badawi. CIA agents kept close track of precision pumps, tubes, and other products from Scomi that would go out on one merchant ship from Malaysia to Dubai and then be transferred to another ship for the final voyage to Libya. Several months after the U.S.-led invasion of Iraq, one such shipment was diverted from Tripoli to Taranto, Italy, where five Libya-bound crates marked agricultural products and containing centrifuge machinery were off-loaded and hauled away in U.S. military trucks. The Western allies now had hard evidence that the Khan network was helping Libyan president Muammar al-Gaddafi build an atomic weapons program. After lengthy negotiations with American and British diplomats, Gaddafi agreed to dismantle the program. The Bush administration claimed, perhaps with some justification, that the American action in Iraq influenced his decision, but the CIA's undercover work was undoubtedly a more potent factor.

Pakistani leaders already realized that Khan was engaged in outside activities, but they were probably unaware of the exquisite detail of his extensive business dealings. For one thing, the cost of his lifestyle far exceeded his modest $30,000-a-year government salary. He owned seven houses in Islamabad, two apartments in London, and a hotel in Timbuktu named after his wife, Hendrina, and he had deposits totaling $8 million in four banks in Karachi, Lahore, Amsterdam, and Dubai.[14] But he had become a national and Muslim hero with the sobriquet "father of the Islamic bomb," and thus a revered figure in Pakistan. Politically, he had to be handled with great care.

After Musharraf came to power in a coup in October 1999, he tried to rein in the freewheeling nuclear scientist by calling for audits and restricting travel, measures that Khan defied. In January 2001 Musharraf relieved Khan of his position at Kahuta and tried to make it look like a retirement by naming him scientific adviser to the president. After 9/11 the United States pressured Musharraf to put Khan out of action. CIA Director George Tenet met twice with the Pakistani president about the activities of the black market network. In a one-on-one session in New York on September 24, 2003—with the vital evidence of the Libyan nuclear buildup still on the high seas—he warned of "devastating consequences" if a nuclear device from Pakistan should be acquired by Libya, Iran, or "God forbid, an organization like al Qaeda." Musharraf told Tenet that he would take care of the problem.[15] The following January he dismissed Khan from his advisory role, and in February, under prolonged questioning, Khan confessed to passing nuclear secrets to Iran, Libya, and North Korea. Reading from a script prepared for him to deliver in English on Pakistani television, he took full responsibility for his actions and absolved Pakistani political and military officials. Hardly anyone outside of Pakistan believed that Khan acted alone, without government knowledge or approval. To keep tensions over the sacking of a national hero from boiling over, the confession was not repeated in Urdu. The greatest nuclear proliferator in history was not formally tried but was placed under house arrest for five years, from which he emerged in 2009.[16]

The end of the Khan network was at hand even before Khan's confession, and key players have had their comeuppance with criminal justice. Tahir was arrested in Malaysia and wrote a detailed confession. He remained in custody until 2008, when Malaysian authorities released him, saying he was no longer a security threat.[17] The Swiss picked up Lerch and then dropped their betrayal charges and extradited him to Germany. There, he was put on trial in 2006 in a case that dragged on for two years until his lawyers negotiated a plea bargain with federal prosecutors. He signed a full confession and was set free with credit for time served in detention. Then he returned to Switzerland. In 2008 he again faced trial in Stuttgart, Germany, for his role in the Khan network. This time he was convicted and sentenced to five-and-a-half years in prison. With credit for time served in detention, he was set free once again.[18] Meyer was indicted in South Africa, but charges against him were dropped when he agreed to turn state's evidence against Wisser.[19] Wisser received a suspended eighteen-year sentence.[20] Friedrich, Urs, and Marco Tinner were taken into custody in Switzerland, but the case against them has been hampered by the CIA's unwillingness to furnish evidence against the family that provided it with vital secrets about the Khan network. At the urging of the United States, the Swiss government further weakened the prosecution's case by destroying computer files and documents about the family's underground operations.[21] If crime doesn't pay, nuclear proliferation, with its dark threat to the survival of mankind, certainly does.

AL QAEDA AND THE A-BOMB

Fear that Osama bin Laden might get his hands on chemical, biological, or nuclear weapons has been an ongoing issue for Western counterterrorism forces. During 1993–94 reports surfaced of al Qaeda efforts to buy a Russian nuclear warhead and other weapons components wherever they could be found on the black market.[22] Bin Laden actually did pay $1.5 million for a cylinder that a Sudanese military officer told him contained weapons-grade uranium, but it turned out to be a fake.[23] Al Qaeda tried again later to buy fissile material in Istanbul, but the material was nothing more than radioactive medical waste.[24]

Clearly, al Qaeda's search for a nuclear weapon has not panned out so far. If it had, bin Laden would surely have used it. One must assume that he's still looking. In an interview with *Time* in 1998 bin Laden said, "Acquiring [chemical and nuclear] weapons for the defense of Muslims is a religious duty."[25] One al Qaeda spokesman, Sulaiman Abu Ghaith, posted a statement on the Internet declaring, "Al Qaeda has the right to kill four million Americans, including one million children, displace double that figure, and injure and cripple hundreds [of] thousands."

Ghaith's numbers were apparently based on his estimate of the number of Muslims killed and injured at the hands of the United States and Israel over the years.[26] Nuclear weapons are the fastest way to reach those numbers. The world is hearing the language of the ancient vendetta with a modern twist. In 2003 bin Laden requested and obtained a fatwa from an Islamist Saudi cleric, Nasser bin Hamad al-Fahd, authorizing the use of weapons of mass destruction to kill American civilians.[27]

One of the Bush administration's main arguments for the invasion of Iraq was an alleged nuclear connection between Iraq and al Qaeda. Bush's advisers pushed the theory that the Iraqis could pass an A-bomb to terrorists who would plant it in an American city. The theory had its roots in a June 1994 meeting during which, through the intercession of Sudanese Islamist Hasan al-Turabi, bin Laden made contact with Iraqi intelligence chief, Faruq al-Hijazi. The meeting turned out to be little more than a chance for the two parties to become acquainted, and there is no evidence that anything came of it. Turabi wanted to forge a cooperative alliance between Iraq and al Qaeda to subvert Arab regimes supported by the United States. Later, when bin Laden moved back to Afghanistan, he had more flirtations with Iraqi intelligence, but they went no further than that. In any case, the issue is moot. However hard Iraq may have tried, it never developed a credible nuclear weapons program.[28]

A more ominous meeting, between al Qaeda leaders bin Laden and Zawahiri and two Pakistani nuclear scientists, Sultan Bashirrudin Mahmood and Chaudiri Abdul Majeed, took place one summer evening around a campfire outside Kandahar about two weeks prior to 9/11. These were not emissaries from A. Q. Khan, who had reportedly rebuffed overtures from al Qaeda. Mahmood and Majeed had their own agenda more closely aligned with al Qaeda's interests. They were leaders of a group called Umma Tameer-e-Nau, which had the stated mission of establishing social welfare programs in Afghanistan. Beneath the surface they trafficked in nuclear advice, and they knew that the conversation above the soothing crackle of the campfire would go beyond alms for the poor. Mahmood, former director for nuclear power at the Pakistan Atomic Energy Commission and an expert on centrifuge technology, was considered an eccentric among Pakistan's nuclear scientists. In 1987 he authored a book, *Doomsday and Life After Death: The Ultimate Fate of the Universe as Seen by the Holy Quran*, in which he predicted a nuclear holocaust that would hasten judgment day and fulfill the prophesies of the Muslim holy book. Reports of the 2001 meeting raised eyebrows at U.S. intelligence and after 9/11 triggered a hastily arranged trip to Islamabad by CIA Director Tenet to inform President Musharraf of America's concern. Musharraf responded by having members of Umma Tameer-e-Nau questioned. Little or nothing came of the investigation, however. These were all respected scientists and engineers, men of high status in Pakistani society. They were treated with kid gloves. Mahmood did confirm the meeting with the al Qaeda leaders and showed the rough sketch of an atom bomb he had drawn for them. He said he told them, "The most difficult part of the process is obtaining the necessary fissile material." To which bin Laden allegedly replied, "What if we already have the material?" Mahmood said he wasn't sure whether bin Laden was asking a purely hypothetical question or declaring possession of fissile material.[29] But it left the intelligence community and policymakers with more to think about.

Hamid Mir, a Pakistani journalist writing a biography of bin Laden, said in an interview on Australian television in 2004 that Zawahiri had told him in November 2001 that al Qaeda had purchased from disgruntled Soviet scientists an unspecified number of suitcase bombs (atomic bombs small enough to carry in large suitcases).[30] Whether Zawahiri's claim was true or not, he wanted Mir to carry the message to the outside world. Saying it is so is not proof, but the world learned from 9/11 (let us hope) not to sell al Qaeda short. If it is not true, at least it demonstrates a high level of skill at manipulating public opinion, and if it is true, the message suggests that the terrorists are looking for a way to deliver the suitcase bombs—a very scary thought. Bin Laden's comment prior to 9/11 that al Qaeda would use chemical or nuclear weapons as a deterrent implies that he favors mutually assured destruction, which is at least better than nuclear holocaust. But this implication is not something the world can count on. In the decade that has passed since he made the statement, bin Laden may have changed his mind—if, indeed, the MAD idea ever occurred to him.

The United States and its allies have responded to the threat of nuclear proliferation with efforts to round up "loose nukes" such as those in former Soviet states, where Zawahiri claimed to have purchased the suitcase bombs. The Nunn-Lugar Act of 1991 (by Senators Sam Nunn and Richard Lugar) authorized steps to keep these weapons out of the hands of terrorists and rogue states. In a bill to update the Nunn-Lugar Act written in 2005, Congress asserted that 6,564 nuclear warheads had been deactivated in the fourteen-year period since the initial act had passed.[31] However, in 2008 Harvard University's Project on Managing the Atom reported that much U.S.-sponsored security updating remains to be completed in the former Soviet Union, and elsewhere in the world. In Russia, the report estimated that about 250 buildings contained stockpiles of nuclear weapons and materials, many of which are poorly secured. While Russia is the largest such nuclear repository, nuclear materials are also stored at lightly guarded sites in China, India, Pakistan, and the former nuclear nation, South Africa.[32] This was especially grim news because the knowledge of how to make a simple uranium bomb is widely available to students of nuclear science—difficult to carry out, but available.

An incident in South Africa in November 2007 highlighted the threat posed by loose nukes. Four armed men attacked a nuclear depository at Pelindaba, where hundreds of pounds of highly enriched uranium were stored. They managed to neutralize the detection system at the perimeter, cut through an electrified fence, and break into the emergency control center. They spent forty-five minutes there before they escaped. If reports are accurate, they did not take any uranium with them, but it makes one wonder what they were doing in those forty-five minutes. The depressing part of the story is that Pelindaba is better protected than many other weapons-grade nuclear storage facilities in other parts of the world.[33]

Rolf Mowatt-Larssen, a career CIA agent and now a scholar at Harvard, spent his last four years in the agency as the leading expert on weapons of mass destruction. He was with Tenet on the visit to Islamabad to warn Musharraf about Umma Tameer-e-Nau. He has offered a controversial plan to covertly acquire nuclear bomb-making material from the black market and smuggle it into the United States as a way of alerting the nation of the nuclear Armageddon threat. It's an interesting idea, but ABC News has already done something like it. In 2002 it borrowed a cylinder of depleted uranium metal from the Natural Resources Defense Council (NRDC) and smuggled it past U.S. Customs. The story was aired on September 11, 2002, the first anniversary of al Qaeda's attack on America. A year later ABC did it again using the same cylinder, and the story aired on September 11, 2003. Although the spent fuel in the cylinder was harmless, according to the NRDC, the operation proved that weapons-grade material could have been smuggled into the country without detection.[34]

It is hard to imagine anything more frightening than a nuclear bomb going off in an American city—or for that matter, in any city anywhere in the world. The threat does not come from a nation but from terrorists who want to save mankind and install God as sovereign over us all. It may be far-fetched, but it is at least plausible that a radicalized Pakistan or a nuclear-armed Iran could secretly hand over one or more nukes to a fanatical organization like al Qaeda, or that al Qaeda could buy one or more in the black market or steal the nuclear material to make their own bombs. With an A-bomb in bin Laden's hands, the rosiest possible scenario would be for him to use it as leverage to negotiate American withdrawal from the Muslim world.

The difficulty of keeping nuclear materials safe from terrorists stood out in November 2010 when the world learned from WikiLeaks that the United States has tried since 2007 to negotiate with Pakistan for the removal of highly enriched uranium from a Pakistani research reactor. The disclosure came from an internal cable sent by Amb. Anne W. Patterson to Washington in May 2009, one of about 250,000 heretofore secret State Department cables—most of them innocuous or outdated, some of them embarrassing—revealing inside information. (Initially, WikiLeaks released only a few dozen State Department cables, but founder Julian Assange threatened to release more "if something happens to us"—like prosecution for espionage in the United States.) Patterson said Islamabad refused to discuss removal of the uranium with American experts for fear expressed by a Pakistani official that if word got out, people "would portray it as the United States taking Pakistan's nuclear weapons."[35] Other WikiLeaks disclosures, these from the Pentagon, are discussed in the next chapter.

8

THINKING
THE UNTHINKABLE

If one were to ask how the Western alliance was doing in the summer of 2010 in its war against the Taliban, and more generally against the Islamist terrorists, the short answer would have to be mixed at best—and that's not good.

In the poppy-growing Helmand Valley district of Marja, where in February American-led forces had driven the Taliban out, about two hundred Taliban had reinfiltrated by May to punish local farmers who dared to cooperate with the Americans. Farmers told the *New York Times* that they knew who among them were Taliban but would not identify them to the Americans for fear of being beaten or even killed. About 150 farm families had already pulled up stakes and moved out of the district.[1] This development represented a setback for the American strategy of isolating the Islamists to eliminate or weaken their influence on the population—demonstrating that the Taliban were not only tough, brave, and ruthless, but also extremely cunning, taking full advantage of local knowledge.

It also amounted to a military reversal for the West. A year earlier U.S. and NATO forces in Helmand had been stalemated because they lacked sufficient numbers to put the Taliban away. In 2010, after President Obama had decided to send thirty thousand troop reinforcements to Afghanistan, the stalemate continued. There is no middle ground in insurgency war. As Henry Kissinger famously said in the Vietnam era, "The conventional army loses if it does not win. The guerrilla wins if he does not lose."[2] Time is on the insurgent's side. In nearby Kandahar the Americans postponed a spring offensive to dislodge the Taliban after residents let it be known that they did not want a bloodbath in their city like those in Ramadi and Fallujah during the occupation of Iraq. The disappointing progress in Marja caused American strategists to revise their game plan in Kandahar, at least temporarily, from direct military force to an emphasis on reconstruction while the Taliban remained in place.[3] The Kissinger aphorism was still relevant. A few weeks later, however, the *New York Times* reported that coalition forces were routing the Taliban with the aid of mobile rocket launchers that could fire missiles with pinpoint accuracy. The Taliban were said to be giving up strong defensive positions and retreating into Pakistan.[4] Later in 2010, for the first time in the Afghan war the United States deployed M1A1 super-tanks in the battle for Kandahar.[5]

Corroboration of a losing war effort came inadvertently on July 25, 2010, from within the U.S. government in the form of about 77,000 classified military secrets released without authorization by the online organization WikiLeaks. Three international news publications—the *New York Times*, the *Guardian* of England, and the German weekly, *Der Spiegel*—received advance copies of the secrets to prepare their coverage, on the condition that they not jump the release date. Initially, WikiLeaks held back about fifteen thousand documents because of security concerns. Generally, the documents, which cover the years 2004 to 2009, rather fragmented as they were, painted a grim picture of growing Taliban power in the face of Western and Afghan army deployments during the Bush years. Most of the information that consisted of raw intelligence from low-level field reports was not new, but some of it was. Documents revealed for the first time that the Taliban may have used heat-seeking missiles (possibly made in China) which, according to civilian eyewitness reports, have shot down allied helicopters. If that is true, and the Pentagon denies it, it could mark a dramatic turn in the war, a conjecture based on the role of American heat-seeking Stinger missiles in beating back the Soviet offensive against the mujahideen in the 1980s. One of the 2010 documents reported on an al Qaeda emissary sent to Iran and North Korea to buy arms. Some confirmed the well-known connection between the Afghan Taliban and Pakistan's ISI. Others gave details of expanded CIA paramilitary operations in Pakistan to spring ambushes, conduct night raids, and order air strikes. Still other documents included information about the Americans' use of drones to assassinate Islamist leaders.[6] The White House strongly condemned WikiLeaks for releasing information that it said put the lives of counterinsurgency troops in danger and threatened U.S. national security.[7]

Steven Aftergood, who writes about the overclassification of official U.S. secrets for the Federation of American Scientists, called the WikiLeaks coup "the largest single unauthorized disclosure of currently classified records that has ever taken place."[8] He gave WikiLeaks a mixed review: praise for its media impact on a global scale, but criticism for its broadside approach. Some documents reportedly contained the names of informants cooperating with the Americans, which imperiled their lives and the lives of their families.[9]

Comparisons with the Pentagon Papers of the Vietnam era, which revealed internal debates and high-level analyses by Defense Department officials, seemed overblown. The shock value then was off the charts. It remains to be seen how much impact the 2010 leaks would have on public opinion and war policy, although a ripple effect was noticeable the very next day when the House of Representatives voted, 308-114, to continue funding the wars in Iraq and Afghanistan. The vote showed that Obama was losing support from within his own party. A hundred and two Democrats broke ranks to vote against the bill, up from only thirty-two rebellious Democrats in the previous war-funding vote. The measure would not have passed without strong Republican support.[10]

WikiLeaks dropped the other shoe in late October 2010 by releasing nearly 400,000 classified documents about the American involvement in Iraq, more than three times the number released on Afghanistan the previous July. Like the Afghanistan leaks, those on Iraq provided details about the grim realities of the war, among them the deaths of fifteen thousand Iraqi civilians that had previously gone unreported and the torture and killing of Iraqi civilians by Iraqi security forces. Many torture incidents were witnessed by American soldiers and duly reported to superior officers, only to have the reports blocked somewhere up the chain of command. The Iraq leaks came late in the game as American troops were finally pulling out, but the documents are sure to be of major importance in future legal proceedings as families seek justice for the deaths and brutal treatment of loved ones.

In the equivalent of a separate war, or a second front of a two-front war, the United States was raining Hellfire missiles from Predator and Reaper drones on Islamist forces in the tribal areas of western Pakistan and to a lesser extent in the wilds of Yemen and Somalia. Unquestionably, the Islamists were hurting from these attacks, and President Obama kept up the pressure despite pleas from the Muslim world and even the United Nations to hold back. But it could hardly be coincidental that during this time of mounting Islamist casualties, terrorist plots that involved targets on American soil were on the rise.

COMMAND DECISION

Shortly after Barack Obama became president and commander in chief of the U.S. armed forces, he authorized the deployment of 21,000 additional combat troops to Afghanistan. This was consistent with his campaign promise to withdraw from Iraq and ratchet up the war against Islamists in Afghanistan and Pakistan. He wished to avenge 9/11 and parry the threat of global terrorism. Nine months after the inauguration, he wrestled with a new request from his handpicked military commander in Afghanistan, Gen. Stanley A. McChrystal, to commit still more troops. The request seemed to echo repeated calls from the military commanders in Vietnam four decades earlier for a constant stream of reinforcements that ultimately built up to more than a half million troops. In Af/Pak, history is not likely to repeat itself to the same degree.

General McChrystal's report, titled "Commander's Initial Assessment" and dubbed the "McChrystal ball" by the *Economist* magazine, was rather a downer. It was submitted to Secretary of Defense Robert M. Gates on August 30, 2009; leaked to author Bob Woodward; and printed with several redactions in the *Washington Post*. McChrystal said the overall situation in Afghanistan was deteriorating, and he gave U.S., NATO, and Afghan National forces one year to reverse the enemy's momentum or "risk an outcome where defeating the insurgency is no longer possible." McChrystal wanted forty thousand more troops, but he did not say so in his written public assessment, which focused instead on Afghan security needs. He projected an increase of Afghan army troops from 92,000 to 134,000 by the fall of 2010 and ultimately to 240,000, and a near-doubling of police from 84,000 to 160,000.[11]

President Obama, amid pressure both for and against the Afghan war, seemed genuinely reluctant to insert more American men and women into the jaws of death halfway around the globe. He spoke to troops at military bases to tell them how much he valued their service. He visited the wounded at Walter Reed Army Medical Center. Once he took a short hop in the middle of the night from Washington to Dover Air Force Base, Delaware, to pay somber tribute to slain soldiers whose bodies arrived in flag-draped coffins. The Bush White House had done its best to cover up any display of dead returning from the war zone.

The White House began its deliberations on September 13. Obama met with top security advisers, including Vice President Joseph Biden, Gates, Secretary of State Hillary Clinton, National Security Adviser James L. Jones, and Adm. Mike Mullen, chairman of the Joint Chiefs of Staff. Gates, Clinton, and Mullen supported McChrystal's request for forty thousand additional American troops. Biden advised against sending any reinforcements. He would ramp up special forces and drone attacks and concentrate U.S. efforts on the defeat of al Qaeda, or in the parlance of the experts, shift the emphasis from counterinsurgency to counterterrorism.[12] His idea seemed to leave the Taliban, both Afghan and Pakistani, out of the equation—a dangerous omission that military advisers and their allies jumped on. The Pakistani Taliban was hell-bent to side with al Qaeda. The Afghan Taliban, while they had not engaged directly in international terrorism, were and still are focused on reclaiming the power they once held in Afghanistan. Although the Afghan Taliban could not be expected to defeat U.S. and NATO troops, they could still wage guerrilla warfare and inflict casualties as long as the West remained in their country. On the other hand, with enough troops, the hawks argued, U.S.-NATO forces might wrest control of the Helmand Valley from the Taliban and deprive them of income from the opium trade.

The ambassador in Kabul, Lt. Gen. Karl W. Eikenberry (Ret.), former commander of U.S. forces in Afghanistan, made a last-minute impact on the deliberations by urging the president to keep reinforcements in check until President Karzai cleaned out the rampant corruption in the Afghan government, fueled in no small measure by the flood of U.S. aid money borrowed at the expense of future American taxpayers. Eikenberry's perception of the Karzai government is strongly supported by the WikiLeaks documents, which contain numerous examples of Afghan government corruption from top to bottom. The Pentagon has spent billions of dollars training Afghan security forces to prepare the way for an American exit beginning in July 2011. "But," according to the *New York Times*, "the police have proved to be an especially risky investment and are often described as distrusted, even loathed, by Afghan civilians. The reports recount episodes of police brutality, corruption petty and large, extortion, and kidnapping." According to the

Times's account of the documents, the Kabul police chief, Brig. Gen. Mir Amanullah Gozar, argued with President Karzai over an effort to have him fired for corruption. Brigadier General Gozar threatened to publicly accuse the president of
engaging in drug trading while associated with the Taliban before 2001. The police
chief of Paktia Province was described as "the axel of corruption" for openly demanding money from officers and troopers under him. The U.S. Army built an
orphanage in Paktia, but few orphans lived in it, and donations of blankets and
warm clothing went missing (possibly sold at the bazaar). A provincial council official told American officers based in Gardez, "The current [corrupt Afghan] government is worse than the Taliban." Another called corruption "a new concept" for
Afghanistan brought by the Americans ("new" being a rather dubious assertion).[13]

After three months of talking, the president announced his decision on December 1, 2009, in a speech to the cadets of the U.S. Military Academy at West
Point. The gist of it was summed up in two short sentences. "As Commander-in-
Chief," he said, "I have determined that it is in our vital national interest to send
an additional thirty thousand U.S. troops to Afghanistan. After eighteen months,
our troops will begin to come home."[14] It had the political effect of trying to appease the hard-liners on the right who wanted an unlimited effort to defeat the
enemy and the hard-liners on the left who sought an immediate and uncondi-
tional pullout.

The plan showed two glaring fundamental weaknesses in the administration's
strategic thinking: the Pakistani army and the Afghan security forces. Pakistan's
army is quite good at domestic politics but less effective at fighting an enemy,
be it the Indian army or the Taliban insurgents. Try as it might, the Obama administration is not likely to achieve decisive results by badgering the Islamabad
government to press on in its campaign against the Taliban–al Qaeda alliance in
FATA. That leaves the United States with pilotless drones and SOF to peck away
at the Islamists.

Prospects for meeting the Afghan security numbers posted by McChrystal are
even dimmer. The Afghans are brave fighters; they fight each other often. But it
stretches credulity to expect the army recruits to shape up as disciplined soldiers,
and the problem of police corruption is well established. When it comes to testing
them against the Taliban, who know how to fight, murder, spring ambushes, and
lay out fields of fire; have the fortitude to lay down their lives with suicide bombs;

and possess a fanatical devotion to divine sovereignty, the government forces in the absence of American support are likely to come up short, just as they did in the 1990s, when the Taliban overran most of the country.

Americans can be forgiven if they take the July 2011 target date for starting withdrawal with a grain of salt. They don't have to doubt Obama's sincerity. But the realities do not augur well for fulfillment. Secretary Gates, in a TV interview, played down the date. "We will have a hundred thousand . . . troops there," he said, "and they are not leaving in July of 2011. Some handful, . . . or whatever the conditions permit, will begin to withdraw at that time."[15] In other words, there will be a token withdrawal. At a news conference in Kabul, Karzai said it would take at least five years for Afghan military and police forces to take full responsibility for Afghan security, and fifteen to twenty years before Afghanistan could afford to pay for it.[16] His assessment might be optimistic. Indeed, in November 2010 the Obama administration floated a plan at the NATO summit to gradually hand over control of combat and police duties to Afghan security forces with the goal of ending the American/NATO combat mission by 2014. That idea obliterates the 2011 date to begin withdrawing.

As the political spin swirls around U.S., NATO, and Afghan government soldiers who put their lives on the line, the Pentagon has begun to worry about the nagging impact of America's longest war. A report released in July 2010 found that military suicides were up, along with the abuse of alcohol and drugs and other "high-risk behavior" that gets soldiers in trouble with the law, whether in the war zones or back in the States. The numbers reported for 2009 were 160 suicides, 146 high-risk deaths, 1,713 suicide attempts, 16,997 drug/alcohol offenses, and 57,503 other criminal offenses.[17] While 60 percent of the military suicides occur in the first enlistment term, Army Vice Chief of Staff Gen. Peter Chiarelli also noted in a televised interview that the increase represented a cumulative effect of on-and-off combat-zone deployments over nearly a decade of war.[18] The Pentagon is well advised to keep track of these trends because in the dying days of America's Vietnam debacle, the Army experienced rampant drug abuse in the ranks and a serious breakdown in discipline that included fragging. Although General Chiarelli insisted that the stressed-out soldiers four decades later were few in number, the danger of a similar implosion cannot be ignored.

Several months after President Obama's decision to send reinforcements to Afghanistan, an article in *Rolling Stone* magazine led to General McChrystal's dismissal. Written by Michael Hastings, who was embedded for about a month with McChrystal and his staff and had virtually unlimited access to outspoken staff officers, the article featured loose comments that one might hear in after-hours bull sessions. For the most part, Hastings quoted unnamed officers who belittled presidential advisers: the dovish Biden was disrespected as "Bite 'em"; Jones, a "clown . . . stuck in [the strategic thinking of] 1985"; Richard Holbrook, a "wounded animal" who wrote endless memos on which McChrystal heaped contempt. Special venom was reserved for Eikenberry, who wrote a classified memo scathingly critical of McChrystal's strategy in Afghanistan and then, according to McChrystal, leaked it to the media. McChrystal considered the leak a "betrayal . . . that covers his [Eikenberry's] flanks for the history books." General McChrystal, by all accounts an outstanding soldier who was Obama's handpicked commander of U.S. and NATO troops in Afghanistan, came out of the reporter's caldron as one who may have lacked the requisite political skills for such a high-level position. The petty bickering seemed to imperil chances for success in the war effort.

Even Obama did not escape the chafe, although it was somewhat less irritating. The president was described as "uncomfortable and intimidated" at a previous meeting with military brass and "didn't seem engaged" when naming McChrystal to the Afghanistan command in 2009.[19] It can be said, however, that Obama was fully engaged in firing McChrystal in 2010 and replacing him with General Petraeus, the hero of Iraq and an architect of the new counterinsurgency strategy. Petraeus stepped down from his higher position as head of Central Command to take the Afghanistan assignment. The Senate approved him at what might be considered the speed of light for congressional action, and in a display of unity Petraeus met the scorned Eikenberry on the way over so that the two of them could arrive together in Kabul. Petraeus took over his new command in a formal ceremony on the Fourth of July with a bold declaration: "We are in this to win."[20] The man who led the turnaround in Iraq would have about one year to achieve "mission improbable" in Afghanistan.

THE OTHER OPTION

History shows that the best way to avoid military quagmires in troubled countries is not to intervene in the first place. Once any great power occupies a small nation and stirs up an insurgency, it is left with no good options. The misguided Bush administration, acting without the support of many of its strongest NATO allies, fell into the great-power trap in Iraq. Within three years of the invasion, the occupiers were facing a chaotic situation. The new counterinsurgency strategy known popularly as the surge saved the occupiers from a humiliating defeat. Obdurate hawks who had advocated war then claimed victory. But what the United States won in Iraq was not victory. Rather, it won the opportunity to leave with American honor intact, contrary to the U.S. departure in Vietnam nearly four decades earlier.

Great power defeats at the hands of insurgents since World War II—the British in Palestine, the French in Vietnam and Algeria, the Americans in Vietnam, the Soviets in Afghanistan, and the Israelis in Lebanon—are too easily forgotten. The British victory in Malaya in the 1950s, the poster child of counterinsurgency, was accomplished after the British turned permanent governance over to the ethnic Malays.[21] The key is self-determination. The message could not be clearer: great power military intervention in the affairs of smaller nations is generally a losing game. Despite what the war apologists say—that it takes time to defeat insurgencies—the contrary is closer to the truth, namely, that it takes time for the interventionists to admit their folly.

Obama has tried to play with the hand he was dealt. America was already in Afghanistan when he took office, and the president has made clear his belief that it should be there because of 9/11. He feels that he cannot walk away from the fight and leave al Qaeda to pursue its agenda of global terrorism. The rightness of the task is not at issue; its difficulty is. It begs the question whether the effort is worth the cost. It puts perhaps the mightiest nation in history face to face with the limits of its power.

For that reason, negotiations with the Taliban must be in the policy mix, no matter how difficult that may seem. The ideal time to negotiate is after a decisive military victory, as happened at the conclusion of the Gulf War in 1991 (despite an American mistake that allowed Saddam Hussein to use helicopters to slaughter rebellious Shiites). Nothing like the Gulf War scenario seems to be in the cards this time around. America is fighting an altogether different kind of warfare and cannot expect more than piecemeal victories in a war of attrition. Which side is more committed? Which side gave ground in the Korengal? Which side is fighting for its own turf?

A major difference between the surge in Iraq and the strategy for Afghanistan is the ethno-religious interplay. In Iraq, Sunni factions found their alliance with Islamists self-defeating, so they went over to the American side. In Afghanistan, the Taliban's beliefs coincide with al Qaeda's. Those Taliban fully invested in Salafist theology are not likely to abandon their fanatical al Qaeda ally because they, too, are fanatical. In one element of the new strategy, McChrystal—later Petraeus—have hoped to lure less committed Taliban fighters into switching sides. Suitcases filled with newly minted $100 bills might help temporarily. In the early days of the American intervention in 2001, such enticements had the desired effect on a unit of several hundred tribesmen fighting on the Taliban side. But hard-core Islamists give no indications that dollars will persuade them to compromise.

If Mullah Omar should come to terms on a coalition Afghan government (unlikely), he would have to agree to shut down al Qaeda training camps on Afghan soil. If Pakistan could somehow make the same arrangement on its territory (also unlikely), al Qaeda would have no choice but to move on—to Kashmir, Yemen, or Somalia, perhaps. Then the United States might have to go through these same gyrations—and on and on. Even if al Qaeda were to disintegrate as an organization, the idea of divine sovereignty would have to play itself out over the years. Given its repressive nature as manifested in past regimes in Afghanistan and Sudan, it would probably not last long as a Muslim belief system. After only three decades the theocracy in Iran with its Shia version of divine sovereignty is struggling to withstand popular unrest. On the other hand, Islamism has made significant gains in Turkey, a NATO member and staunch American ally, so far without damaging its Western alliance. (Turkey, however, showed signs of impatience with Israel in a 2010 blockade-running incident off Gaza that involved Turkish citizens.[22]) The idea of divine sovereignty seems to have staying power, and the West must learn to live with it.

More to the immediate problem, withdrawal may be the ultimate solution in Afghanistan. If possible, for domestic consumption Obama must find a way out that will allow him to leave behind the impression that he has won, as in Iraq. For that, he now depends on Petraeus. Withdrawal does not have to be considered as losing if it shifts the strategic advantage in America's favor. In the right circumstances, an American pullout could be interpreted as a rational strategic maneuver rather than inglorious defeat. By stepping back, the United States would deflate the Islamist argument that the world's hegemon was repressing Muslim freedom. Islamism might fall of its own accord if the United States would stop propping it up by trying to destroy it militarily. As a practical matter, a U.S. withdrawal would leave Afghanistan's problems in the hands of the Afghans, and Pakistan's in the hands of the Pakistani, where they belong.

Robert A. Pape, a University of Chicago professor of political science, argues that the rise of suicide bombings in Afghanistan—none in 2002, two in 2003, five in 2004, nine in 2005, ninety-seven in 2006, 142 in 2007, and 148 in 2008— parallels the growth of the U.S. and NATO presence from the few who helped the Northern Alliance chase al Qaeda and the Taliban out of the country to about twenty thousand troops in 2005 to more than a hundred thousand in 2009. He cites a similar pattern for roadside bomb attacks. Consequently, he asserts, the Western troops are the cause of the rising violence, and the Afghan people increasingly view them as occupiers. His remedy—similar to Vice President Biden's position—is to significantly reduce the level of U.S. and NATO forces in Afghanistan and train local opposition groups to fight the Islamists, an initiative already under way. However, Pape offers the dubious idea of holding Western troops cooped up on ships offshore in the Persian Gulf and Indian Ocean (with boots off Muslim soil) to be ready when necessary to strike the enemy in cooperation with friendly local forces.[23]

An imperfect plan, perhaps, but at least Pape recognizes that withdrawal is the neglected option, unthinkable to war hawks such as former vice president Cheney and the neocons. It might have to be a unilateral move, the way Israel pulled out of Lebanon in 2000 and Gaza in 2005 because the Israeli leaders determined that Israel had more to gain from withdrawal than from staying the course. These were not perfect moves by any stretch of the imagination, especially in Gaza, where Hamas continued for a time to rain rockets down on Israel. Despite the flaw in the Gaza withdrawal, Ariel Sharon, the Israeli leader at the time and hardly a dove, obviously came to the conclusion that it was the lesser evil. So it was also for the Soviet leadership in 1989, when Soviet troops pulled out of Afghanistan.

Withdrawal, however, seems destined to remain on the back burner because President Obama has decided that escalation is the better choice. Or does the president have something else up his sleeve? Is he looking for opportunities to withdraw with honor? *Washington Post* columnist David Ignatius suggests that back-channel contacts are in order, contacts that will leave the public in the dark until a peace agreement is reached. General Petraeus, he argues, is the ideal man for that sort of mission because of his experience in Iraq of putting on strong military pressure while exploring political opportunities behind the scenes.[24] The American people can only hope that the Obama administration is headed in that direction.

Most Americans, in particular the neocons and like-minded hawks, fail to acknowledge the deleterious role that the U.S. global reach has played in the growth of al Qaeda and its Islamist allies. America would have been well advised to suppress its hegemonic instincts and pay more attention to the principle of self-determination. Leading a broad coalition to turn back the 1990–91 Iraqi aggression against Kuwait was one thing. Keeping a more or less permanent air base on Saudi territory afterward was quite another. The Western defense of Saudi oil made bin Laden angry; staying behind on "sacred" Saudi soil made him go mad. Not that America should appease bin Laden. Simply put, a great power should do the right thing: respect other peoples, leave ancient cultures to determine their own fate, and avoid wasting its power in small wars. In the 1950s President Eisenhower won points in the Muslim world by halting a joint British-French-Israeli advance on the Suez Canal. A similar show of evenhandedness in the 1990s might have stayed bin Laden's hand. He might not have resorted to jihad or declared war on America. All that is hindsight, of course, but it is also insight for the future. The history cannot be changed, but it is never too late to learn from past mistakes.

Notes

PROLOGUE: THAT AWFUL DAY

1. "Notes Found After the Hijackings," *New York Times*, September 29, 2001.
2. Philip D. Zelikow, Ernest R. May, and Bonnie Jenkins, *The 9/11 Commission Report: Final Report of the National Commission on Terrorist Attacks upon the United States*, authorized ed. (New York: Norton, 2004), 5–6.
3. Carol J. Williams, John-Thor Dahlburg, and H. G. Reza, "Mainly, They Just Waited," *Los Angeles Times*, September 27, 2001.
4. Peter Finn, "Hijackers Depicted as Elite Group," *Washington Post*, November 5, 2001. According to website BuzzFlash.com, Senate Republicans removed this article from the Internet.
5. "Notes Found After the Hijackings."
6. Osama bin Laden, "Ladenese Epistle: Declaration of War Against the Americans Occupying the Land of the Two Holy Places," Part 3, *Washington Post Online*, October 11, 2001.
7. Williams and others, "Mainly, They Just Waited"; Associated Press, "Atta Does Not Fit Terrorist Mold," *Milwaukee Journal Sentinel*, September 28, 2001.
8. Peter Finn and Charles Love, "Will Gives a Window into Suspect's Mind: Czechs Say Atta Met with Iraqi Official," *Washington Post*, October 6, 2001.
9. Two Muslim scholars from Brandeis and Harvard universities find the concept of "martyr" proclaimed in the letter to be a distortion of the Muslim tradition because it fails to mention any communal purpose for the attacks. See Kanan Makiya and Hassan Mneimneh, "Manual for a 'Raid,'" *New York Review of Books* 49, no. 1 (January 17, 2002): 18–21.

10. Zelikow and others, *9/11 Commission Report*, 6–7.
11. Amy Goldstein, Lena H. Sun, and George Lardner Jr., "Hanjour a Study in Paradox," *Washington Post*, October 15, 2001.
12. Jim McKinnon, "The Phone Line from Flight 93 Was Still Open When a GTE Operator Heard Todd Beamer Say: 'Are You Guys Ready? Let's Roll,'" *Pittsburgh Post-Gazette*, September 16, 2001, http://www.post-gazette.com /headlines/20010916phonecallnat3p3.asp.
13. Jodi Wilgoren and Edward Wong, "On a Doomed Jet, Passengers Vowed to Perish Fighting," *New York Times*, September 13, 2001.
14. Ibid.
15. Ibid.
16. McKinnon, "Phone Line from Flight 93."
17. Jere Longman, "Cockpit Tape Offers Few Answers but Points to Heroic Efforts," *New York Times*, March 27, 2002.
18. Charter of the United Nations, Chapter VII, Article 51.
19. Transcript, *New York Times*, September 21, 2001.
20. Manuel Perez-Rivas, "Bush vows to rid the world of 'evil-doers,'" CNN.com, September 16, 2001.
21. President's remarks, "America's New War: President Bush Talks with Reporters at Pentagon," CNN.com, September 17, 2001.
22. Peter Ford, "Europe Cringes at Bush 'Crusade' Against Terrorists," *Christian Science Monitor*, September 19, 2001.

PREFACE

1. Barbara W. Tuchman, *The Pursuit of Folly: From Troy to Vietnam* (New York: Ballantine Books, 1984), 4.

INTRODUCTION: A MORE NUANCED FOLLY

1. Madeleine Albright on *Today*, NBC, February 19, 1998.
2. Colin L. Powell, *My American Journey*, with Joseph E. Persico (New York: Random House, 1995), 576.
3. Chalmers Johnson, *The Sorrows of Empire: Militarism, Secrecy, and the End of the Republic* (New York: Metropolitan Books, 2004), 236.
4. Barack Obama, "Remarks by the President in Address to the Nation on the Way Forward in Afghanistan and Pakistan" (speech, Eisenhower Hall Theatre, U.S. Military Academy, West Point, NY, December 1, 2009), http:// www.whitehouse.gov/the-press-office/remarks-president-address-nation-way -forward-afghanistan-and-pakistan.

5. Johnson, *Sorrows of Empire,* 64, 65.

6. Andrew J. Bacevich, *The New American Militarism: How Americans Are Seduced by War* (New York: Oxford University Press, 2005), 2.

7. See the author's account of the lead-up to the Iraq War, James Gannon, *Military Occupations in the Age of Self-Determination: The History Neocons Neglected* (Westport, CT: Praeger Security International, 2008), 10–27.

8. "Operation Iraqi Freedom," *iCasualties: Iraq Coalition Casualty Count,* http://icasualties.org/Iraq/.

9. Ibid.

10. Elizabeth Ferris and Michael E. O'Hanlon, "Iraq's Displaced Millions," *Washington Times,* June 1, 2009; Steve Coll, "The General's Dilemma," *New Yorker,* September 8, 2008, 36.

11. "Total Cost of Wars Since 2001," National Priorities Project, accessed November 10, 2010, http://costofwar.com/numbers.html.

12. Linda J. Bilmes and Joseph E. Stiglitz, "The Iraq War Will Cost Us $3 Trillion, and Much More," *Washington Post,* March 9, 2008.

13. Quoted in Ahmed Rashid, *Descent into Chaos: The U.S. and the Disaster in Pakistan, Afghanistan, and Central Asia* (New York: Penguin Books, 2009), 245.

14. Thomas E. Ricks, *The Gamble: General David Petraeus and the American Military Adventure in Iraq, 2006–2008* (New York: Penguin Press, 2009).

15. Extrapolated by the author from "Operation Iraqi Freedom," *iCasualties.*

16. David Kilcullen, *The Accidental Guerrilla: Fighting Small Wars in the Midst of a Big One* (New York: Oxford University Press, 2009), 117.

17. Barack Obama, speech at an antiwar rally (Chicago, October 2, 2002), http://www.barackobama.com/2002/10/02/remarks_of_illinois_state_sen.php.

18. Taliban in the Pashtu language is the plural of *talib,* or "student." They were students in radical madrassas. Therefore, the plural word "Taliban" takes a plural verb.

19. "White Paper of the Interagency Policy Group's Report on U.S. Policy toward Afghanistan and Pakistan," White House, March 27, 2009, http://www.whitehouse.gov/assets/documents/afghanistan_pakistan_white_paper_final.pdf.

20. The Viet Cong used this tactic in the early 1960s. Natural leaders of a South Vietnamese village who might oppose Communist rule were wiped out by assassination. See Douglas Pike, *War, Peace, and the Viet Cong* (Cambridge, MA: MIT Press, 1969), 63.

21. Kilcullen, *Accidental Guerrilla,* 34–38.

CHAPTER 1: A PARADOX OF POWER

1. George Santayana, *The Life of Reason*, Vol. 1, ch. 12 (1905; repr., Bel Air, California: Old Landmark Publishing, 2005), from *The Oxford Dictionary of Quotations*, 5th ed., ed. Elizabeth Knowles (Oxford: Oxford University Press, 1999), 644.

2. Niall Ferguson, *Colossus: The Price of America's Empire* (New York: Penguin Press, 2004), 46.

3. Department of Defense, *Base Structure Report Fiscal Year 2008 Baseline* (Washington, DC: Office of the Deputy Undersecretary of Defense, 2007); and Department of Defense, *Base Structure Report Fiscal Year 2003 Baseline* (Washington, DC: Office of the Deputy Undersecretary of Defense, 2002).

4. Coll, "General's Dilemma," 36.

5. Johnson, *Sorrows of Empire*, 153.

6. William E. Odom and Robert Dujarric, *America's Inadvertent Empire* (New Haven, CT: Yale University Press, 2004), 68–80.

7. Accounts of Iraqi armor losses during the Gulf War vary widely. Florida-based U.S. Central Command, which has overall command in that part of the world, reported 2,159 Iraqi tanks destroyed or captured, 451 (21 percent) from air attacks and 1,708 (79 percent) from ground attacks, according to the think tank Global Security, http://www.globalsecurity.org/military/world /iraq/ground-equipment-intro.htm.

8. "HIMARS High Mobility Artillery Rocket System, USA," Army-technology .com, http://www.army-technology.com/projects/himars/.

9. Carlotta Gall, "Coalition Forces Routing Taliban in Key Afghan Region," *New York Times,* October 20, 2010.

10. Steven Aftergood, "Al Qaida: Western Spies Multiply 'Like Locusts,'" *Secrecy News*, July 13, 2009, http://www.fas.org/blog/secrecy/2009/07/al_libi_spies .html.

11. Chalmers Johnson, *Blowback: The Costs and Consequences of American Empire* (New York: Henry Holt, 2000), 35–36.

12. Noel Villalba, "Philippines: A Subjective View of the U.S. Bases Issue," *Human Rights Solidarity*, December 31, 1991, http://www.hrsolidarity.net/main file.php/1991vol01no01/1984/.

13. Katharine H. S. Moon, *Sex Among Allies: Military Prostitution in U.S.-Korea Relations* (New York: Columbia University Press, 1997), 7, quoted in Johnson, *Blowback,* 35.

14. Johnson, *Blowback*, 35.

15. Ibid., 42.
16. Ibid., 34.
17. *Heart of Darkness: The Vietnam War Chronicles, 1945–1975*, directed by Edward Feuerherd (New York: KOCH Vision, September 5, 2006); Philip Shenon, "20 Years After Victory, Vietnamese Communists Ponder How to Celebrate," *New York Times*, April 23, 1995.

CHAPTER 2: THE ROOTS OF ISLAMISM

1. Seyyed Hossein Nasr, *The Heart of Islam: Enduring Values for Humanity* (New York: HarperSanFrancisco, 2002), 270–71.
2. *The Holy Bible, containing the Old and New Testaments,* New Revised Standard Edition (Iowa Falls: World Bible Publishers, 1989).
3. Karen Armstrong, *Holy War: The Crusades and Their Impact on Today's World* (New York: Doubleday, 1991), 30–31.
4. Maxime Rodinson, *Mohammad* (New York: Pantheon Books, 1980), 14.
5. Quoted in Karen Armstrong, *Muhammad: A Biography of the Prophet* (New York: HarperCollins, 1992), 168.
6. Anonymous, *Imperial Hubris: Why the West Is Losing the War on Terror* (Washington, DC: Brassey's, Inc., 2004), 11, from Dr. Mohammed Abd-al-Halim Umar, "The United States Has Begun Its War Against Islam," *Lailatalqadr* (Internet version), March 21, 2002. (Michael Scheuer is the author of *Imperial Hubris*. When the book was published, he was the CIA's leading expert on Osama bin Laden. He has since resigned.)
7. Quoted in Robin Wright, *Sacred Rage: The Wrath of Militant Islam* (New York: Linden Press, 1985), 36.
8. Sir John Bagot Glubb, *The Life and Times of Muhammad* (New York: Stein & Day, 1970), 185; Rodinson, *Mohammad*, 167. This is an often-told story. Rodinson's version is slightly different from Glubb's. Their original source was Ibn Hisham, an Arab biographer who lived two centuries after Muhammad. Ibn Hisham was translated into German in the mid-nineteenth century. Sira Ibn Hisham, *Das Leben Muhammeds,* ed. F. Wuestenfeld (Göttingen, 1859–60), 445.
9. Rodinson, *Mohammad*, 286.
10. All Muslims accept the Koran and Hadith as sharia sources. Other sources can be considered based on consensus and analogy to a known case, as can fairness and the public interest, as long as they are consistent with the objectives of the lawgiver, i.e., God. But acceptance of these other sources is not universal.

Wahhabists, for their part, are strict constructionists of the sharia. See Nasr, *The Heart of Islam*, 120–21; Robert Van de Weyer, *The Shared Well: A Concise Guide to Relations between Islam and the West* (Washington, DC: Brassey's, Inc., 2002), 46–47.

11. Robert Lacey, *The Kingdom* (New York: Harcourt Brace Jovanovich, 1981), 56.

12. David Holden and Richard Johns, *The House of Saud: The Rise and Rule of the Most Powerful Dynasty in the Arab World* (New York: Holt, Rinehart, and Winston, 1981), 69–70.

13. Helen Chapin Metz, ed., "Wahhabi Theology," *Country Studies, Saudi Arabia* (Washington, DC: Library of Congress, 1992), 2, http://countrystudies.us /saudi-arabia/.

14. Domingo Badia y Leyblich (Ali Bey), *Travels of Ali Bey in Morocco, Tripoli, Cyprus, Egypt, Arabia, Syria and Turkey between the Years 1803 and 1807* (London: Gregg, 1970), 2:60–63, quoted in F. E. Peters, *Mecca: A Literary History of the Muslim Holy Land* (Princeton, NJ: Princeton University Press, 1994), 295–97.

15. Ibid.

16. For a fuller biography of Hasan al-Banna see Richard P. Mitchell, *The Society of Muslim Brothers* (New York: Oxford University Press, 1993), 1–6.

17. Dore Gold, *Hatred's Kingdom: How Saudi Arabia Supports the New Global Terrorism* (Washington, DC: Regnery Publishing, 2003), 54–55.

18. Mitchell, *Society of Muslim Brothers*, 6.

19. Ibid., 8.

20. Ibid., 165.

21. Amira Howeidy, "Politics in God's Name," *Al-Ahram Weekly Online*, no. 247 (November 16–22, 1995), http://weekly.ahram.org.eg/archives/parties /muslimb/polgod.htm.

22. Ibid.

23. Mitchell, *Society of Muslim Brothers*, 14–15.

24. "Islam: A Threat to World Stability," *Intelligence Review*, no. 1 (February 14, 1946): 24–35, http://www.fas.org/irp/agency/army/intelreview1.pdf.

25. Howeidy, "Politics in God's Name."

26. Ibid., 9.

27. Ibid., 47–49.

28. Sayyid Qutb, *Milestones*, trans. Ahmad Zaki Hammad (Indianapolis: American Trust Publications, 1990), 8.

29. Gilles Kepel, *Jihad: The Trail of Political Islam*, trans. Anthony F. Roberts

(Cambridge, MA: Harvard University Press, 2002), 31–32.

30. Mitchell, *Society of Muslim Brothers*, 140–41.

31. Ibid., 173–74.

32. Ahmed Rashid, *Taliban: Militant Islam, Oil and Fundamentalism in Central Asia* (New Haven, CT: Yale Nota Bene, 2001), 88.

33. Charles J. Adams, "Mawdudi and the Islamic State," in *Voices of Resurgent Islam*, ed. John L. Esposito (New York: Oxford University Press, 1983), 100.

34. Ibid., 101.

35. Kepel, *Jihad*, 32–36.

36. In Islam the closest thing to a religious hierarchy is the Ulema, the body of religious scholars who protect and interpret divine law, and the first Ulema to rule in a major Islamic country was in Iran in 1979. Nasr, *Heart of Islam*, 148–49.

37. For a fuller analysis, see Adams, "Mawdudi and the Islamic State," 111–31; and John L. Esposito, *Islam and Politics*, 3rd ed. (Syracuse, NY: Syracuse University Press, 1991), 143–51.

CHAPTER 3: THE ENEMIES

1. The picture of two Taliban drawn in the following paragraphs is based on reporting by Pakistani journalist Rashid, *Descent into Chaos*, 265–92, 358–71, 402–8.

2. Jason Burke, *Al Qaeda: Casting a Shadow of Terror* (London: I. B. Tauris, 2003), 7–22.

3. Steve Coll, *Ghost Wars: The Secret History of the CIA, Afghanistan, and Bin Laden, from the Soviet Invasion to September 10, 2001* (New York: Penguin Press, 2004), 202–4.

4. Ibid., 400–401.

5. Burke, *Al Qaeda*, 149–50.

6. Osama bin Laden, "Manifesto of the World Islamic Front," February 22, 1998, in *Holy War, Inc.: Inside the Secret World of Osama bin Laden*, by Peter L. Bergen (New York: Free Press, 2001), 96.

7. Rashid, *Descent into Chaos*, 89.

8. Kepel, *Jihad*, 142–43.

9. John L. Esposito, *Unholy War: Terror in the Name of Islam* (New York: Oxford University Press, 2002), 107.

10. Kepel, *Jihad*, 144.

11. Rashid, *Descent into Chaos*, 90–91.

12. Gold, *Hatred's Kingdom*, 131.
13. Rashid, *Descent into Chaos*, 89.
14. Kepel, *Jihad*, 226.
15. Rashid, *Descent into Chaos*, 90.
16. Kepel, *Jihad*, 226.
17. Rashid, *Descent into Chaos*, 29.
18. Rashid, *Taliban*, 31–33.
19. Ibid., 31–48.
20. Ibid., 1–4.
21. Kepel, *Jihad*, 220–31.
22. Rashid, *Descent into Chaos*, 268–69.

CHAPTER 4: INSIDE THE SURGE

1. Kilcullen, *Accidental Guerrilla*, 34–38.
2. Douglas Pike, "The Vietcong Secret War," in *War in the Shadows: The Vietnam Experience*, ed. Samuel Lipsman (Boston: Boston Publishing, 1988), 11.
3. Alistair Horne, *A Savage War of Peace: Algeria, 1954–1962* (New York: Viking Press, 1977), 119–22.
4. K. G. Tregonning, *A History of Modern Malaya* (New York: David McKay, 1964), 287–302.
5. Ricks, *Gamble*, 60.
6. Niel Smith and Sean MacFarland, "Anbar Awakens: The Tipping Point," *Military Review*, March–April 2008, 41–52.
7. Ellen Knickmeyer and I. K. Ibriham, "Bombing Shatters Mosque in Iraq," *Washington Post*, February 23, 2006.
8. Ricks, *Gamble*, 21–22.
9. U.S. Department of the Army, *The U.S. Army/Marine Corps Counterinsurgency Field Manual: U.S. Army Field Manual No. 3-24: Marine Corps Warfighting Publication No. 3-33.5* (Chicago: University of Chicago Press, 2007), 51.
10. Kilcullen, *Accidental Guerrilla*, 133–35.
11. Ricks, *Gamble*, 169–70.
12. Ibid., 168.
13. Ibid., 169–70.
14. Kilcullen, *Accidental Guerrilla*, 144–45.
15. "Operation Iraqi Freedom," *iCasualties*.
16. Tim Cocks, "U.S. Military Says Iraq Troop Surge Has Ended," Reuters, July

22, 2008.

17. "Operation Iraqi Freedom," *iCasualties.*

18. Ernesto Londono and Greg Jaffe, "Iraq Carnage Shows Sectarian War Goes On," *Washington Post,* August 20, 2009.

19. Kilcullen, *Accidental Guerrilla,* 46.

20. Griff Witte, "Afghan Promises to Insurgents Often Empty," *Washington Post,* December 14, 2009.

21. Kilcullen, *Accidental Guerrilla,* 71.

22. Sebastian Junger, "Into the Valley of Death," *Vanity Fair,* January 2008, http://www.vanityfair.com/politics/features/2008/01/afghanistan200801.

23. Rashid, *Descent into Chaos,* 411.

24. Christina Lamb, "Stop Bombing Us: Osama Isn't Here, Says Pakistan," *Times Online,* July 12, 2009, http://www.timesonline.co.uk/tol/news/world/asia /article6689741.ece.

25. ABC World News, "Is the Troop Surge Too Little Too Late?: Martha Raddatz is in Afghanistan to see if the surge can make a difference," December 3, 2009, http://abcnewsgo.com/video/playerIndex?id=9244286.

26. Rashid, *Descent into Chaos,* 363–64.

27. Ibid., 361.

28. Ann Scott Tyson, "'Skittish' Afghans Wary of Marines, Taliban," *Washington Post,* August 15, 2009.

29. Karen DeYoung, "Taliban Surprising U.S. Forces with Improved Tactics," *Washington Post,* September 2, 2009.

30. Kilcullen, *Accidental Guerrilla,* 39–40.

31. K. Alan Kronstadt, "Pakistan-U.S. Relations," *Congressional Research Service,* May 9, 2006. These figures can only be approximate because the figures for FY2007 are the amounts requested from Congress; for FY2006, estimated; for FY2001–FY2005, actual.

32. Rashid, *Descent into Chaos,* 91–93.

33. Ibid., 270–72.

34. Ibid., 274–75.

35. "Bomb blast kills 20 in NW Pakistan," Xinhua, August 22, 2008; "Taliban torched over 200 schools in Swat in 2yrs: Report," Indian Express.com, May 24, 2009, http://www.indianexpress.com/news/taliban-forched-over-200 -schools-in-2-yrs-report/465093/0; Zulfiqar Ali and Laura King, "Pakistani officials allow Sharia in volatile region," *Los Angeles Times,* February 17, 2009, http://articles.latimes.com/2009/feb/17/world/fg-pakistan-pact17; Declan

Walsh, "Inside the Taliban's besieged Swat fortress as battle rages," *The Observer,* May 10, 2009.

36. Aftergood, "Al Qaida: Western Spies Multiply 'Like Locusts.'"

37. Karen DeYoung and Walter Pincus, "Success Against al Qaeda Cited," *Washington Post,* September 30, 2009.

38. Pir Zubair Shah and Jane Perlez, "Car Bomb Kills at Least 41 in Restive Region of Pakistan," *New York Times,* October 13, 2009, http://www.nytimes .com/2009/10/13/world/asia/13pstan.html.

39. "Pakistan reels from fresh attack," *BBC News,* October 12, 2009, http://news. bbc.co.uk/2/hi/south_asia/8302055.stm.

CHAPTER 5: SHADES OF RAMBO

1. Michael Smith, *Killer Elite: The Inside Story of America's Most Secret Special Operations Team* (New York: St. Martin's Press, 2006), 11.

2. Ibid., 20.

3. Rod Powers, "U.S. Military Special Operations Forces," About.com, http:// usmilitary.about.com?od/jointservices/a/specialops.htm?p=1.

4. Eric L. Haney, *Inside Delta Force: The Story of America's Elite Counterterrorism Unit* (New York: Delacourte Press, 2002), 25–83.

5. Steven Emerson, *Secret Warriors: Inside the Covert Military Operations of the Reagan Era* (New York: G. P. Putnam's Sons, 1988), 16.

6. Haney, *Inside Delta Force,* 89–90.

7. Mark Bowden, *Black Hawk Down: A Story of Modern War* (New York: Signet, 1999), 39.

8. Ibid.

9. Elite UK Forces, Special Air Service, Special Boat Service, http://www.elite ukforces.info/.

10. Leigh Neville, *Special Operations Forces in Afghanistan* (Oxford, UK: Osprey Publishing, 2008), 29–32.

11. Smith, *Killer Elite,* 30–32.

12. Col. Mark E. Kipphut, USAF, *Crossbow and Gulf War Counter-Scud Efforts: Lessons from History,* The Counterproliferation Papers Future Warfare Series No. 15 (Maxwell Air Force Base, AL: Air University, 2003), 11.

13. Smith, *Killer Elite,* 165–67.

14. Sentencing Judgment of Trial Chamber III in the Todorovic Case, The Hague, July 31, 2001.

15. Bin Laden, "Ladenese Epistle: Declaration of War."

16. Bin Laden, "Manifesto of the World Islamic Front."

17. Coll, *Ghost Wars*, 389–96.

18. Burke, *Al-Qaeda*, 143–45, 153–54, 160.

19. Zelikow and others, *9/11 Commission Report*, 115–21; Richard A. Clarke, *Against All Enemies: Inside America's War on Terror* (New York: Free Press, 2004), 184.

20. Coll, *Ghost Wars*, 422.

21. Ibid., 446–52.

22. Sean D. Naylor, "SpecOps Unit Nearly Nabs Zarqawi," ArmyTimes.com, April 28, 2006, http://www.armytimes.com/legacy/new/1-292925-1739387. php; "Task Force 145 (TF 145)," GlobalSecurity.org, August 6, 2006, http:// www.globalsecurity.org/military/agency/dod/tf-145.htm.

23. Smith, *Killer Elite*, 212–13.

24. John Pike and Steven Aftergood, "Military Analysis Network," Federation of American Scientists, March 24, 2004, http://www.fas.org/man/dod-101/sys /dumb/blu-82.htm.

25. Rashid, *Descent into Chaos*, 93–94.

26. Neville, *Special Operations Forces in Afghanistan*, 16–18.

27. Seth G. Jones, *In the Graveyard of Empires: America's War in Afghanistan* (New York: Norton, 2009), xxii.

28. Gary Berntsen and Ralph Pezzullo, *Jawbreaker: The Attack on Bin Laden and Al-Qaeda: A Personal Account by the CIA's Key Field Commander* (New York: Crown Publishers, 2005), 157–60.

29. Neville, *Special Operations Forces in Afghanistan*, 19–20.

30. Smith, *Killer Elite*, 222–23; Bernstein and Pezzullo, *Jawbreaker*, 314–15.

31. Smith, *Killer Elite*, 219–20.

32. Ibid., 235–39.

33. Naylor, "SpecOps Unit."

34. Rashid, *Descent into Chaos*, 272.

35. "Blast 'kills al Qaeda commander,'" BBC News, December 3, 2005, http:// news.bbc.co.uk/2/hi/south_asia/4494428.stm.

36. Rashid, *Descent into Chaos*, 276.

37. Declan Walsh, "Air strike kills Taliban leader Baitullah Mehsud," *Guardian*, August 7, 2009, http://www.guardian.co.uk/world/2009/aug/o7/baitullah-mehsud-dead-taliban-pakistan.

38. Luis Rodriguez and Martha Raddatz, "Al-Qaeda Operations Manager Saleh al-Somaleh Believed Dead in Drone Strike," ABC News, December 11, 2009, http://abcnews.go.com/International/Terrorism/al-qaeda-operation.

39. David Kilcullen, "Death from Above, Outrage Down Below," *New York Times*, May 16, 2009, http://www.nytimes.com/2009/05/17/opinion/17exum .html?_r=1.

40. Peter Bergen and Katherine Tiedemann, "Pakistan Drone War Takes a Toll on Militants—and Civilians" CNN, October 29, 2009, http://www.peterbergen.com/services/print.aspx?id=410.

41. Karen DeYoung, "Al-Qaeda Seen as Shaken in Pakistan," *Washington Post*, June 1, 2009.

42. Jeremy Scahill, "Blackwater's Secret War in Pakistan," *Nation*, November 23, 2009.

43. James Risen and Mark Mazzetti, "Blackwater Guards Tied to Secret Raids by the C.I.A.," *New York Times*, December 11, 2009.

44. Neville, *Special Operations Forces in Afghanistan*, 43–44.

45. Sean D. Naylor, "Surviving SEAL Tells Story of Deadly Mission," Army Times.com, June 18, 2007. Luttrell wrote of the failed mission in his book, *Lone Survivor: The Eyewitness Account of Operation Redwing and the Lost Heroes of SEAL Team 10*, with Patrick Robinson (Boston: Little, Brown. 2007).

46. Neville, *Special Operations Forces in Afghanistan*, 45–46.

47. Sean Naylor, "Exclusive: Inside a U.S. Hostage Rescue Mission," ArmyTimes .com, November 10, 2008, http://www.armytimes.com/news/2008/11/ military_air_rescue_11070.

48. Field Manual, Army Special Operations Forces, FM3-05-130, Washington, DC: Army Publishing, 2006.

CHAPTER 6: GLOBAL TERRORISM

1. Rashid, *Descent into Chaos*, 265.

2. Kepel, *Jihad*, 237.

3. Gold, *Hatred's Kingdom*, 143–44.

4. Steven Schwartz, *The Two Faces of Islam: The House of Saud from Tradition to Terror* (New York: Doubleday, 2002), 215.

5. "Chechens 'Confirm' Warlord's Death," BBC News, April 29, 2002, http:// news.bbc.co.uk/2/hi/europe/1957411.stm.

6. Michael Wines, "Chechens Seize Moscow Theater, Taking as Many as 600 Hostages," *New York Times*, October 24, 2002, http://www.nytimes.com /2002/10/24/world/chechens-seize-moscow-theater-taking-as-many-as-600 -hostages.html; Michael Wines, "Hostage Drama in Moscow: The Aftermath; Hostage Toll in Russia Over 100; Nearly All Deaths Linked to Gas,"

New York Times, October 28, 2002, http://www.nytimes.com/2002/10/28 /world/hostage-drama-moscow-aftermath-hostage-toll-russia-over-100 -nearly-all-deaths.html.

7. Peter Finn, "New Report Puts Blame on Local Officials in Beslan Siege," *Washington Post*, December 29, 2005.

8. C. J. Chivers and Steven Lee Myers, "Rebels in Russia Had Precise Plan," *New York Times*, September 6, 2004, 1, 9.

9. "Rebels' Dilemma After Basayev Death," BBC News, July 12, 2006, http:// news.bbc.co.uk/2/hi/europe/5168984.stm.

10. Raymond Bonner, "Bali Suicide Bombers Said to Have Belonged to Small Gang," *New York Times*, October 7, 2005, 3.

11. "Country Reports on Terrorism," Office of the Coordinator for Counterterrorism, U.S. Department of State, April 30, 2007, http://www.state.gov/s/ct /rls/crt/2006/82738.htm.

12. "India: Gujarat Officials Took Part in Anti-Muslim Violence," *Human Rights News*, April 30, 2002, http://www.hrw.org/en/news/2002/04/29/india -gujarat-officials-took-part-anti-muslim-violence.

13. World Factbook, "India," *Central Intelligence Agency*, October 27, 2010, http://www.cia.gov/library/publications/the-world-factbook/.

14. "Ayodhya: India's religious Flashpoint," CNN.com, December 6, 2002, http://edition.cnn.com/2002/WORLD/asiapcf/south/12/06/ayodhya.

15. Santosh Digal, "After seven years, courts can rule on Godhra massacre," AsiaNews.it, October 29, 2010.

16. Karl Vick, "Al-Qaeda's Hand in Istanbul Plot," *Washington Post,* February 13, 2007.

17. Alfred B. Prados, "Saudi Arabia: Current Issues and U.S. Relations," CRS Issues Brief for Congress, Congressional Research Service, August 4, 2003, http://www.fas.org/man/crs/IB93113.pdf.

18. Scott MacLeod and Bruce Crumley, "Saudi Arabia's New Terror," *Time,* November 16, 2003.

19. "Saudi car bomb attack kills four," BBC News, April 22, 2004, http://news .bbc.co.uk/2/hi/middle_east/3646195.stm.

20. Neil MacFarquhar, "Saudi Military Storms Complex to Free Hostages," *New York Times*, May 31, 2004.

21. Brian Dakss, "U.S. Hostage Beheaded," CBS News, June 18, 2004.

22. "Saudi Arabia issues new list of wanted 'terrorist' suspects," asharq alawsat, June 29, 2005, http://aawsat.com/english/news.asp?id=613&section=1.

23. "Terror blasts rock Casablanca," BBC News, May 17,2003, http://news.bbc
    .co.uk/2/hi/africa/3035803.stm.
24. "Madrid train attacks," BBC News, Attacks/Investigation.
25. "7 July Bombings," BBC News, In Depth: What Happened/The Investigation.
26. "21 July attacks," BBC News, In Depth: What Happened/The Investigation.
27. Daniel Williams, "Egyptian Police Kill Suspect in Red Sea Attacks," *Washington Post*, May 10, 2006.
28. Ellen Knickmeyer and Jonathan Finer, "Insurgent Leader al-Zarqawi Killed in Iraq," *Washington Post*, June 8, 2006.
29. "Khalid Sheikh Mohammed," GlobalSecurity.org, April 27, 2005, http://www.globalsecurity.org/military/world/para/ksm.htm.
30. Vikram Dodd, "Three Terrorists Convicted of Plotting to Blow Up Jets over Atlantic," *Guardian*, September 7, 2009, http://www.guardian.co.uk/world/2009/sep/07/terrorists-plot-atlantic-liquid-bombs.
31. William K. Rashbaum and Karen Zraick, "Government Says Al Qaeda Ordered N.Y. Plot," *New York Times*, April 23, 2010.
32. Clifford Krauss, "Defendant in Court for Hearing at Ft. Hood," *New York Times*, October 12, 2010.
33. Dana Priest and William M. Arkin, "Top Secret America: A *Washington Post* Investigation," *Washington Post Online*, July 19, 2010, http://projects.washingtonpost.com/top-secret-america/.
34. "Obama's top intelligence adviser resigns," CNN, May 20, 2010; Greg Miller, "Muslim Cleric Aulaqi is 1st U.S. Citizen on List of Those CIA Is Allowed to Kill," *Washington Post,* April 7, 2010.
35. "Times Square Bomb Attempt, May 1, 2010," *New York Times,* May 6, 2010.
36. "Civil Justice, Military Justice," *New York Times*, October 5, 2010.
37. Peter Finn and Julie Tate, "Package Bomb Could Have Downed Plane Over Canada, Data Show," *Washington Post*, November 10, 2010.
38. Mark Mazzetti, Robert F. Worth, and Eric Lipton, "Bomb Plot Shows Key Role Played by Intelligence," *New York Times*, October 31, 2010.
39. Jason Burke, "How the Perfect Terrorist Plotted the Ultimate Crime," *Observer*, April 7, 2002, http://www.guardian.co.uk/world/2002/apr/07/september11.terrorism.
40. Craig Whitlock, "Jordan's Spy Agency: Holding Cell for the CIA," *Washington Post*, December 1, 2007
41. Syed Saleem Shahzad, "A Chilling Inheritance of Terror," *Asia Times*, October 30, 2002.

42. Erik Eckholm, "Pakistanis Arrest Qaeda Figure Seen as Planner of 9/11," *New York Times*, March 2, 2003.
43. Rashid, *Descent into Chaos*, 226.
44. Mark Mazzetti and Margot Williams, "In Tribunal Statement, Confessed 9/11 Plotter Burnishes His Image as a Soldier," *New York Times*, March 16, 2007.
45. Verbatim Transcript of Combatant Status Review Tribunal Hearing for ISN 10024, U.S. Naval Base Guantánamo Bay, Cuba, March 10, 2007, http://www.defense.gov/news/transcript_isn10024.pdf.
46. "Statement of Levin and Graham on Trip to Guantanamo Bay," Levin press release, March 16, 2007, http://levin.senate.gov/newsroom/release.cfm?id=270804.
47. Josh White, "Al-Qaeda Suspect Says He Planned Cole Attack," *Washington Post*, March 20, 2007
48. Simon Elegant, "The Terrorist Talks," *Time*, October 5, 2003.
49. Scott Horton, "Renditions Buffoonery," *Harper's Magazine*, February 2, 2009, http://www.harpers.org/archive/2009/02/hbc-90004326. See also "Fact Sheet: Extraordinary Rendition," American Civil Liberties Union, December 6, 2005, http://www.aclu.org/national-security/fact-sheet-extraordinary-rendition; Peter Bergen and Katherine Tiedemann, "Disappearing Act: Rendition by the Numbers," *New American Foundation*, March 3, 2008, http://www.newamerica.net/node/9093, first published in *Mother Jones* (March 3, 2008). Bergen and Tiedemann compiled a useful partial list of extraordinary renditions before and after September 11, 2001. Their list is consistent with the ACLU definition of extraordinary rendition but would seem to put them at odds with Horton, who argued that no extraordinary renditions occurred prior to 9/11. Berger and Tiedemann defined the term differently from Horton as "the extrajudicial transfer of an individual to a country where there is reasonable probability he will be tortured." That definition (and the ACLU's) puts the emphasis on torture rather than submission to a criminal justice system. Based on that definition, Bergen and Tiedemann named fourteen victims of extraordinary rendition prior to September 11, 2001. Of these, seven were either executed or received prison terms, which indicates a judicial judgment, and so they would fit Horton's definition of the purpose of ordinary rendition: to deliver the suspect to a criminal justice system. The disposal of the other seven individuals listed was either unknown or indefinite. Therefore, the seven firm findings of Bergen and Tiedemann support Horton's point that extraordinary renditions occurred only after 9/11, if you accept Horton's defi-

nition. If the seven pre-9/11 individuals named were tortured, their treatment was inhumane but irrelevant in the Horton context.

50. Dana Priest, "Wrongful Imprisonment: Anatomy of a CIA Mistake," *Washington Post*, December 4, 2005.

51. Evan Wallach, "Waterboarding Used to Be a Crime," *Washington Post*, November 4, 2007.

52. Scott Shane, "Waterboarding Used 266 Times on 2 Suspects," *New York Times*, April 19, 2009. Shane cites Marcy Wheeler of the blog *emptywheel* for the discovery and notes, "The sentences in the [Justice] memo containing that information appear to have been redacted from some copies but are visible in others."

53. Stephen G. Bradbury, Principal Deputy Attorney General, U.S. Department of Justice, Office of Legal Counsel, memorandum to John A. Rizzo, Senior Deputy General Counsel, Central Intelligence Agency, May 30, 2005, redacted, http://luxmedia.com.edgesuite.net/aclu/olc_05302005_bradbury.pdf.

54. Mark Mazzetti, "Interrogation Memos Detail Harsh Tactics by the C.I.A.," *New York Times*, April 17, 2009.

55. Peter Finn, Joby Warrick, and Julie Tate, "Administration Releases More of a Long-Classified CIA Report on Interrogations," *Washington Post*, August 24, 2009.

56. Jane Perlez, Raymond Bonner, and Salman Masood, "An Ex-Detainee of the U.S. Describes a 6-Year Ordeal," *New York Times*, January 6, 2009, http://www.nytimes.com/2009/01/06/world/asia/06iqbal.html.

57. "Terror Watch List Counter: A Million Plus," American Civil Liberties Union, http://www.aclu.org/privacy/spying/watchlistcounter.html. The watch list was bloated with innocent people, including the late Senator Edward M. Kennedy of Massachusetts. It grows at a rate of about twenty thousand per month, and by 2009 it exceeded 1.1 million individuals.

58. Jane Mayer, "Outsourcing Terror: The Secret History of America's 'Extraordinary Rendition' Program," *New Yorker*, February 14, 2005; Michael Bilton, "Post-9/11 Renditions: An Extraordinary Violation of International Law," Center for Public Integrity, May 22, 2007, http://projects.publicintegrity.org/MilitaryAid//report.aspx?aid=855.

59. Priest, "Wrongful Imprisonment."

60. Peter Bergen, "Exclusive: I Was Kidnapped by the CIA," *Mother Jones*, March 3, 2008, http://www.motherjones.com/print/15664.

61. Agence France Presse, "Court Convicts 23 Ex-CIA Agents in Imam Kidnapping Trial," France 24, November 4, 2009, http://www.france24.com /en/20091104-italy-convicts-23-ex-cia-agents-imam-kidnapping-trial -justice-prison.

CHAPTER 7: NUCLEAR JIHADISM

1. Graham Allison, *Nuclear Terrorism: The Ultimate Preventable Catastrophe* (New York: Henry Holt, 2004), 4.
2. Abdul Qadeer Khan, interview by Nadeem Malik on *Islamabad Tonight*, Aaj Television News, August 31, 2009, cited in Steven Aftergood, "A. Q. Khan Discusses Pakistan's Nuclear Program," *Secrecy News*, September 8, 2009, http://www.fas.org/blog/secrecy/2009/09/page/2.
3. "Status of World Nuclear Forces," Federation of American Scientists, November 8, 2010, http://www.fas.org/programs/ssp/nukes/nuclearweapons/nukestat.
4. Douglas Frantz and Catherine Collins, *The Nuclear Jihadist: The True Story of the Man Who Sold the World's Most Dangerous Secrets—and How We Could Have Stopped Him* (New York: Twelve, 2007), 55.
5. Amir Oren, "U.S. Army Document Describes Israel as 'a Nuclear Power,'" *Haaretz*, March 18, 2009, http://www.haaretz.com/hasen/spages/1069303. html.
6. "Dirty Bombs," Council on Foreign Relations Backgrounder, October 19, 2006, http://www.cfr.org/publication/9548/dirty_bombs.html.
7. Frantz and Collins, *Nuclear Jihadist*, 45–46.
8. Ibid., 127.
9. Ibid., 154–61.
10. "Iraq Nuclear File: key findings," International Atomic Energy Agency, http://www.iaea.org/OurWork/SV/Invo/factsheet.html.
11. Frantz and Collins, *Nuclear Jihadist*, 198.
12. Ibid., 235–41.
13. William J. Broad and David E. Sanger, "In the Nuclear Net's Undoing, a Web of Shadowy Deals," *New York Times*, August 25, 2008, http://www.nytimes. com/2008/08/25/world/25nuke.html; Frantz and Collins, *Nuclear Jihadist*, 247–51.
14. Frantz and Collins, *Nuclear Jihadist*, 253–54.
15. George Tenet, *At the Center of the Storm: My Years at the CIA*, with Bill Harlow (New York: HarperLuxe, 2007), 436.
16. Frantz and Collins, *Nuclear Jihadist*, 340.

17. "B.S.A. Tahir Released; Many More Still Detained Under ISA," *Aliran*, June 25, 2008.

18. "Special Report: The A.Q. Khan Network: German Case Highlights Difficulties of Prosecuting Nuclear Smugglers," *WMD Insights*, January 2010.

19. Mark Shapiro, "South Africa's Nuclear Underground," Center for Investigative Reporting, April 10, 2008, http://www.centerforinvestigativereporting .org/node/3608; Leonard S. Spector, Nilsu Goren, and Sammy Salama, "Special Report: The A. Q. Khan Network: Crime . . . and Punishment?" *WMD Insights*, March 2006, http://www.wmdinsights.com/I3/G1_SR_AQK _Network.htm.

20. Adam P. Williams, "South Africa, Germany Announce Significant Developments in Prosecution of Suspected Khan Network Participants," *WMD Insights*, December 2007–January 2008, http://www.wmdinsights.com/I21 /I21_AF1_SouthAfricaGermany.htm.

21. Broad and Sanger, "In the Nuclear Net's Undoing."

22. Anonymous (Michael Scheuer), *Through Our Enemies' Eyes: Osama bin Laden, Radical Islam, and the Future of America* (Washington, DC: Brassey's, Inc., 2003), 124.

23. Zelikow and others, *9/11 Commission Report*, 60.

24. Frantz and Collins, *Nuclear Jihadist*, 263.

25. *Time*, December 23, 1998, quoted in "Osama bin Laden v. the U.S.: Edicts and Statements," *Frontline*, PBS, http://www.pbs.org/wgbh/pages/frontline /shows/binladen/who/edicts.html.

26. Tenet, *At the Center of the Storm*, 410.

27. House Committee on the Judiciary, *Hearing on the Department of Justice*, 108th Cong., 1st sess., 2003, serial 59.

28. Lawrence Wright, *The Looming Tower* (New York: Knopf, 2008), 295–96.

29. Tenet, *At the Center of the Storm*, 397–408.

30. Hamid Mir, interview by Andrew Denton, *Enough Rope with Andrew Denton*, ABC (Australian Broadcasting Corporation), March 22, 2004.

31. *Nunn-Lugar Cooperative Threat Reduction Act of 2005*, S 313, 109th Cong., 1st sess. (February 8, 2005).

32. David E. Hoffman, "Report on Nuclear Security Urges Prompt Global Action," *Washington Post*, November 18, 2008.

33. Matthew Bunn, "Securing the Bomb 2008," Project on Managing the Atom, Belfer Center for Science and International Affairs, Harvard Kennedy School

and Nuclear Threat Initiative, November 18, 2008, http://belfercenter.ksg
.harvard.edu/publication/18672/securing_the_bomb_2008.html.

34. Frantz and Collins, *Nuclear Jihadist*, 269–70; Allison, *Nuclear Terrorism*, 105–6.

35. Scott Shane and Andrew W. Lehren, "Leaked Cables Offer Raw Look at U.S. Diplomacy," *New York Times*, November 28, 2010.

CHAPTER 8: THINKING THE UNTHINKABLE

1. Carlotta Gall, "Taliban Hold Sway in Area Taken by U.S., Farmers Say," *New York Times*, May 16, 2010, http://www.nytimes.com/2010/05/17/world/asia /17marja.html?_r=1.

2. Henry Kissinger, *Foreign Affairs*, January 1969, quoted in *Oxford Dictionary of Quotations*, 441.

3. Rod Nordland, "Afghanistan Strategy Focuses on Civilian Effort," *New York Times*, June 9, 2010.

4. Gall, "Coalition Forces Routing Taliban in Key Afghan Region," *New York Times*, October 20, 2010.

5. Rajiv Chandrasekaran, "U.S. Deploys Heavily Armored Battle Tanks for First Time in Afghan War," *Washington Post*, November 19, 2010.

6. C. J. Chivers, Carlotta Gall, Andrew W. Lehren, Mark Mazzetti, Jane Perlez, and Eric Schmitt, "View Is Bleaker than Official Portrayal of War in Afghanistan," *New York Times*, July 25, 2010, http://www.nytimes.com/2010/07/26/ world/asia/26warlogs.html; Mark Mazzetti, Jane Perlez, Eric Schmitt, and Andrew W. Lehren, "Pakistan Aids Insurgency in Afghanistan, Reports Assert," *New York Times*, July 25, 2010, http://www.nytimes.com/2010/07/26/ world/asia/26isi.html; Greg Jaffe and Karen DeYoung, "Leaked Files Lay Bare War in Afghanistan," *Washington Post*, July 26, 2010.

7. Chivers and others, "View Is Bleaker."

8. Steven Aftergood, "Can the Secrecy System Be Fixed?" *Secrecy News*, July 28, 2010, http://www.fas.org/blog/secrecy/2010/07.

9. "From One Transparency Advocate to Another," *On the Media*, NPR, July 30, 2010.

10. Gail Russell Chaddock, "WikiLeaks controversy hovers, but House passes war funding bill," *Christian Science Monitor*, July 28, 2010.

11. Gen. Stanley A. McChrystal, "COMISAF's Initial Assessment," report to Secretary of Defense Robert M. Gates, August 30, 2009, http://media.wash-

ingtonpost.com/wp-srv/politics/documents/Assessment_Redacted_092109. pdf?sid=ST2009092003140.

12. Peter Baker and Elizabeth Bumiller, "Obama Considers Strategy Shift in Afghan War," *New York Times*, September 23, 2009.

13. Chivers and others, "View Is Bleaker."

14. This and subsequent quotes from the president are taken from the official transcript of his speech at West Point: Obama, "Remarks by the President," December 1, 2009.

15. Robert Gates on *Meet the Press*, NBC, December 6, 2009.

16. Richard A. Oppel and Elisabeth Bumiller, "Afghan Says Army will Need Help Until 2024," *New York Times*, December 8, 2009, http://www.nytimes .com/2009/12/09/world/asia/09gates.html.

17. Gen. Peter W. Chiarelli, *Army Health Promotion, Risk Reduction, Suicide Prevention: Report 2010* (U.S. Army, 2010), http://usarmy.vo.llnwd.net/e1 /HPRRSP/HP-RR-SPReport2010_v00.pdf.

18. Gen. Peter Chiarelli on *This Week with Christiane Amanpour*, ABC, August 8, 2010.

19. Michael Hastings, "Stanley McChrystal: The Runaway General: Obama's Top Commander in Afghanistan Never Takes His Eye off the Real Enemy," *Rolling Stone*, June 22, 2010.

20. Joshua Partlow, "Petraeus Takes Command in Afghanistan, Pledging Victory," *Washington Post*, July 5, 2010.

21. See Gannon, *Military Occupations in the Age of Self-Determination*, 58–59, 166.

22. "Turkey to Israel: Lift blockade of Gaza," Haaretz.com, May 25, 2010.

23. Robert A. Pape, "To Beat the Taliban, Fight from Afar," *New York Times*, October 15, 2009, http://www.nytimes.com/2009/10/15/opinion/15pape .html.

24. David Ignatius, "Where Is President Obama's Machiavelli?" *Washington Post*, July 8, 2010.

Bibliography

BOOKS

Adams, Charles J. "Mawdudi and the Islamic State." In *Voices of Resurgent Islam*, edited by John L. Esposito. New York: Oxford University Press, 1983.

Allison, Graham. *Nuclear Terrorism: The Ultimate Preventable Catastrophe.* New York: Henry Holt, 2004.

Anonymous (Michael Scheuer). *Imperial Hubris: Why the West Is Losing the War on Terror.* Washington, DC: Brassey's, Inc., 2004.

———. *Through Our Enemies' Eyes: Osama bin Laden, Radical Islam, and the Future of America.* Washington, DC: Brassey's, Inc., 2003.

Armstrong, Karen. *Holy War: The Crusades and Their Impact on Today's World.* New York: Doubleday, 1991.

———. *Muhammad: A Biography of the Prophet.* New York: HarperCollins, 1992.

Bacevich, Andrew J. *The New American Militarism: How Americans Are Seduced by War.* New York: Oxford University Press, 2005.

Bergen, Peter L. *Holy War, Inc.: Inside the Secret World of Osama bin Laden.* New York: Free Press, 2001.

Berntsen, Gary, and Ralph Pezzullo. *Jawbreaker: The Attack on Bin Laden and Al-Qaeda: A Personal Account by the CIA's Key Field Commander.* New York: Crown Publishers, 2005.

Bowden, Mark. *Black Hawk Down: A Story of Modern War.* New York: Signet, 1999.

Burke, Jason. *Al Qaeda: Casting a Shadow of Terror.* London: I. B. Tauris, 2003.

Clarke, Richard A. *Against All Enemies: Inside America's War on Terror.* New York: Free Press, 2004.

Coll, Steve. *Ghost Wars: The Secret History of the CIA, Afghanistan, and Bin Laden, from the Soviet Invasion to September 10, 2001.* New York: Penguin Press, 2004.

Emerson, Steven. *Secret Warriors: Inside the Covert Military Operations of the Reagan Era.* New York: G. P. Putnam's Sons, 1988.

Esposito, John L. *Islam and Politics.* 3rd ed. Syracuse, NY: Syracuse University Press, 1991.

———. *Unholy War: Terror in the Name of Islam.* New York: Oxford University Press, 2002.

Ferguson, Niall. *Colossus: The Price of America's Empire.* New York: Penguin Press, 2004.

Frantz, Douglas, and Catherine Collins. *The Nuclear Jihadist: The True Story of the Man Who Sold the World's Most Dangerous Secrets . . . and How We Could Have Stopped Him.* New York: Twelve, 2007.

Gannon, James. *Military Occupations in the Age of Self-Determination: The History Neocons Neglected.* Westport, CT: Praeger Security International, 2008.

Glubb, Sir John Bagot. *The Life and Times of Muhammad.* New York: Stein & Day, 1970.

Gold, Dore. *Hatred's Kingdom: How Saudi Arabia Supports the New Global Terrorism.* Washington, DC: Regnery Publishing, 2003.

Haney, Eric L. *Inside Delta Force: The Story of America's Elite Counterterrorism Unit.* New York: Delacourte Press, 2002.

Holden, David, and Richard Johns. *The House of Saud: The Rise and Rule of the Most Powerful Dynasty in the Arab World.* New York: Holt, Rinehart, and Winston, 1981.

Horne, Alistair. *A Savage War of Peace: Algeria, 1954–1962.* New York: Viking Press, 1977.

Johnson, Chalmers. *Blowback: The Costs and Consequences of American Empire.* New York: Henry Holt, 2000.

———. *The Sorrows of Empire: Militarism, Secrecy and the End of the Republic.* New York: Metropolitan Books, 2004.

Jones, Seth G. *In the Graveyard of Empires: America's War in Afghanistan.* New York: Norton, 2009.

Kepel, Gilles. *Jihad: The Trail of Political Islam.* Translated by Anthony F. Roberts. Cambridge, MA: Harvard University Press, 2002.

Kilcullen, David. *The Accidental Guerrilla: Fighting Small Wars in the Midst of a Big One.* New York: Oxford University Press, 2009.

Lacey, Robert. *The Kingdom.* New York: Harcourt Brace Jovanovich, 1981.

Mitchell, Richard P. *The Society of Muslim Brothers.* New York: Oxford University Press, 1993.

Moon, Katharine H. S. *Sex Among Allies: Military Prostitution in U.S.-Korea Relations.* New York: Columbia University Press, 1997.

Nasr, Seyyed Hossein. *The Heart of Islam: Enduring Values for Humanity.* San Francisco: HarperSanFrancisco, 2002.

Naylor, Sean. *Not a Good Day to Die: The Untold Story of Operation Anaconda.* New York: Berkeley Books, 2005.

Neville, Leigh. *Special Operations Forces in Afghanistan.* Oxford, UK: Osprey Publishing, 2008.

Odom, William E., and Robert Dujarric. *America's Inadvertent Empire.* New Haven, CT: Yale University Press, 2004.

Peters, F. E. *Mecca: A Literary History of the Muslim Holy Land.* Princeton, NJ: Princeton University Press, 1994.

Pike, Douglas. "The Vietcong Secret War." In *War in the Shadows: The Vietnam Experience,* edited by Samuel Lipsman. Boston: Boston Publishing, 1988.

———. *War, Peace, and the Viet Cong.* Cambridge, MA: MIT Press, 1969.

Powell, Colin L. *My American Journey.* With Joseph E. Persico. New York: Random House, 1995.

Qutb, Sayyid. *Milestones.* Translated by Ahmad Zaki Hammad. Indianapolis: American Trust Publications, 1990.

Rashid, Ahmed. *Descent into Chaos: The U.S. and the Disaster in Pakistan, Afghanistan, and Central Asia.* New York: Penguin Books, 2009.

———. *Taliban: Militant Islam, Oil and Fundamentalism in Central Asia.* New Haven, CT: Yale Nota Bene, 2001.

Ricks, Thomas E. *The Gamble: General David Petraeus and the American Military Adventure in Iraq, 2006–2008.* New York: Penguin Press, 2009.

Risen, James. *State of War: The Secret History of the CIA and the Bush Administration.* New York: Free Press, 2006.

Rodinson, Maxime. *Mohammad.* New York: Pantheon Books, 1980.

Schwartz, Steven. *The Two Faces of Islam: The House of Saud from Tradition to Terror.* New York: Doubleday, 2002.

Smith, Michael. *Killer Elite: The Inside Story of America's Most Secret Special Operations Team.* New York: St. Martin's Press, 2006.

Tenet, George. *At the Center of the Storm: My Years at the CIA.* With Bill Harlow. New York: HarperLuxe, 2007.

Tregonning, K. G. *A History of Modern Malaya.* New York: David McKay, 1964.

Tuchman, Barbara W. *The Pursuit of Folly: From Troy to Vietnam.* New York: Ballantine Books, 1984.

Van de Weyer, Robert. *The Shared Well: A Concise Guide to Relations between Islam and the West.* Washington, DC: Brassey's, Inc., 2002.

Wright, Robin. *Sacred Rage: The Wrath of Militant Islam.* New York: Linden Press, 1985.

Zelikow, Philip D., Ernest R. May, and Bonnie Jenkins. *The 9/11 Commission Report: Final Report of the National Commission on Terrorist Attacks upon the United States,* Authorized Edition. New York: Norton, 2004.

NEWSPAPERS, MAGAZINES, AND JOURNALS

"7 July Bombings." BBC News, In Depth: What Happened/The Investigation.

"21 July Attacks." BBC News, In Depth: What Happened/The Investigation.

Ali, Zulfigar, and Laura King. "Pakistan officials allow Sharia in volatile region." *Los Angeles Times,* February 17, 2009. http://articles.latimes.com/2009/feb/17/world/fg-pakistan-pact17.

"Arafat Horrified by Attacks, but Thousands of Palestinians Celebrate; Rest of World Outraged." Fox News, September 12, 2001.

Associated Press. "Atta Does Not Fit Terrorist Mold." *Milwaukee Journal Sentinel,* September 28, 2001.

"Attacks in Past Week." In "Pakistan reels from fresh attacks." BBC News, October 12, 2009. http://news.bbc.co.uk/2/hi/south_asia/8302055.stm.

"Ayodhya: India's Religious Flashpoint." CNN.com, December 6, 2002. http://articles.cnn.com/2002-12-06/world/ayodhya.background_1_ayodhya-world-hindu-council-vhp?_s=PM:asiapcf.

Baker, Peter, and Elizabeth Bumiller. "Obama Considers Strategy Shift in Afghan War." *New York Times,* September 23, 2009.

Bergen, Peter. "Exclusive: I Was Kidnapped by the CIA." *Mother Jones,* March 3, 2008. http://www.motherjones.com/print/15664.

Bergen, Peter, and Katherine Tiedemann. "Disappearing Act: Rendition by the Numbers." *New American Foundation,* March 3, 2008. http://www.newamerica.net/node/9093. First published in *Mother Jones,* March 3, 2008.

Bilmes, Linda J., and Joseph E. Stiglitz. "The Iraq War Will Cost Us $3 Trillion, and Much More." *Washington Post,* March 9, 2008.

"Blast 'kills al Qaeda commander.'" BBC News, December 3, 2005. http://news.bbc.co.uk/2/hi/south_asia/4494428.stm.

"Bomb blast kills 20 in NW Pakistan," *China View, Xinhua,* August 23, 2008.

Bonner, Raymond. "Bali Suicide Bombers Said to Have Belonged to Small Gang." *New York Times*, October 7, 2005.

Broad, William J., and David E. Sanger. "In the Nuclear Net's Undoing, a Web of Shadowy Deals." *New York Times*, August 25, 2008. http://www.nytimes .com/2008/08/25/world/25nuke.html.

Burke, Jason. "How the Perfect Terrorist Plotted the Ultimate Crime." *Observer*, April 7, 2002. http://www.guardian.co.uk/world/2002/apr/07/september11 .terrorism.

Chaddock, Gail Russell. "WikiLeaks controversy hovers, but House passes war funding bill." *Christian Science Monitor*, July 28, 2010.

Chivers, C. J., Carlotta Gall, Andrew W. Lehren, Mark Mazzetti, Jane Perlez, and Eric Schmitt. "View Is Bleaker than Official Portrayal of War in Afghanistan." *New York Times*, July 25, 2010. http://www.nytimes.com/2010/07/26/world /asia/26warlogs.html.

Chivers, C. J., and Steven Lee Myers. "Rebels in Russia Had Precise Plan." *New York Times*, September 6, 2004.

Choudhury, Ishfaq Ilahi. "Pakistan: Into the Vortex of Violence." *New Nation* (Bangladesh), November 13, 2009. http://nation.ittefaq.com/issues/2009/11/13/ news0376.htm.

"Civil Justice, Military Justice." *New York Times*, October 5, 2010.

Coll, Steve. "The General's Dilemma." *New Yorker*, September 8, 2008.

Dakss, Brian. "U.S. Hostage Beheaded." CBS News, June 18, 2004.

DeYoung, Karen. "Al-Qaeda Seen as Shaken in Pakistan." *Washington Post*, June 1, 2009.

———. "Taliban Surprising U.S. Forces with Improved Tactics." *Washington Post*, September 2, 2009.

DeYoung, Karen, and Walter Pincus. "Success Against al Qaeda Cited." *Washington Post*, September 30, 2009.

Digal, Santosh. "After seven years, courts can rule on Godhra massacre." AsiaNews .it, October 29, 2010. http://www.asianews.it/news-en/After-seven-years -courts-can-rule-on-Godhra-massacre-19856.html.

Dodd, Vikram. "Three Terrorists Convicted of Plotting to Blow Up Jets over Atlantic." *Guardian*, September 7, 2009. http://www.guardian.co.uk/world /2009/sep/07/terrorists-plot-atlantic-liquid-bombs.

Donaldson-Evans, Catherine. "Palestinian Officials Quash Pictures of Arab Celebrations." Fox News, September 13, 2001. http://www.foxnews.com/story /0,2933,34346,00.html.

Eckholm, Erik. "Pakistanis Arrest Qaeda Figure Seen as Planner of 9/11." *New York Times*, March 2, 2003.

Elegant, Simon. "The Terrorist Talks." *Time*, October 5, 2003.

Ferris, Elizabeth, and Michael E. O'Hanlon. "Iraq's Displaced Millions." *Washington Times*, June 1, 2009.

Finn, Peter. "Hijackers Depicted as Elite Group." *Washington Post*, November 5, 2001.

———. "New Report Puts Blame on Local Officials in Beslan Siege." *Washington Post*, December 29, 2005.

Finn, Peter, and Charles Love. "Will Gives a Window into Suspect's Mind: Czechs Say Atta Met with Iraqi Official." *Washington Post*, October 6, 2001.

Finn, Peter, Joby Warrick, and Julie Tate. "Administration Releases More of a Long-Classified CIA Report on Interrogations." *Washington Post*, August 24, 2009.

Finn, Peter, and Julie Tate. "Package Bomb Could Have Downed Plane Over Canada, Data Show." *Washington Post*, November 10, 2010. http://www.washingtonpost.com/wp-dyn/content/article/2010/11/10/AR2010111003725.html.

Gall, Carlotta. "Coalition Forces Routing Taliban in Key Afghan Region." *New York Times,* October 20, 2010.

———. "Taliban Hold Sway in Area Taken by U.S., Farmers Say." *New York Times*, May 16, 2010. http://www.nytimes.com/2010/05/17/world/asia/17marja.html?_r=1.

Goldstein, Amy, Lena H. Sun, and George Lardner Jr. "Hanjour a Study in Paradox." *Washington Post*, October 15, 2001.

Hastings, Michael. "Stanley McChrystal: The Runaway General: Obama's Top Commander in Afghanistan Never Takes His Eye off the Real Enemy." *Rolling Stone*, June 22, 2010.

Hoffman, David E. "Report on Nuclear Security Urges Prompt Global Action." *Washington Post*, November 18, 2008.

Horton, Scott. "Renditions Buffoonery." *Harper's Magazine*, February 2, 2009. http://www.harpers.org/archive/2009/02/hbc-90004326

Howeidy, Amira. "Politics in God's Name." *Al-Ahram Weekly Online*, no. 247 (November 16–22, 1995). http://weekly.ahram.org.eg/archives/parties/muslimb/polgod.htm

Ignatius, David. "Where Is President Obama's Machiavelli?" *Washington Post*, July 8, 2010.

Jaffe, Greg, and Karen DeYoung. "Leaked Files Lay Bare War in Afghanistan." *Washington Post*, July 26, 2010.

Junger, Sebastian. "Into the Valley of Death." *Vanity Fair*, January 2008. http://www.vanityfair.com/politics/features/2008/01/afghanistan200801.

Kilcullen, David. "Death from Above, Outrage Down Below." *New York Times*, May 16, 2009. http://www.nytimes.com/2009/05/17/opinion/17exum.html?_r=1.

Knickmeyer, Ellen, and I. K. Ibriham. "Bombing Shatters Mosque in Iraq." *Washington Post*, February 23, 2006.

Knickmeyer, Ellen, and Jonathan Finer. "Insurgent Leader al-Zarqawi Killed in Iraq." *Washington Post,* June 8, 2006.

Krauss, Clifford. "Defendant in Court for Hearing at Ft. Hood." *New York Times,* October 12, 2010.

Lamb, Christina. "Stop Bombing Us: Osama Isn't Here, Says Pakistan." *Times Online*, July 12, 2009. http://www.timesonline.co.uk/tol/news/world/asia/article6689741.ece.

Londono, Ernesto, and Greg Jaffe. "Iraq Carnage Shows Sectarian War Goes On." *Washington Post*, August 20, 2009.

Longman, Jere. "Cockpit Tape Offers Few Answers but Points to Heroic Efforts." *New York Times*, March 27, 2002.

MacFarquhar, Neil. "Saudi Military Storms Complex to Free Hostages." *New York Times*, May 31, 2004.

MacLeod, Scott, and Bruce Crumley. "Saudi Arabia's New Terror." *Time,* November 16, 2003.

Makiya, Kanan, and Hassan Mneimneh. "Manual for a 'Raid.'" *New York Review of Books* 49, no. 1 (January 17, 2002): 18–21.

Mayer, Jane. "Outsourcing Terror: The Secret History of America's 'Extraordinary Rendition' Program." *New Yorker*, February 14, 2005.

Mazzetti, Mark. "Interrogation Memos Detail Harsh Tactics by the C.I.A." *New York Times*, April 17, 2009.

Mazzetti, Mark, and Margot Williams. "In Tribunal Statement, Confessed 9/11 Plotter Burnishes His Image as a Soldier." *New York Times*, March 16, 2007.

Mazzetti, Mark, Robert F. Worth, and Eric Lipton. "Bomb Plot Shows Key Role Played by Intelligence." *New York Times*, October 31, 2010. http://nytimes.com/2010/11/01/world/01terror.html?_r=1&nl=&emc=a1.

McKinnon, Jim. "The Phone Line from Flight 93 Was Still Open When a GTE Operator Heard Todd Beamer Say: 'Are You Guys Ready? Let's Roll.'" *Pittsburgh Post-Gazette*, September 16, 2001. http://www.postgazette.com/headlines/20010916phonecallnat3p3.asp.

Miller, Greg. "Muslim Cleric Aulaqi is 1st U.S. Citizen on List of Those CIA Is Allowed to Kill." *Washington Post,* April 7, 2010.

Naylor, Sean D. "Exclusive: Inside a U.S. Hostage Rescue Mission." ArmyTimes .com, November 10, 2008. http://www.armytimes.com/news/2008/11 /military_air_rescue_11070.

———. "SpecOps Unit Nearly Nabs Zarqawi." ArmyTimes.com, April 28, 2006. http://www.armytimes.com/legacy/new/1-292925-1739387.php.

———. "Surviving SEAL Tells Story of Deadly Mission." ArmyTimes.com, June 18, 2007.

Nordland, Rod. "Afghanistan Strategy Focuses on Civilian Effort." *New York Times,* June 9, 2010.

"Notes Found After the Hijackings." *New York Times,* September 29, 2001.

"Obama's top intelligence adviser resigns." CNN.com, May 20, 2010. http:// articles.cnn.com/2010-05-20/politics/intelligence.director.resigns.

Oppel, Richard A., and Elisabeth Bumiller. "Afghan Says Army will Need Help Until 2024." *New York Times,* December 8, 2009. http://www.nytimes.com /2009/12/09/world/asia/09gates.html.

Oren, Amir. "U.S. Army Document Describes Israel as 'a Nuclear Power.'" *Haaretz,* March 18, 2009. http://www.haaretz.com/hasen/spages/1069303.html.

Pape, Robert A. "To Beat the Taliban, Fight from Afar." *New York Times,* October 15, 2009. http://www.nytimes.com/2009/10/15/opinion/15pape.html.

Partlow, Joshua. "Petraeus Takes Command in Afghanistan, Pledging Victory." *Washington Post,* July 5, 2010.

Perez-Rivas, Manuel. "Bush vows to rid the world of 'evil-doers.'" CNN.com, September 16, 2001.

Perlez, Jane, Raymond Bonner, and Salman Masood. "An Ex-Detainee of the U.S. Describes a 6-Year Ordeal." *New York Times,* January 6, 2009. http://www .nytimes.com/2009/01/06/world/asia/06iqbal.html.

Pincus, Walter. "From Clinton, Plain Talk on Afghanistan." *Washington Post,* December 8, 2009.

President's remarks. "America's New War: President Bush Talks to Reporters at Pentagon." CNN, September 16, 2001.

"President's Remarks on the South Lawn of the White House." CNN, September 16, 2001.

Priest, Dana. "Wrongful Imprisonment: Anatomy of a CIA Mistake." *Washington Post,* December 4, 2005.

Priest, Dana, and William M. Arkin. "Top Secret America: A *Washington Post* Investigation: Part 1: A Hidden World, Growing Beyond Control." *Washington*

Post Online, July 19, 2010. http://projects.washingtonpost.com/top-secret -america/articles/a-hidden-world-growing-beyond-control/.

Rashbaum, William K., and Karen Zraick. "Government Says Al Qaeda Ordered N.Y. Plot." *New York Times,* April 23, 2010.

Risen, James, and Mark Mazzetti. "Blackwater Guards Tied to Secret Raids by the C.I.A." *New York Times*, December 11, 2009.

Rodriguez, Luis, and Martha Raddatz. "Al-Qaeda Operations Manager Saleh al-Somaleh Believed Dead in Drone Strike." ABC News, December 11, 2009. http://abcnews.go.com/International/Terrorism/al-qaeda-operation.

"Saudi Arabia issues new list of wanted 'terrorist' suspects." asharq alawsat, June 29, 2005. http://aawsat.com/english/news.asp?id=613&section=1.

"Saudi car bomb attack kills four." BBC News, April 22, 2004, http://news.bbc .co.uk/2/hi/middle_east/3646195.stm.

Scahill, Jeremy. "Blackwater's Secret War in Pakistan." *Nation*, November 23, 2009.

Shah, Pir Zubair, and Jane Perlez. "Car Bomb Kills at Least 41 in Restive Region of Pakistan." *New York Times*, October 13, 2009. http://www.nytimes.com/ 2009/10/13/world/asia/13pstan.html.

Shahzad, Syed Saleem. "A Chilling Inheritance of Terror." *Asia Times*, October 30, 2002.

———. "Seven Steps to Peace in Afghanistan." *Asia Times*, August 22, 2009. http://www.atimes.com/atimes/South_Asia/KH22Df03.html.

Shane, Scott. "Waterboarding Used 266 Times on 2 Suspects." *New York Times*, April 19, 2009.

Shenon, Philip. "20 Years After Victory." *New York Times*, April 22, 1995.

Smith, Niel, and Sean MacFarland. "Anbar Awakens: The Tipping Point." *Military Review*, March–April 2008, 41–52.

Spector, Leonard S., Nilsu Goren, and Sammy Salama. "Special Report: The A. Q. Khan Network: Crime . . . and Punishment?" *WMD Insights*, March 2006. http://www.wmdinsights.com/I3/G1_SR_AQK_Network.htm.

"Taliban torched over 200 schools in Swat in 2 yrs: Report." Indian Express.com, May 24, 2009. http://www.indianexpress.com/news/taliban-torched-over-200-schools-in-2-yrs-report/465093/0.

"Terror blasts rock Casablanca." BBC News, May 17, 2003, http://news.bbc.co .uk/2/hi/africa/3035803.stm.

Tyson, Ann Scott. "'Skittish' Afghans Wary of Marines, Taliban." *Washington Post*, August 15, 2009.

Vick, Karl. "Al-Qaeda's Hand in Istanbul Plot." *Washington Post*, February 13, 2007.

Villalba, Noel. "Philippines: A Subjective View of the U.S. Bases Issue." *Human Rights Solidarity*, December 31, 1991. http://www.hrsolidarity.net/mainfile.php/1991vol01no01/1984/.

Wallach, Evan. "Waterboarding Used to Be a Crime." *Washington Post*, November 4, 2007.

Walsh, Declan. "Air strike kills Taliban leader Baitullah Mehsud." *Guardian*, August 7, 2009. http://www.guardian.co.uk/world/2009/aug/o7/baitullah-mehsud-dead-taliban-pakistan.

———. "Inside the Taliban's besieged Swat fortress as battle rages." *Observer*, May 10, 2009.

White, Josh. "Al-Qaeda Suspect Says He Planned Cole Attack." *Washington Post*, March 20, 2007.

Whitlock, Craig. "Jordan's Spy Agency: Holding Cell for the CIA." *Washington Post*, December 1, 2007.

Wilgoren, Jodi, and Edward Wong. "On a Doomed Jet, Passengers Vowed to Perish Fighting." *New York Times*, September 13, 2001.

Williams, Adam P. "South Africa, Germany Announce Significant Developments in Prosecution of Suspected Khan Network Participants." *WMD Insights*, December 2007–January 2008. http://www.wmdinsights.com/I21/I21_AF1_SouthAfricaGermany.htm.

Williams, Carol J., John-Thor Dahlburg, and H. G. Reza. "Mainly, They Just Waited." *Los Angeles Times*, September 27, 2001.

Williams, Daniel. "Egyptian Police Kill Suspect in Red Sea Attacks." *Washington Post*, May 10, 2006.

Witte, Griff. "Afghan Promises to Insurgents Often Empty." *Washington Post*, December 14, 2009.

———. "Taliban Shadow Officials Offer Concrete Alternative." *Washington Post*, December 8, 2009.

DOCUMENTS, REPORTS, AND SPEECHES

Aftergood, Steven. "Al Qaida: Western Spies Multiply 'Like Locusts.'" *Secrecy News*, July 13, 2009. http://www.fas.org/blog/secrecy/2009/07/al_libi_spies.html.

———. "Can the Secrecy System Be Fixed?" *Secrecy News*, July 28, 2010. http://www.fas.org/blog/secrecy/2010/07

Agence France Presse. "Court Convicts 23 Ex-CIA Agents in Imam Kidnapping

Trial." France 24, November 4, 2009. http://www.france24.com/en/20091104 -italy-convicts-23-ex-cia-agents-imam-kidnapping-trial-justice-prison.

"Baath Ground Forces Equipment." Global Security. http://www.globalsecurity .org/military/world/iraq/ground-equipment-intro.htm.

Bergen, Peter, and Katherine Tiedemann. "Pakistan Drone War Takes a Toll on Militants—and Civilians." CNN, October 29, 2009. http://www.peter bergen .com/services/print.aspx?id=410.

Bilton, Michael. "Post-9/11 Renditions: An Extraordinary Violation of International Law." Center for Public Integrity, May 22, 2007. http://projects.public integrity.org/MilitaryAid//report.aspx?aid=855.

Bin Laden, Osama. "Ladenese Epistle: Declaration of War Against the Americans Occupying the Land of the Two Holy Places." Part 3. *Washington Post Online*, October 11, 2001.

———. "Manifesto of the World Islamic Front." February 22, 1998. In *Holy War, Inc.: Inside the Secret World of Osama bin Laden*, by Peter L. Bergen, 96. New York: Free Press, 2001.

Bradbury, Stephen G., Principal Deputy Attorney General, U.S. Department of Justice, Office of Legal Counsel. Memorandum for John A Rizzo, Senior Deputy General Counsel, Central Intelligence Agency, May 30, 2005, redacted. http://luxmedia.com.edgesuite.net/aclu/olc_05302005_bradbury.pdf.

Bunn, Matthew. "Securing the Bomb 2008." Project on Managing the Atom, Belfer Center for Science and International Affairs, Harvard Kennedy School and Nuclear Threat Initiative, November 18, 2008. http://belfercenter.ksg .harvard.edu/publication/18672/securing_the_bomb_2008.html.

Charter of the United Nations, Chapter VII, Article 51.

"Chechens 'Confirm' Warlord's Death." BBC News, April 29, 2002. http://news .bbc.co.uk/l/hi/world/europe/1957411.stm.

Chiarelli, Gen. Peter W. *Army Health Promotion, Risk Reduction, Suicide Prevention: Report 2010.* U.S. Army, 2010. http://usarmy.vo.llnwd.net/e1/HPRRSP /HP-RR-SPReport2010_v00.pdf.

Cocks, Tim. "U.S. Military Says Iraq Troop Surge Has Ended." Reuters, July 22, 2008.

"Country Reports on Terrorism." Office of the Coordinator for Counterterrorism, U.S. Department of State, April 30, 2007.

Department of Defense. *Base Structure Report Fiscal Year 2003 Baseline.* Washington, DC: Office of the Deputy Undersecretary of Defense, 2002.

———. *Base Structure Report Fiscal Year 2008 Baseline.* Washington, DC: Office of the Deputy Undersecretary of Defense, 2007.

"Dirty Bombs." Council on Foreign Relations Backgrounder, October 19, 2006. http://www.cfr.org/publication/9548/dirty_bombs.html.

Elite UK Forces. Special Air Service, Special Boat Service. http://www.eliteuk forces.info/.

"Fact Sheet: Extraordinary Rendition." American Civil Liberties Union, December 6, 2005. http://www.aclu.org/national-security/fact-sheet-extraordinary -rendition.

Field Manual. Army Special Operations Forces, FM3-05-130. Washington, DC: Army Publishing, 2006.

"From One Transparency Advocate to Another." *On the Media.* NPR, July 30, 2010.

Heart of Darkness: The Vietnam War Chronicles, 1945–1975. Directed by Edward Feuerherd. New York: KOCH Vision, September 5, 2006.

"HIMARS High Mobility Artillery Rocket System, USA." Army-technology.com. http://www.army-technology.com/projects/himars/.

"India: Gujarat Officials Took Part in Anti-Muslim Violence." *Human Rights News,* April 30, 2002. http://www.hrw.org/en/news/2002/04/29/india -gujarat-officials-took-part-anti-muslim-violence.

"Iraq Nuclear File: Key Findings." International Atomic Energy Agency. http:// www.iaea.org/OurWork/SV/Invo/factsheet.html.

"Islam: A Threat to World Stability." *Intelligence Review,* no. 1 (February 14, 1946): 24–35. http://www.fas.org/irp/agency/army/intelreview1.pdf.telreview/pdf.

"Karzai: I'd Talk with Taliban." Associated Press, December 3, 2009.

Khan, Abdul Qadeer. Interview by Nadeem Malik on *Islamabad Tonight.* Aaj Television News, August 31, 2009. Cited in Aftergood, Steven. "A. Q. Khan Discusses Pakistan's Nuclear Program." *Secrecy News,* September 8, 2009. http:// www.fas.org/blog/secrecy/2009/09/page/2.

Kipphut, Col. Mark E. *Crossbow and Gulf War Counter-Scud Efforts: Lessons from History.* The Counterproliferation Papers Future Warfare Series No. 15. Maxwell Air Force Base, AL: Air University, 2003.

Kronstadt, K. Alan. "Pakistan-U.S. Relations." *Congressional Research Service,* May 9, 2006.

"Madrid train attacks." BBC News, Attacks/Investigation.

McChrystal, Gen. Stanley A. "COMISAF's Initial Assessment." Report to Secretary of Defense Robert M. Gates, August 30, 2009. http://media.washington

post.com/wp-srv/politics/documents/Assessment_Redacted_092109 .pdf?sid=ST2009092003140.

Meet the Press. NBC, December 6, 2009.

Metz, Helen Chapin, ed. "Wahhabi Theology." *Country Studies, Saudi Arabia.* Washington, DC: Library of Congress, 1992. http://countrystudies.us/saudi -arabia/.

Mir, Hamid. Interview by Andrew Denton. *Enough Rope with Andrew Denton.* ABC (Australian Broadcasting Corporation), March 22, 2004.

Nunn-Lugar Cooperative Threat Reduction Act of 2005. S 313. 109th Cong., 1st sess. (February 8, 2005).

Obama, Barack. "Remarks by the President in Address to the Nation on the Way Forward in Afghanistan and Pakistan." Speech, Eisenhower Hall Theatre, U.S. Military Academy, West Point, NY, December 1, 2009. http://www .whitehouse.gov/the-press-office/remarks-president-address-nation-way -forward-afghanistan-and-pakistan.

———. Speech at an antiwar rally. Chicago, October 2, 2002. http://www .barackobama.com/2002/10/02/remarks_of_illinois_state_sen.php.

Pike, John, and Steven Aftergood. "Military Analysis Network." Federation of American Scientists, March 24, 2004. http://www.fas.org/man/dod-101/sys /dumb/blu-82.htm.

Powers, Rod. "U.S. Military Special Operations Forces." About.com. http://us military.about.com?od/jointservices/a/specialops.htm?p=1.

Prados, Alfred B. "Saudi Arabia: Current Issues and U.S. Relations." CRS Issues Brief for Congress, Congressional Research Service, August 4, 2003. http:// www.fas.org/man/crs/IB93113.pdf.

"Rebels' Dilemma After Basayev Death." BBC News, July 12, 2006. http://news .bbc.co.uk/2/hi/europe/5168984.stm.

Sentencing Judgment of Trial Chamber III in the Todorovic Case. The Hague, July 31, 2001.

Shapiro, Mark. "South Africa's Nuclear Underground." Center for Investigative Reporting, April 10, 2008. http://www.centerforinvestigativereporting.org /node/3608.

"Six al-Qaeda Killed at Hospital Siege." BBC News, January 28, 2002. http:// news.bbc.co.uk/2/hi/south_asia/1786011.stm.

"Special Report: The A.Q. Khan Network: German Case Highlights Difficulties of Prosecuting Nuclear Smugglers." *WMD Insights*, January 2010.

"Statement of Levin and Graham on Trip to Guantanamo Bay." Levin press release, March 16, 2007. http://levin.senate.gov/newsroom/release.cfm?id=270804.

"Status of World Nuclear Forces." Federation of American Scientists, November 8, 2010. http://www.fas.org/programs/ssp/nukes/nuclearweapons/nukestat.

"Terror Watch List Counter: A Million Plus." American Civil Liberties Union. http://www.aclu.org/privacy/spying/watchlistcounter.html.

This Week with Christiane Amanpour. ABC, August 8, 2010.

Time, December 23, 1998. Quoted in "Osama bin Laden v. the U.S.: Edicts and Statements." *Frontline.* PBS. http://www.pbs.org/wgbh/pages/frontline/shows/binladen/who/edicts.html.

"Times Square Bomb Attempt, May 1, 2010." *New York Times,* May 6, 2010.

Today. NBC, February 19, 1998.

"Total Cost of Wars Since 2001." National Priorities Project. Accessed November 10, 2010. http://costofwar.com/numbers.html.

"Turkey to Israel: Lift blockade of Gaza." Haaretz.com, May 25, 2010.

U.S. Department of the Army. *The U.S. Army/Marine Corps Counterinsurgency Field Manual: U.S. Army Field Manual No. 3-24: Marine Corps Warfighting Publication No. 3-33.5.* Chicago: University of Chicago Press, 2007.

U.S. House. Committee on the Judiciary. *Hearing on the Department of Justice.* 108th Cong., 1st sess., 2003, serial 59.

Verbatim Transcript of Combatant Status Review Tribunal Hearing for ISN 10024. U.S. Naval Base Guantánamo Bay, Cuba, March 10, 2007. http://www.defense.gov/news/transcript_isn10024.pdf.

"White Paper of the Interagency Policy Group's Report on U.S. Policy toward Afghanistan and Pakistan." White House, March 27, 2009. http://www.whitehouse.gov/assets/documents/afghanistan_pakistan_white_paper_final.pdf.

World Factbook. "India." *Central Intelligence Agency,* October 27, 2010. http://www.cia.gov/library/publications/the-world-factbook/.

Index

ABC News, 137
Abdulmutallab, Umar Farouk, 109
Abu Sayyaf, 39
Afghanistan, xvii, xxv, xxvi, xxvii, xxx, 6,
    9, 89, 93, 94, 96, 117, 118, 135, 141,
    146, 148
    corruption, 63, 143, 144
    Hazara ethnics, 45–46, 52, 82
    Jalalabad, 84
    Kabul, 42, 43, 83, 84
    Kandahar, 42, 43, 44, 83, 85, 140
    Korengal, 63, 147
    Kunar, 62–63, 89
    Kunduz, 68, 82
    Logar, 63–64, 84
    Mazar–e Sharif, 82, 83
    Pashtun ethnics, xx, xxviii, 43, 44,
        52, 60, 61–62, 72, 82
    security forces, 140, 142, 143,
        144–45
    surge, 59–67
    Tajik ethnics, 42, 43, 45, 52
    Taliban rule, xvi, xxix, 1–2
    Taloqan, 82
    Tora Bora, xix, 84–85, 89
    two-front war, xxviii, xxix, 61
    Uzbek ethnics, 45–46, 52, 82
    U.S. troop reinforcements in, xvii,
        139, 142, 144
Ahmedzay, Zarein, 108
al-Asiri, Ibriham Hassan, 111

al-Aulaqi, Anwar, 108, 109
al-Banna, Hasan, 19, 22–26
al-Fahd, Nasser bin Hamad, 135
al-Gamaa al-Islamiya, 118
Algeria, 51
al-Hijazi, Faruq, 135
al-Libi, Abu Yahya, 71
al Qaeda, xvii, xxvii, xxix, 9, 35, 52, 60,
    70, 72, 84, 88, 89, 90, 117, 118 140,
    143, 148, 149, 150
    and the A–bomb, 125, 126, 127,
        133, 134, 135, 136, 138
    AQAP (al Qaeda on the Arabian
        Peninsula), 93, 108, 109
    in Iraq, 86–87
    and 9/11, xi, xxv, xix, 2, 147
    origins, 37–39
    Pakistan sanctuary of, xviii, 36, 37,
        46–48
    world terrorism, 93–115
al-Nashiri, Abd al-Rahim, 117
al-Somali, Saleh, 87–88, 108
al-Suwaylim, Samir ibn (Khattab), 96–97
al-Turabi, Hasan, 135
al-Wahhab, Muhammad Abd, 19–20, 44
al-Zarqawi, Abu Musab, 9, 86–87, 104,
    107, 117–18
al-Zawahiri, Ayman, xix, 38, 39, 60, 69,
    79, 87, 89–90, 127, 135, 136
American Civil Liberties Union, 116
Amos, James F., 56

Ansar al-Islam, 39
Arafat, Yasir, 25, 94
Arar, Maher, 117
Atta, Mohammed, x–xi, 104
Attash, Walid Mohammed bin, 115
Australia, 104
Aziz, Abu Abdul (Barbarossa), 95
Aznar, Jose Maria, 104–5
Azzam, Abdullah, 38, 95

Balkans, 94–95
    Bosnia-Herzegovina, 94–95
    el-Muzhahidun, 95
Barrett, Richard, 71
Basayev, Shamil, 96, 98
Berlusconi, Silvio, 119
Benyaich, Abdelaziz, 104
Berger, Sandy, 80–81
Berntsen, Gary, 83–84
Bhutto, Benazir, 41, 42, 70
Bhutto, Zulfikar Ali, 40, 127, 128
Biden, Joseph, 143, 146
Binalshibh, Ramzi, 113, 115, 121
bin Laden, Osama, xxvi, 38–39, 63, 69,
    79–81, 87, 93, 94, 95, 99, 117, 150
    and the A-bomb, 127, 134, 138
    declarations of war on U.S., 39, 79
        and 9/11, xi
    from piety to terrorism, 38–39, 60
    retaliation for 9/11, xv, xvi, xix,
Blackwater USA (Xe Services), 88–89
Blair, Dennis C., 109
Britain, 65, 70, 77, 78, 104, 147
    airline bomb plots, 107
    army, 65
    London transit bombings, 105–6
    MI-6 (Intelligence), 70, 81
    special operations, 77, 78, 85
Bush, George W. (administration), xiii,
    xix, xxvi–xxvii, xxx, 60, 140,
    143, 147
        and the A-bomb, 135
        excessive rhetoric, xvi–xvii, 12–13,
        and extraordinary renditions, 115,
        119,
Butt, Siddique, 128

Calhoun, Luke, 57
Carter, Jimmy, 114
Chechnya, 68, 88, 95–98, 126

Beslan school, 97–98
    Dubrovka theater, 97
Cheney, Dick, xiii, 149
China, xv, xxiii, 5, 68, 137
Chiarelli, Peter, 145
Clarke, Richard A., 79, 80, 81
Clinton, Bill, 60, 79, 80, 81, 114, 115
Clinton, Hillary, 143

de Klerk, F. W., 129
Dostum, Rashid, 45, 83
drones, xxviii, xxix, 9, 35, 37, 48, 61,
    70, 72, 87, 88, 110, 121, 140, 141,
    143, 144
Dudayev, Dzhokhar, 95, 96

Efflandt, Scott, 57
Egypt, 22–29
    Sharm el-Sheikh bombings, 106–7
    Taba bombings, 106–7
Eikenberry, Karl W., 143, 146
Eisenhower, Dwight David, 150
el-Masri, Khalid, 117–18

Farooq, Mohammed, 130
France, 147
Franks, Tommy, 82, 84–85

Gaith, Sulaiman Abu, 134–35
Gates, Robert M., 142, 143, 145
Gaza, 88
Germany, 128, 134
Gozar, Mir Amanullah, 144
Graham, Lindsay O., 114
Guantanamo Bay, 113, 114, 117, 119–20
Gulf war, 39, 147

Haney, Eric L., 75–76
Haqqani, Jalaluddin, 36, 46–47, 63
Harkat-ul-Mujahideen, 39
Hasan, Nidal Malik, 108–9
Hekmatyar, Gulbuddin, 40, 41–42, 43,
    63, 90, 112
Holbrook, Richard, 146
Holder, Eric H., Jr., 110, 120–21
Horton, Scott, 115
Howe, Paul, 76
Husayn, Zayn al-Abidin Muhammad
    (Abu Zubaydah), 112, 115, 116, 121
        waterboarding, 116

Hussein, Saddam, xxvi, 9, 39, 85, 86, 126, 130
Hussein, Uday and Qusay, 85–86

IAEA (International Atomic Energy Agency), 130
India, 98, 99–101, 127
    Ayodhya, 101
    Godhra train fire, 100–101
    Kashmir, 99
    Mumbai, 100
    New Delhi, 100
    nuclear development, 127, 137
    Srinagar, 100
Indonesia, 98, 99
    Bali, 99
IEDs (improvised explosive devices), 13
International Islamic Front (IIF), 39, 79, 100
Iqbal, Muhammad Saad, 117
Iran, xvi, 13, 129, 130, 133, 140
Iraq, xvii, xx, xxiv, xxv, xxvii, xxix, xxx, 9, 12–13, 52–59, 89, 129, 130, 135, 141, 147, 150
    Baghdad, 57–59
    Ramadi, 53–54, 57, 140
    Sunni insurgency, 13
    Tal Afar, 52–53, 56
    war casualties in, xxv
    war cost, xxvi
Islamic Combat Group, 39
Islamist theology, xxvii, xxviii, 15–19, 148, 149–50
    Deobandism, 30–32, 40, 42, 44
    heritage, 16
    jihad, xxx, 17
    martyrdom (suicide), xxx, 15–16, 17–18, 20
    umma, 18
    vendetta, xxx, 16–17, 39, 135
    Wahhabism, xxix, 20–21, 95, 96
Isomuddin, Riduan bin (Hambali), 99, 114
Israel, 88, 114, 147, 148, 149
Italy, 104, 118
    Imam Rapito case, 118, 119, 120
    SISMI (Military Intelligence and Security Service), 119

Jaish-e-Mohammed, 39, 100
Jamaah Islamiyah, 39, 98–99

Jamiat-e-Ulema-Islam (JUI), 39–40, 41, 68–69
    madrassas, 40
Japan, 104
Johnson, Paul Marshall, Jr., 102
Jones, James L., 143, 146
Jordan, 107, 113
    bombings, 107
    prison, 113

Karzai, Hamid, 47, 83, 143, 144, 145
Kashmir, 68
Khan, A. Q., 126–29, 130–31
    access to nuclear secrets, 127
    downfall, 133
    and Iran, 131
    power and prestige, 133
    uranium enrichment program, 128
    at Urenco, 127
Khan, Ismael, 43
Kilcullen, David, xxvii, xxix, 49–50, 56, 61–63, 88
Kissinger, Henry, xxiii, 139–40
Korea, 5, 10–11, 12

Lady, Robert Selden, 119
Lashkar-e-Toiba, 39, 100
Lerch, Gotthard, 129, 131, 134
    And Iran, 129–30
Levin, Carl M., 114–15
Libyan nuclear project, 131, 132, 133
Lugar, Richard, 136
Lutrell, Marcus, 89

MacFarland, Sean, 53–54, 55
Mahmood, Bashirrudin, 135
Majeed, Chaudiri Abdul, 135
Malaya (British counterinsurgency), 51, 147
Malaysia, 132
Maskhadov, Aslan, 96, 98
Massoud, Ahmed Shah, 38, 43
Mawdudi, Mawlana, 19, 22, 32–33, 39–40
McChrystal, Stanley A., 91, 142, 145–46, 148
McMaster, H. R., 52–53, 55, 56
Medunjanin, Adis, 108
Mehsud, Baitullah, 35, 70, 87, 110
Meyer, Johan, 131, 134
Mohammed, Khalid Sheikh (KSM), 38, 99, 115, 116, 120

multiple bomb plots, 107
    capture, 113
    testimony at Guantanamo, 113–14
    torture, 116
Morocco, 98
    Moroccan Islamic Combat Group
      (GICM), 103
Mowatt-Larssen, Rolf, 137
Mullen, Mike, 143
Musharaf, Pervez, 68, 69, 114, 133
Muslim Brotherhood, 22–29
    expansion, 29–30
    founding, 23–24
    growth, 24
    militant wing, 24–26
    outlawed, 26

Nasr, Hassan Mustafa Osama (Abu
    Omar), 118–19, 120
Nasser, Gamal Abdul, 26, 28
National Resources Defense Council, 137
NATO (North Atlantic Treaty Organiza-
    tion), xv, xxvii, xxix, 5, 6, 9, 36, 47,
    64, 68, 70, 72, 87, 89, 101, 118, 139,
    142, 143, 145, 145, 147, 148, 149
Netherlands (Holland), 127, 128, 129
Northern Alliance, xvi, xix, 81–83, 149
North Korea, 131, 133, 140
nuclear threat, xvii, xxx, 4, 123
    black market (Pakistani pipeline),
      129, 131–33
    dirty bomb, 126
    Hiroshima and Nagasaki, 123–24
    MAD (Mutually Assured Destruc-
      tion), 4, 124, 136
    New York scenario, 123
    plutonium and uranium bombs,
      125–26
    Project on Managing the Atom, 137
    proliferation, 124–25, 136
Nunn-Lugar Act, 136, 137
Nunn, Sam, 136

Obama, Barack, xvii, xxvi–xxvii, xxviii,
    xxx, 47, 65, 91, 109, 115, 139, 141,
    142, 145, 146, 147, 148
Odierno, Ray, 56
Okinawa, 11, 12
Omar, Mohammad, xvi, 42, 60, 64, 68,
    87, 148

Padilla, Jose, 126
Pahlawan, Malik, 45
Pakistan, xvi, xvii, xxviii, 2, 84, 88, 120,
    127, 130, 131, 136, 138, 141, 142, 148
    army, 36–37, 68, 69–70, 72, 88,
      131, 144
    ISI (InterService Intelligence Di-
      rectorate), 36, 37, 41–42, 45,
      47, 60, 64, 68,112, 140
    Nuclear development, 37, 126,
      128, 137
      Kahuta enrichment plant, 128,
        129, 133
    police action, 112–15, 121
      Attash arrest, 114
      Binalshibh arrest, 112–13
      KSM arrest,
      Zubaydah arrest, 112
    sanctuaries in, xvii, xix, 9, 37, 47,
      71, 72, 87
    sovereignty issue, 37, 47, 72, 87
    U.S. aid, 67
Pearce, David, 56
Pearl, Daniel, 102, 113
Pentagon Papers, 141
PETN (explosive), 110–11
Petraeus, David, xxvii, 51, 55–56, 146,
    148, 150
Philippines, 3, 10
Poland, 104
Pope John Paul II, 114
Putin, Vladimir, 97

Qutb, Sayyid, 19, 26–29
    Milestones, 27–29
    execution, 29

Rauf, Rashid, 107, 108
Reid, Richard, 113
Rumsfeld, Donald, 47, 51, 64
Russia, xv, 88, 95–98, 124, 137,

Salafist Group for Call and Combat, 39
Saqlain, Raja, 113
Saudi Arabia, 19–22, 40–41, 93, 98,
    102, 131
Saydullayev, Abdul-Khalim, 98
Sayyaf, Abdul Rasul, 40
Schroen, Gary, 81, 83
Schuringa, Jasper, 109

self-determination, xx, 1, 121, 147, 150
Shahzad, Faisal, 110
Sherzai, Gul Agha, 83
Somalia, 141, 148
South Africa, 129, 134, 137
    Pelindaba, 137
Soviet Union, 4–5, 6, 41, 51, 60, 94,
    124, 136, 137, 147, 149
Spain, 98, 104
    Madrid train bombings, 103–5
    political fallout, 104–5
Sudan, 38, 148
surge, xxvii, xxix, 37, 49–51
    in Afghanistan, 61–63, 72
        Dahaneh, 66
        Kunar road, 62–63
        Helmand, 65–66
        Mianposhteh, 66
    in Iraq, 52–59
        Anbar awakening, 54
        Baghdad, 56–59
        Ramadi, 53–54, 55
        Tal Afar, 52–53, 55
        Tarmiyah, 57
Switzerland, 129, 134
Syria, 131

Tahir, Buhary Sayed Abu, 130, 131
    Malaysian connection, 132, 133–34
Taliban (original), xvi, xvii, xix, xxvii,
    xxix, 2, 9, 41, 96, 112, 144, 148, 149
    Afghanistan campaigns, 42–44,
        45–46
    defeat (2001–2), 81–85
    justice system, xxix, 44–45
Taliban, Afghan (Quetta Shura), xxviii,
    xxix, 35, 36, 37, 47, 60, 61, 72, 139,
    140, 143, 147
    drug trade, 65
    Helmand, 64, 65–66, 139, 143
    Kandahar, 64–65, 140
    Marja, 139, 140
    Now Zad, 65–66
    Uruzgan, 67
Taliban, Pakistani (post 9/11), xxviii, 9,
    35–37, 46–47, 60, 67, 68, 69–71, 72,
    88, 89, 90, 110, 143
    Buner, 70
    North Waziristan, 69

South Waziristan, 68, 69, 71
Swat Valley, 70, 71
Waygal, 67
Tenet, George, 80, 81, 133, 136
terrorism, xxvi, 94, 95, 97–111,
    attack on America (9/11), ix–
      xv, xvii, xix, xx, xxv, xxvii, 2, 38,
      94, 98, 112, 115, 121, 136, 147
    Bali, 98, 99, 114, 115
    Egypt, 106–7
    India, 100–101
    Jakarta, 99, 114, 115
    Jordan, 107
    Kashmir, 99–100, 148
    London, 105–6
    Madrid, 103–5
    Morocco, 103
    Turkey, 98, 101–2, 114
    Saudi Arabia, 102
    U.S. East Africa embassies, 80
    USS *Cole*, 94, 113, 114
Tinner, Friedrich, 130, 131, 132, 134
Tinner, Marco, 132, 134
Tinner, Urs, 131–32, 134
torture, 116–17, 118, 119, 121, 141
    waterboarding, 116, 121
    legality, 119–20
Turkey, 131, 148

Umma Tameer-e-Nau, 135, 136
United Arab Emirates, 131
United Nations, 142
United States, ix–xv, 2–10, 114, 135, 139,
    142, 143, 145, 146, 147, 148, 149
    aid to Mujahideen, 41
    bases, 6–7
    CIA, 70, 73, 81, 83–84, 89, 109,
      112, 113, 114, 119, 128, 140
      abductions, 116, 118
      "black sites" (secret prisons),
        115, 116, 117, 118, 120
      extraordinary rendition, 112,
        113, 115, 117, 118, 119, 120
      and nuclear black market,
        131–34
      and Tinner family, 132, 134
    Eagle Claw (failed Iran hostage
      rescue), 73–74
    FBI, 113, 117
    Fort Hood shootings, 108–9

four failed bomb plots, 108–11
  cargo planes plot, 110–11
  Christmas Day plot, 109, 111
  New York subway plot, 108
  Times Square bomb, 110
growth, 2–4
Gulf war performance, 7–8
insurgency wars, xxv, 1, 6
militarism, xxiv
power, xxx, 4–10
Special Operations Forces (SOF),
    73, 77–78, 82, 83, 85, 89, 91,
    121, 143, 144
  Amariya, 78
  Balkans, 78–79
  Delta Force, 73, 75–77
  Green Berets, 75
  Iraq, 85–87
  ISA (Intelligence Support Ac-
    tivity), 73, 77, 78
  Mogadishu, 76–77
  Rangers, 75, 77
  scuds, 77–78

SEALs, 73, 75, 79, 89–90
terrorist watch list, 117
training, 75–77
weapons, high tech, 9–10, 70
withdrawal issues, 146–50

Vietnam, xxiii, 5–6, 11–12, 50–51, 142,
    145, 147

WikiLeaks, 138, 140–41, 143
Wisser, Gerhard, 131, 134

Yarkas, Imad Eddin Barakat (Abu Dah-
    dah), 104
Yeltsin, Boris, 96
Yemen, 93, 141, 148
Yousef, Ramsi, 114, 120

Zardari, Asif Ali, 70
Zapatero, José Luis Rodrigues, 104–5
Zazi, Najibullah, 108
Zia-ul-Haq, Mohammad, 40, 60, 128
Zougam, Jamal, 103

About the Author

James Gannon is a journalist and former producer-writer of documentaries for NBC News. He is the author of *Stealing Secrets, Telling Lies: How Spies and Codebreakers Helped Shape the Twentieth Century* and *Military Occupations in the Age of Self-Determination: The History Neocons Neglected*. Gannon lives in Stony Point, New York.